RAISING KIDS TO THRIVE

Balancing Love With Expectations and Protection With Trust

KENNETH R. GINSBURG, MD, MS ED, FAAP

ILANA GINSBURG AND TALIA GINSBURG

American Academy of Pediatrics

DEDICATED TO THE HEALTH OF ALL CHILDREN™

American Academy of Pediatrics Publishing Staff

Director, Department of Publishing
Mark Grimes
Director, Division of Professional and Consumer Publishing
Jeff Mahony
Manager, Consumer Publishing
Kathryn Sparks
Coordinator, Product Development
Holly Kaminski
Director, Division of Editorial and Production Services
Sandi King, MS

Editorial Specialist
Amanda Cozza
Publishing and Production Services Specialist
Shannan Martin
Manager, Art Direction and Production
Linda Diamond
Director, Department of Marketing and Sales
Mary Lou White
Manager, Consumer Product Marketing
Mary Jo Reynolds

Published by the American Academy of Pediatrics
141 Northwest Point Blvd, Elk Grove Village, IL 60007-1019
847/434-4000
Fax: 847/434-8000
www.aap.org

About the American Academy of Pediatrics
The American Academy of Pediatrics is an organization of 62,000 primary care pediatricians, pediatric medical subspecialists, and pediatric surgical specialists dedicated to the health, safety, and well-being of infants, children, adolescents, and young adults.

Raising Kids to Thrive: Balancing Love With Expectations and Protection With Trust was created by Kenneth R. Ginsburg, MD, MS Ed, FAAP, Ilana Ginsburg, and Talia Ginsburg.

Cover design by Daniel Rembert
Lighthouse illustration on front cover © GoGraph.com/csp_maximus2566
Book design by Linda Diamond

Library of Congress Control Number: 2014949301
ISBN: 978-1-58110-867-5
eBook: 978-1-58110-871-2
EPUB: 978-1-58110-920-7
Kindle: 978-1-58110-919-1

The recommendations in this publication do not indicate an exclusive course of treatment or serve as a standard of medical care. Variations, taking into account individual circumstances, may be appropriate.

Statements and opinions expressed are those of the authors and not necessarily those of the American Academy of Pediatrics.

Products and Web sites are mentioned for informational purposes only. Inclusion in this publication does not imply endorsement by the American Academy of Pediatrics. The American Academy of Pediatrics is not responsible for the content of the resources mentioned in this publication. Web site addresses are as current as possible but may change at any time.

Every effort is made to keep *Raising Kids to Thrive: Balancing Love With Expectations and Protection With Trust* consistent with the most recent advice and information available from the American Academy of Pediatrics.

This book has been developed by the American Academy of Pediatrics. The authors, editors, and contributors are expert authorities in the field of pediatrics. No commercial involvement of any kind has been solicited or accepted in the development of the content of this publication.

Special discounts are available for bulk purchases of this book. Email our Special Sales Department at aapsales@aap.org for more information.

CB0081

9-356   1 2 3 4 5 6 7 8 9 10

Also Available From the American Academy of Pediatrics

Other Books by Dr Kenneth Ginsburg

Building Resilience in Children and Teens:
Giving Kids Roots and Wings

For Youth-Serving Professionals

Reaching Teens: Strength-Based
Communication Strategies to Build
Resilience and Support Healthy
Adolescent Development

Common Conditions

ADHD: What Every Parent Needs to Know

Allergies and Asthma: What Every Parent
Needs to Know

The Big Book of Symptoms: A–Z Guide
to Your Child's Health

Mama Doc Medicine: Finding Calm
and Confidence in Parenting, Child
Health, and Work-Life Balance

My Child Is Sick! Expert Advice for
Managing Common Illnesses
and Injuries

Sleep: What Every Parent Needs to Know

Waking Up Dry: A Guide to Help Children
Overcome Bedwetting

Developmental, Behavioral, and Psychosocial Information

Autism Spectrum Disorders: What Every
Parent Needs to Know

CyberSafe: Protecting and Empowering
Kids in the Digital World of Texting,
Gaming, and Social Media

Mental Health, Naturally: The Family Guide to
Holistic Care for a Healthy Mind and Body

Newborns, Infants, and Toddlers

Caring for Your Baby and Young Child:
Birth to Age 5*

Dad to Dad: Parenting Like a Pro

Guide to Toilet Training*

Heading Home With Your Newborn:
From Birth to Reality

Mommy Calls: Dr. Tanya Answers Parents'
Top 101 Questions About Babies
and Toddlers

New Mother's Guide to Breastfeeding*

Newborn Intensive Care: What Every Parent
Needs to Know

Raising Twins: Parenting Multiples From
Pregnancy Through the School Years

Retro Baby: Cut Back on All the Gear and
Boost Your Baby's Development With
More Than 100 Time-tested Activities

Your Baby's First Year*

Nutrition and Fitness

Food Fights: Winning the Nutritional
Challenges of Parenthood Armed With
Insight, Humor, and a Bottle of Ketchup

Nutrition: What Every Parent Needs to Know

A Parent's Guide to Childhood Obesity:
A Road Map to Health

Sports Success R$_x$! Your Child's Prescription for
the Best Experience

School-aged Children and Adolescents

Less Stress, More Success: A New Approach
to Guiding Your Teen Through College
Admissions and Beyond

For additional parenting resources, visit the HealthyChildren bookstore at
shop.aap.org/for-parents/.

shop.aap.org

*This book is also available in Spanish.

WHAT PEOPLE ARE SAYING

In *Raising Kids to Thrive*, Dr Ken Ginsburg's eloquent, insightful, and compassionate new book on adolescence, the views of both parents and teens are artfully woven into a narrative that models collaboration and mutual respect. Co-written with Dr Ginsburg's teen daughters, Talia and Ilana, *Raising Kids to Thrive* cleverly offers parents the views of hundreds of teenagers from across the country on the topics teens care about most—love, independence, trust, safety, honesty, and freedom. As an expert in adolescent medicine, and a renowned public speaker, Dr Ginsburg is unmatched in his ability to synthesize the latest research and drill down to the core essentials of any parenting issue. His love for teenagers, his respect for their innate goodness and beauty, and his fervent advocacy for healthy parent-teen relationships are evident in every chapter. To have the added benefit of Talia and Ilana Ginsburg's clear, intelligent perspectives, and to read through the thought-provoking opinions and observations culled from hundreds of teens nationwide, is a gift. Everything a parent needs is right here—clear, powerful, and workable.

> Lonnie Stonitsch
> Executive Director
> Family Action Network

America's favorite pediatrician, colleague, and expert on resilience is thankfully back. Dr Ginsburg reminds us once again that the sine qua non of effective parenting is unconditional love and high expectations, not only because they promote success but, just as important, because they promote resilience. Here he synthesizes research with practical expert-driven advice and weaves it together with the views from more than 500 youth to help us learn how to apply these foundational principles in our complicated world. *Raising Kids to Thrive* is equally accessible to parents and youth.

> Madeline Levine, PhD
> Stanford Graduate School of Education
> Author, *The Price of Privilege* and *Teach Your Children Well*

Parenting is as much an art as it is a science. In *Raising Kids to Thrive*, Dr Ginsburg masterfully synthesizes 2 decades of research on best practices with suggestions on how parents can creatively apply these principles to help their kids make real-life decisions in real time. This easy-to-navigate book provides a deeper dive into how parents can give unconditional love while holding kids to high expectations for effort, character, and morality, as well as how we can protect our kids while letting them learn from life's lessons. His sensible "lighthouse parenting" strategy is a balanced approach in which parents can be a stable source of inspiration and guidance. The book includes actionable concepts such as defining success as a family, emphasizing growth rather than perfection, and helping youth discover and build their "spikes"—the areas of excellence from which their unique contributions will flow.

Perhaps what I like best is that he wrote this book with his 2 teenaged daughters, Ilana and Talia. Their perspective, and that gleaned from interviews of more than 500 diverse young people across the country, is infused throughout. In this way, *Raising Kids to Thrive* resonates with SpeakUp!'s long-held belief that youth can be our teachers and that listening to other people's children is a great starting point for really hearing our own.

I have read all of Dr Ginsburg's books and think that this is the perfect complement to his portfolio of work. On behalf of the thousands of youth and families we serve, we are grateful that he has dedicated his life to promoting healthy youth development and resilience.

Martie Bernicker
SpeakUp!
St. David's, PA

Wading through conflicting "expert" parenting advice is challenging. Applying that knowledge in a way that works for your own family in real time can be downright overwhelming. How do you know when you've used those parenting skills to do the "right thing" or whether you've "blown it"? We can always count on Dr Ginsburg to translate the best of research and clinical practice into language we can understand and to coach us on structured strategies we can use at home. However, what takes this book to the next level is the richness of the youth-to-adult voices included in these pages. What do we sound like to our teens when we say "Stop that!" And how do they hear it when we say, "I love you, but I'm going to have to draw a line here." And what do they think of us when we back down to our own peer pressure because other kids' parents are doing something different from what we would prefer? And possibly most important, what do our children learn from us in those day-to-day moments when we quietly and simply "get it right"? Chances are your own kid won't tell you in those moments. But these kids have. Dr Ken's books are required reading for parents in our practice; we are thrilled to add *Raising Kids to Thrive* to our library.

Susan Sugerman, MD, MPH
President and Cofounder
Girls to Women Health and Wellness
Dallas, TX

This is a book for parents and children of any age. This book is about the stuff that really matters in our lives. Dr Ginsburg sure gets it right saying, "Kids have a real stake in parenting." We all want articulate, savvy advice for providing a stable emotional bond for our children. *Raising Kids to Thrive* provides real-life tools wed with science-based tips to make it happen.

There's beauty in this book; the list of what you'll learn reads like poetry, and the threads of advice and woven-in quotations from teens make fair parenting with thoughtful love feel very possible. The real parenting expert today is our social network, helping us shape decisions (in real life and online), so inviting Dr Ginsburg and his contributors into yours makes sense. Dr Ginsburg's approach blended to science, anecdotes, and expertise from all angles can help us parent with the love we want while providing the protection we know is essential.

Wendy Sue Swanson, MD, MBE, FAAP
Pediatrician
Seattle Children's, The Everett Clinic
Author, *Mama Doc Medicine*

With love to the one person in our home
who was not an author but without whom
we would not be a family.

Celia Pretter has offered her children the security rooted in
unconditional love, the sense of wonder to explore the world
around them, and the vision to work toward improving it.
She inspires us because she is dedicated not only to her
own family but to the well-being of all children.

We are blessed to have her
in our lives.

CONTENTS

ACKNOWLEDGMENTS

It would not be possible to thank all of the people who supported me in writing this book or inspired me to feel it should be written. First, I have to thank the American Academy of Pediatrics for its commitment to publishing the kind of credible books parents know they can always rely on and for considering me worthy of being one of their messengers. In particular, I am deeply appreciative to Mark Grimes for the vision to make this happen and to Kathryn Sparks for shepherding it through every step of the process with a real commitment to the message.

I also must thank Elyse Salek, MEd, our project manager, for working with Talia and Ilana to process the wisdom from more than 500 youth. This book, quite simply, could not have happened without Elyse's help. We are so appreciative of the critical review offered by Amy Newell of Texas and Angela Piccione of Pennsylvania, both of whom have given tremendous thought to being the kind of parent who would raise her own children to thrive.

I thank my professional mentors, Gail B. Slap, MD, and Donald Schwarz, MD, FAAP, who have had the experience to guide me, the knowledge to enlighten me, and the passion and love of youth to transmit to me. Above all, they have repeatedly demonstrated they care not just about my academic career but about me. I also thank the best teacher I ever had, Judith Lowenthal, PhD, who inspired me (when I was an adolescent) to grasp the potential in every young person. I also need to thank my colleagues at the Craig-Dalsimer Division of Adolescent Medicine at The Children's Hospital of Philadelphia for teaching me so much and being uniformly supportive of these efforts. In particular, one could only dream of having a division chief like Carol Ford, MD, who is so deeply supportive of work that supports youth and families.

I have been blessed to work in regional, national, and international settings to promote resilience. I must highlight, however, the opportunity I have had to work with an inspirational group of strength-based youth development organizations in Philadelphia. I am learning from colleagues in each of these organizations how best to engage youth and families in strategies that will help them *thrive*. We hope to take all we are learning to help programs throughout the nation understand the power of respectful, loving adult relationships in the lives of youth. Joanna Berwind, Catherine Murphy, and Trean Bock are my partners along this journey. None of it would be possible without Joanna's vision to explore the power of connections rooted in unconditional love.

My first mentors and first teachers, of course, were my parents, Arnold and Marilyn Ginsburg. I learned much of what I have come to see as good parenting in their home. I was also blessed to learn about the strength of family from my grandmother, Belle Moore, who demonstrated unconditional love better than anyone I have known, except for her daughter Marilyn. They were 2 of a kind. I hope I have passed along, in some small measure, what I learned from them to my own daughters.

I thank the young people and their families who have let me into their lives. I am awed by the love I see in parents who bring their children to me at The Children's Hospital of Philadelphia, and I hope I have served them well. I am moved by the resilience of many of my patients, in particular the youth of Covenant House Pennsylvania, who serve as a constant reminder of the tenacity and strength of the human spirit.

Finally, but most importantly, I am grateful to Celia Pretter, my wife, for raising the kind of kids who would have the passion and wherewithal to work with their father on a book that would help other families thrive as we hope to.

Ken Ginsburg

We are so grateful to the time and energy that more than 500 young people committed to this project. Their involvement concretely demonstrates how much adolescents care about healthy relationships with their parents. Members of the teen panel were integral to the writing of this book, as they helped us develop and build upon the teen-generated ideas. We are particularly appreciative of Jakub Zegar, chair of the teen panel, whose dedication throughout this project made him a valued and irreplaceable member of the team.

Ken, Ilana, and Talia Ginsburg

PREFACE

We all *want* our children to be happy, but we *need* them to be resilient. We wish we could guarantee a future for them with bountiful opportunities and manageable bumps. Because we lack this control over the future, we must prepare our children to successfully handle both good and challenging times.

I have been working to promote the healthy development and resilience of children and adolescents for more than 2 decades and have been fortunate to partner with the American Academy of Pediatrics to produce educational materials for both parents and professionals. My book *Building Resilience in Children and Teens: Giving Kids Roots and Wings* synthesizes the best of what is known about building resilience and offers many strategies parents can use to raise resilient young people.

If resilience were a trait, something you had or didn't have, there would be little we could do to foster it in our children. Part of what is so exciting—and important—about the work of youth development is that children's resilience is largely determined by how parents and communities raise them.

There are numerous strategies I and others have proposed, but there are 2 fundamental principles we all agree are at the root of resilience. First, a parent's unconditional love is the most important force in a child's life. It offers the unwavering security that helps young people develop the confidence to walk through life's puddles. The unconditional love has to be coupled with high expectations for effort, character, and morality. Otherwise, a child will feel nurtured but not learn to hold himself to high standards. Second, a child will never learn life's lessons if he is protected from experiencing them. This point has to be tempered with the fact that children need protection from challenges that can bring irreparable harm.

I have had the privilege of teaching resilience to parents and professionals throughout the world. The described principles are so fundamental to resilience that I teach them while standing on one foot to emphasize their simplicity. The clarity of this message resonates nearly universally; it tells parents what they already know in their parental bone marrow. Once they learn these core principles, parents understand that all other strategies are just details. This frees them to take comfort that they don't need an encyclopedia of parenting to raise secure kids or the latest gadget to raise successful ones. To raise their kids well, they need to do what their instinct prepares them to do.

Once parents are grounded in these core principles, I go on to teach the communication and parenting strategies that flesh out a comprehensive approach to building resilience. Because the core of resilience building is so simple and there are so many strategies to implement them, my books and presentations focus on the details.

I have taught hundreds of thousands of parents over the years in my office, through my books, and during my visits to communities. Over time, it has become increasingly clear that the questions people have are rarely about those details. Instead, they struggle to better understand the simple points, because they recognize they are really anything but simple. They want to know how to apply these core principles in a complicated world. It doesn't matter what they *know* to be right; what they wrestle with is how to *do* it.

I have come to understand there are 2 questions over which parents wrestle as they consider how to build resilience in their children.

How do I give my child the unconditional love needed to thrive while also holding him to the high expectations needed for success?
We know kids need both, but on some level these 2 concepts are in opposition to each other. Doesn't holding expectations somehow undermine the unconditional nature of love?

How do I protect my child while letting her learn life's lessons?
We parents all know intellectually that we have to get out of the way to let life be the teacher it is meant to be. We know coddled children lack the confidence to handle challenges. Yet it is absolutely our job to protect our children, and even letting our children experience emotional discomfort goes against our ingrained desire to protect them. We struggle with when to protect and when to get out of the way and watch from the sidelines.

Countless parents have asked for my guidance in reconciling their conflicting feelings about the core principles of resilience. *Raising Kids to Thrive: Balancing Love With Expectations and Protection With Trust* offers the answers parents seek. It takes a deeper dive into the essential building blocks of resilience presented earlier in *Building Resilience*. *Raising Kids to Thrive* will allow parents to think through how to put these 2 core principles into action while also learning concrete strategies to build resilience.

It will not always be able to offer definitive answers, because those answers are tightly tied to your child's unique circumstances. But I believe it will frame all of the questions clearly, so you will be able to find your own comfort zone.

If you can resolve the tension these 2 principles of resilience pose, your child will have the security she can only gain from you and the confidence she can only develop from experience. She will be more than resilient; she will be poised to thrive.

INTRODUCTION

"Tiger moms," helicopter parents, snowplow parenting, free-range parenting—these approaches grab headlines but are no way to raise your children. Other books often play on your anxiety by implying teens are out of their minds. Parenting is not a fad to be approached as the flavor of the month, and adolescence is a time to be celebrated, not feared.

When you approach parenting from the balanced perspective, you guarantee safety and foster independence, and you prepare your child to navigate the world and develop the parent-child relationship you both deserve.

Wherever there are extremes, the truth is usually found somewhere in the middle. Parenting is about finding the approaches that fit your child's temperament, needs, and circumstances. So you shouldn't hover like a helicopter, but you should watch carefully. You shouldn't pressure like a tiger mom, but with respect to your child's capabilities, you should hold her to high expectations. You shouldn't clear an obstacle- free path like a snowplow, but you must look ahead for dangers. You don't want your children to encounter the world freely with limitless freedoms, but you must understand their ingrained need to forge their own paths successfully.

Child and adolescent development has its fits and starts, but never interpret that as craziness. Never forget that each child possesses the inner wisdom to navigate life's journey. We, however, are blessed to be their guides.

We should be like lighthouses for our children—beacons of light on a stable shoreline from which they can safely navigate the world. We must make certain they don't crash against the rocks but trust they have the capacity to learn to ride the waves on their own.

Sometimes striking the right balance is harder than choosing an extreme position. The lighthouse metaphor serves as a reminder of the type of balanced parenting known to lead to the best behavioral outcomes and strongest parent-child relationships. Balance means you want to be consistently loving but authoritative when necessary. Balance means you always have to be thoughtful of and responsive to your child's needs, as well as prepared to consider an adjustment in your practice to meet changing circumstances. Sometimes balance means negotiating with another person who also cares deeply about your children but doesn't fully agree with how to raise them.

In this book, we dive deeply into 2 of the toughest questions with which we parents wrestle.

1. How do I give my child the unconditional love needed to thrive while also holding him to the high expectations needed for success?

2. How do I protect my child while letting her learn life's lessons?

If we can strike the right balance when answering these questions, we will raise resilient children who are poised to thrive through good and challenging times.

I wish I could promise you that after reading this book, you'll get everything right because I had delivered the definitive answers to these overarching questions. But these questions are far too complex to have universally appropriate answers. And nobody gets everything right, partly because there isn't always a right. "Cookbooks" for parenting almost always fall flat because the authors know neither your kids nor your circumstances. Only you can make decisions responsive to the needs of your child and household. My daughters and I, therefore, hope to further empower you to give thoughtful, informed consideration to these toughest of questions.

And for the record, I write books on parenting, but I don't get everything right…not nearly so. Ask my girls.

This book offers 3 approaches to help you build the perspective that will allow you to make well-informed decisions.

- It offers you science. There are real answers to some of these questions. We know how some approaches to parenting affect children's emotional and behavioral well-being.

- It offers clearly framed questions. We hope the clarity with which these struggles are illuminated will foster reflection and start honest conversations in your home and community.

- It exposes you to adolescent viewpoints. Adolescents are the people who are experiencing your parenting right now. They may not have lived many years, but they understand the world they interact with better than we ever could. They know when they feel supported and when they feel controlled. They know what they need to thrive. Sometimes our own kids do a good job of communicating in a way that shuts down our ability to hear them. Here is an opportunity to listen to youth and imagine your child sharing his thoughts and experiences. You'll be surprised by how thoughtful kids are when they are given an opportunity to be our teachers, as well as how much easier it can be to hear other people's kids when what they say doesn't feel quite so personal. That doesn't mean you'll always agree with their views, but it may be helpful to hear their thoughts as a starting point for better communication with your own child.

Why Include Adolescents as Experts Here?

Parenting books rarely, if ever, include youth insights and perspectives, but this one does.

Kids have a real stake in parenting. They may not have gone to parenting seminars or read volumes on raising children, but they know what it feels like to be parented. They know what they need. Kids may not grasp the worry we feel and why we so desperately want to protect them. They may not comprehend the guilt so many of us feel for not being able to be as available to them as we had hoped. They may not understand the fear we have for their futures and our desire to give them a leg up, but what they fully grasp is their own lives, the environment they need to plot a course through, and how they react to our guidance, support, and criticism.

Put simply, youth lack the wisdom of years but nonetheless are the authorities on their own lives.

This book is about exploring 2 fundamental questions with which we struggle. There is some useful information to guide us, but these questions are so vast that good parents will continue to wrestle with them on a case-by-case basis. None of us are alone. Parents before us and alongside of us have considered these same issues and did the best they could, sometimes striking the right balance and sometimes missing the mark entirely. Each parenting decision ultimately had its greatest impact on children and youth.

When parenting styles miss the mark wildly, the next generation raises their children in a way that tries to correct for the "failings" of their parents. (As they do so, they may learn their parents didn't fail as much as they had thought, as well as discover that parenting is the most challenging, gratifying job imaginable.) There are serious limitations to drawing from the successes or challenges of our parents. First, it takes a generation to make the corrections. Second, we are putting too much emphasis on our personal experience. Third, we sometimes overcorrect, going in an opposite and uncharted direction.

Real-life decisions have to be made in real time. You do not have a generation to correct ill-fated approaches; you will make decisions today for your child's tomorrow. Why not get immediate feedback from those who can directly report how different approaches to parenting affect kids?

Ultimately, I want you to get to the point at which you and your own children can have thoughtful discussions about these issues. A step in that direction is hearing from other kids first. More than 500 young people participated in writing this book. My 18-year-old daughters, Ilana and Talia, synthesize these young people's views in Chapter 16 and 17. Simultaneously, these young people's ideas "float" throughout the book. They are there to reinforce points, give an alternative view, or offer a poignant moment of reflection. Let me underscore the point: although I am generally humbled by their wisdom, I do not always agree with everything these young people say. Regardless of whether or not a given point of theirs reinforces my views, I know a critical step for each of us in reaching our own child is understanding how she views the world. The breadth of views in this book may help you better understand your child's vantage point. (If you wish to learn about how the youth were recruited, as well as read some descriptions of who they are before you take in their thoughts, see Chapter 15.)

When Is the Right Time to Read This Book?

Now. Whether you have a toddler or a teen, this book can offer insights and information on how to be the kind of parent you want to be.

Many points we discuss come to a head during adolescence. It is during the teen years you'll have a sense of whether or not your child is poised for success. It is then you'll know whether or not your child can bounce from adversity and grow from failure. Any behavioral concerns take on more dangerous proportions during this time. For this reason, many of our examples are drawn from the teen years.

If your child is an adolescent now, your added support can make a big difference in guiding him in a positive direction. Never believe it is too late to reboot your relationship. This book ends with thoughts on how to improve communication between the 2 of you and increase your potential to effectively guide your child.

If you have a toddler or young child, now is the time to put into place the parenting style and communication strategies that will prepare her for happiness and success far into the future. Now is the time to help her develop a wide repertoire of coping strategies to manage life's stressors. Equipped with those healthy means of managing life's challenges, she will be less likely to turn to worrisome quick fixes later. Now is the time to create the kind of relationship that assures safety while honoring her growing independence. Children who feel secure, without feeling controlled, have less to rebel against in the teen years and may be more comfortable managing their own lives throughout adulthood.

It is never too early (or too late!) to put into place the parenting strategies that prepare your child to *thrive* far into the future.

Thoughts From Teens

My mom always says, "You are who you hang with," "You are what you eat," etc. She says it so much that those sayings pop in my head all the time. My advice is for parents to say your sayings; know I listen, even though you think I don't.

—16-year-old female, Alaska

Please, please, please be patient with [your kids], and don't yell at them or show that you are exasperated with them. Just take a deep breath and get through it. Please love them with all your heart.

—13-year-old female, Illinois

If I am standing on the cliff of my wildest dreams, please let me jump. I know I might get a few cuts and bruises along the way, but at least I had the courage to jump. And that courage comes from knowing you will always be there when I need you.

—15-year-old female, Kentucky

I hope that I can always be that rock for my children, as my mother has been for me. I hope to be a role model of "feeling." As much as I share joy, triumph, and accomplishment, I also want to share tears and sadness. I want them to understand that I am not someone who wants to "control" them; I am here to "guide" them through the crazy journey of life. I will support them no matter the situation, because I know the importance of having support when I was trying to figure out who I was in this world.
—Stephanie Lefthand, 19-year-old, Texas

I want to be the kind of father who has a son that says, "I want to be the kind of father my dad was."
—18-year-old male, Texas

I want to be the kind of parent that…leads by example, not by threats and disappointment.
—17-year-old male, New Jersey

I want my children to be able to tell me EVERYTHING and ANYTHING. I never want them to feel like I am not there for them.
—15-year-old female, California

Sometimes a parent just has to listen. Make sure they have someone to talk to. Sometimes I say, "Mom, I need you to shut up and just listen to me, because I need someone to talk to." Parents have to be more willing to listen and judge less.
—Anonymous

PART

1

Unconditional Love Versus High Expectations

How do I give my child the unconditional love needed to thrive while also holding him to the high expectations needed for success?

We know our unconditional love is the fundamental protective force in our children's lives. We also know that because kids live up or down to our expectations, we had better set them high.

These 2 forces seem to be in direct opposition. Doesn't our need to set expectations mean we must apply conditions? Let's reconcile this contradiction.

What You Will Learn

We hope to build the case that you can give unconditional love *and* hold your child to high expectations. It is about what those high expectations are and how they are conveyed. I invite you to wrestle over the points I make and to discuss them with your partner, relatives, friends, and children.

This is not a suspense novel, so here is a summary of the points I will make over the next few chapters.

- Love does not spoil kids; it only makes them sweeter.

- Unconditional love is a protective force that is the foundation of emotional security.

- When conditions are put on love in the home in which we are raised, they can make us question our worth over our entire lifetime.

- No parent intentionally makes love conditional, but if we are not thoughtful about how we communicate our expectations, it can feel judgmental. Judgment, by its simplest definition, sets a condition, acceptable or not.

- Our connection to our children is the most protective factor in their lives. But a connection that makes them reliant on us to meet their every need undermines their long-term well-being.

- To wisely convey expectations, it is important first to remind ourselves that our goal is to raise a child who will become a successful, moral adult.

- Unrestrained praise is not the way to show our unconditional love. It can make kids anxious about disappointing us and worried about trying things that may not gain accolades.

- We should hold our children to the highest expectations in terms of character. By doing so, we help them remain stable, centered, and self-aware as they navigate life's waves.

- We must be careful when we use performance standards as expectations. A focus on grades, scores, and awards can make a young person feel as if she is not acceptable unless she meets those standards. This unstable footing can undermine the key ingredients needed for success and even for healthy moral development.

- When we accept that people are uneven and learn to celebrate our children's strengths and accept their limitations, those areas in which they are destined to make their greatest contributions will naturally reveal themselves.

- Sometimes children who are not meeting our expectations are reacting to standards they cannot achieve and choosing to pretend they don't care. More pressure doesn't help.

- We want our kids to know our expectations include setbacks, even failures, and all we want is for them to grow from each stumble. Our expectation is growth, not perfection.

- When we expect our children to put their greatest effort toward all endeavors, they will develop confidence in their talents and learn to accept their unevenness (if we do).

- We must expect behavior that is safe and moral, no exceptions. The borders must be clear. Children will have the opportunity within those boundaries to take chances, so they can learn self-control and how to recover from inevitable mistakes.

CHAPTER

1

The Protective Force of Parental Love

From the moment your baby grasped your finger, you knew you were forever connected. You felt a kind of love people tried to explain to you but was unimaginable until you held this sacred being in your arms. As you put your child in the infant seat to leave the hospital, suddenly you became instinctually aware of your baby's vulnerability and knew it was your job to protect her. Any dreams you ever had for yourself paled in comparison to those you now held for your child.

A supportive nurturing connection between parent and child offers the deep-seated security so critical to well-being and healthy development. This connection is the bedrock of the serve-response relationship that starts in infancy. First, babies (toddlers, children, and even adolescents!) do something to get our attention (serve). Then, when we respond to their action, they learn what they do matters, and this is an underpinning of the sense of control over their lives that healthy children need. As we respond with awe to the miracles of development and affectionately to the excitement our children experience with every new discovery, we reinforce their curiosity and love of learning. In turn, their passion for knowledge will build their intelligence. Parental nurturing has even been found to be highly protective through the worst of times. Adverse childhood experiences have been shown to negatively affect health and well-being far into adulthood, *unless* a responsive loving adult stands solidly alongside the child through even traumatic circumstances. This makes our parental role as resilience-builders crucial to helping our children remain strong, and even to gain wisdom, through life's challenges.

> Always promise love. That's the promise you made when you decided to have a child.
>
> —16-year-old female, New Jersey

Love Without Conditions

Love only offers security if it is given without conditions. This is certainly true for children, but it remains true for people throughout their lifespans. When children are loved unconditionally, they know they are worthy based on their being, not their doing. Unconditional love allows people to take chances when they need to adapt to new circumstances because they needn't fear disapproval, recrimination, or abandonment. They are safe. They are acceptable. They are valued, even when they doubt themselves. Ideally, parents are an unwavering source of this essential ingredient of stability and well-being, but the more supportive adults are in a child's life, the more firmly rooted and unshakeable his security.

Unconditional love doesn't mean unconditional approval. Part of being a loving parent is being clear about what is acceptable and what is not. But we can reject a behavior entirely while simultaneously loving the child fully. Love must never be withdrawn or threatened to be withheld based on a behavior or disappointing performance. Rather, part of loving is being present to mold our children into their best selves—not our vision of who they should be but who they are. Unconditional love is not based on performance; it is based on a child's inherent worth. Our children cannot be seen as reflections of us. Frankly, when we see them as representing us, we may never find them satisfactory, especially if we have doubts of our own value. We must be proud of who they truly are and not of the bumper stickers we place on our cars based on what they do.

Your child must know that you are not going anywhere, no matter what. Your presence is the one thing to be counted on, even if the rest of the world seems unpredictable.

" Remind them that you loved them from the moment they were born—when they were tiny, feeble, and useless. If you loved them then, you can love them now. **"**

—18-year-old female, Texas

What Happens When We Put Conditions on Our Affection and Attention?

Just as unconditional love is the root of security, questioning whether one is genuinely loved is a source of pain and uneasiness. We are designed to need others; we are driven to reinforce the sense that we belong. From the moment children gaze into their parents' eyes, they need to draw the comfort that comes from a stable attachment. When we were infants and toddlers, we did whatever it took to gain our parents' attention. We did the same as teenagers, for better or worse. Our fundamental need was to know we were cared about. Our moments of greatest angst, or perhaps ongoing sources of internal conflict, derive from questioning whether we were acceptable.

We hope children perform well because it generates self-satisfaction. Ideally, they put in their greatest effort because they are internally motivated to achieve growth. When, on the other hand, their performance is to gain approval, it generates anxiety. This unsettling anxiety might translate into perfectionism or a young person choosing to feign indifference. Perfectionism destroys many of the elements a person needs to be successful. On the other hand, young people who invest their energy in pretending they don't care, usually because they care too much, will shun the very effort needed to ensure their success. Or worse, they will take on risky behaviors that deaden their senses so they need not experience their real feelings.

It Is Not About What You Feel But Rather How Your Child Interprets Your Messages

There is not a single parent reading these words who does not deeply love her child. Not one reader is intentionally putting conditions on his love. To the extent that any of us are holding our children to strict standards, it is undoubtedly with the best of intentions to make our expectations clear.

The last thing I would ever do is imply I could offer you advice on how to love your child unconditionally. The best I can do is underscore the vital importance of such love and gently guide you to reflect on the possibility that your child may be misinterpreting your intentions as you guide her toward success.

> 66 Families should make time to be together. They have to slow down and get back to basics. 99
>
> —14-year-old male, Texas

Your love is not in question. But you may want to consider if the way in which you convey your high expectations might inadvertently convey a message of conditional acceptance. Your messages of disappointment can be conveyed by word, deed, or body language. Your intention is the starting point, but what really matters are the messages your child receives.

If your child feels like his behaviors elicit judgment, good or bad, he will feel his relationship with you is on shaky ground; he will view the security of his connection as dependent on his performance (for more on the importance of not judging performance, see Chapter 5, High Expectations Gone Awry: The Problem With Focusing Mainly on Academic Performance). I am not suggesting you can never praise or criticize but that you do so in a way that is loving and honors the potential for growth.

It Is Not About What You Feel But Rather if Your Child Knows What You Feel

Some parents feel love is something that is shown, never discussed. They worry words such as *I love you* will spoil their child. Rest assured that loving words and displays of affection do not spoil children; they only make them sweeter.

One mother shared a story of why it is so important to her that she consistently and clearly communicates her affection toward her teenaged son and daughter:

As a child, I never heard the comforting words I love you from my mother, and I missed them terribly. After I became a parent, I summoned the courage to ask her why she never told me how she felt. She replied, "Well, my mother taught me to never say that to your child. If you do, your child will take advantage of you." My mother went on to tell me that she showed me she loved me by how she cared for me. That may be, but I remember longing for those words as a child. I choose to tell my children I love them every day, and as a result I have 2 beautiful, confident children. There is no price tag on the words I love you. Today, as adults, my mother and I now say, "I love you," to each other every day. I believe she is now no longer afraid to say it because she saw how secure and gracious my kids turned out to be.

“ Parents should always have love that's unconditional for their child. It doesn't matter what their kid did or does; a parent should alwaaaaaaays have unconditional love for their child, and they should tell them that. **”**

—17-year-old female, Pennsylvania

66 Unconditional love should always be there, no matter what they do, because if children's parents don't love them, they might think that they are unlovable and that if no one loves them there is no point in living. Children should feel that no matter what they do, their parents will always love them, because that is what parents are for. 99

—14-year-old female, Massachusetts

Men, in particular, might have trouble with the language of love. There is no doubt in my mind that men have the same capacity to love their children as women do. Nevertheless, society's traditional views of masculinity do not include nurturance. Thankfully, our culture is evolving, and men are now freer to show the intensity of their feelings toward their children. In my view, we will have a stronger and emotionally healthier society when caring for and about children is considered the pinnacle of masculinity.

Many men were raised by fathers who may have displayed loving actions but rarely, if ever, expressed their feelings verbally. Their affection was understood by the physicality of their presence. They stood solidly at the sports games and beamed with pride at the recitals. They were human jungle gyms, wrestled with their kids, tousled their daughters' hair, and gave their sons attaboy squeezes on their neck. Loving words were absent.

The challenge for men raised this way is they may not have learned how powerful and meaningful loving words can be. This becomes a problem when they are separated by distance from their children, whether because of divorce, military deployment, or frequent business travel. Neither the physicality of presence, nor a reassuring pat on the shoulder, works through Skype. Words are sometimes all we have. Again, there is nothing more masculine than a man who knows how to tell his children they are cherished.

There is nothing more any parent can do to raise a successful, moral child or to foster a secure, long-standing connection than to express love for that child unconditionally.

66 As someone who struggles with the fear of disappointment, I always know that even if I do make perhaps not the best decision, as I have done before, my mother is always there to back me up. After some explanation of why this may or may not have been the best choice for me, she will always tie it back to her love and support for me. 99

—19-year-old female, Texas

More Thoughts From Teens

My parents expecting me to do well makes me want to do even better than they think I will. Knowing that whatever I choose to do well won't affect my parents' love for me is what motivates me to follow my dreams. Yes, my parents might want me to do certain things, but they don't FORCE me to do it. Forcing your teen to do something makes them want to do the opposite. An example of how a parent could communicate in a way that both offers unconditional love and holds their child to high expectations would be saying, "Of course I'll support anything you choose to do, but I want you to always do your best in what you choose, and choose it for the right reason."

—17-year-old female, Pennsylvania

Parents should understand that things they love will fail at times, so they must be forgiving but not accepting of the failure. Parents should be allies and always willing to support their child but not be a friend. So they should also encourage them positively. It is nice when a parent leaves a little "love you" Post-it or says that they are proud of how he or she is handling setbacks.... Sometimes parents' love gets lost in translation over time, and we kids just need to hear it once in a while.

—17-year-old female, Illinois

I think unconditional love should function like the confidentiality clauses at doctors—unconditional support and committed confidentiality unless there is a risk of harm to oneself or others. My B on my report card won't ruin my life; it doesn't mean it should be ignored, but it also doesn't mean that I need to be yelled at over it. If I don't get into the college of my dreams, that is MY problem, not my parents'. The expectations of unconditional love should be clear: if you hurt or consider hurting yourself or someone around you, the love is put on hold until safety and equilibrium are reached. A teen is constantly feeling like no one likes them, and the last thing they need to think is that their parents won't love them or will think less of them if they don't make varsity or get a 5.0 and a full ride. There are things I didn't tell my father because I didn't want him to look down on me; I thought that he'd love me less if he knew about the indiscretions I'd made in my personal life. I feared that he'd cut off communication if I admitted I'd snuck out and gone to a party or that I'd kissed a guy I barely knew. I feared that the person I was wasn't the person my dad wanted me to be, and, thus, I ended up lying to cover. Parents need to make clear where they stand on morals and expectations, but they need to make clearer that their love won't cease unless someone is in harm's way.

—Anonymous

I was raised to who I am through unconditional love, tough love, and high expectations. To this day, I do not want to disappoint my parents with anything that I do, even if it's a bad grade. It is more of my own conscience that I do not want to disappoint my parents, because they have always told me as long as I am happy with who I am, they will be too. But I can't help but want to make them happy, go to college, graduate, and become a child they are proud of. I think parents need to realize that setting high expectations is sometimes a lot of pressure on their kids. A parent should always have unconditional love for their kids and never "revoke" it when they mess up. Children, teens especially, need to know that through everything, whether it is a rebelling stage, drugs, partying, grades slipping, relationship problems, drama—whatever it is—they need to know parents will always provide them with unconditional love and help them with whatever it may be.

—19-year-old female, Texas

CHAPTER

2

Why Does Love Sometimes Feel Like a One-way Street?

It might be frustrating for you to hear me preaching about the power of unconditional love, while your teen daughter sometimes finds the way you breathe embarrassing.

If you are a parent of a preteen, I want you to be prepared that there may be a period of time coming when you will be asked to practice being invisible. During these moments, your child's behavior can push you away or make you reflexively withhold your love just because it is often unrequited. I am covering this here so you will never make the expression of your love conditional on how your teen is treating you.

If you understand the following 4 key points, you'll make it through this phase and remain as close as ever with your child, even as she works to convince herself that you are not needed.

Point 1
They Have to Distinguish Themselves From Us

It is hard to fathom how your loving, huggable child who had consistently expressed he wanted to be you when he grew up suddenly finds you totally awkward. A good starting point is to remember that adolescents need to focus on figuring out the answer to the all-encompassing "Who am I?" question. Part of that answer has to be, "Not you!" It's hard to come up with that answer when your child knows he looks like you, talks like you, walks like you, and may even agree with your political views. All teens are also answering the "Am I normal?" question by looking around and comparing themselves to others. They exist in the imaginary theater ("all the world's a stage, and I am the main actor"), believing that others must be scrutinizing them the same way they are observing others. Your teen has enough trouble constantly managing being on display, without also having to worry about what other people might be thinking about you. Therefore, your teen believes it would be easier if you could learn to be around ("to drive and stuff") without being seen.

Point 2
Sometimes They Have a Right to Be Mad at Us

Adolescence is a time when an individual moves from having concrete to abstract thought. Concrete thinkers see the world as it is presented to them. Abstract thinkers can see the what-ifs and sometimes get frustrated by what is. It is, therefore, a time of great idealism, as well as righteous indignation. Sometimes we are the objects of the accompanying frustration.

Although we might long for the time when our kids saw us as perfect, isn't it kind of exciting that they now view everything, including us, as more complex? They seem to have "what is wrong" sensors so they can begin imagining how to fix it. This is exactly why adolescents are our future; our progress depends on their imagination. However, it's not always easy when they are expressing how much fixing they think we need.

How you handle this criticism may make a difference in your child's development. People are a work in progress, including you and your teen. When you reject your teen's advice/criticism outright, you are communicating that feedback is uniformly destructive. When you listen, gently guiding how the message can be delivered, you communicate that advice can be constructive. For example, you might say, "I hear what you are saying, but it's hard to listen when I am being yelled at. Say it again, a bit calmer, so I can try to learn from this." As importantly, you communicate that growth is a lifelong process and one to celebrate. Your teen will absorb this message and feel safer being imperfect now *and* in the future.

This is also a great opportunity to facilitate further conversation in which your teen can grow and you both can benefit. If your teen is spot-on, thank her for the advice and say you will reflect on it and try to improve. If your teen feels you have treated him unfairly, and after consideration you agree, start with an apology. You could say, "You know what. You're right. I'm really sorry. Tell me what I could have done differently." If he is calm enough, you can add, "All I want is for you to be safe, responsible, and happy. But it sounds like what I said didn't get that across at all." This is an amazing opportunity to reboot your relationship. See Part 4, Rebooting: Moving Toward the Relationship You Hope to Have, for getting important conversations started.

❝ At a young age, we rarely see the flaws in our parents; we believe that whatever our parents tell us is right. Therefore, it is much easier for younger children to accept whatever parents say. ❞

—17-year-old female, unknown state

Point 3
Development Is a Tough Process, and They Have to Do It (Mostly) on Their Own

You might notice that when our children are going through something and should need us the most, they sometimes push us away the hardest. Children mature in fits and starts. Whenever an important, new milestone is about to be crossed, your child may regress a bit or be uncontrollably moody. Sometimes you will be on the receiving end of her moodiness. This is frustrating but normal.

Imagine every developmental milestone as a chasm that needs to be crossed. It is 12 feet wide and 100 feet deep—far enough to see across but not so close that you know how to get to the other side confidently. There are crocodiles crawling along the bottom and, of course, rusty metal spikes. You've got to get to the other side, but you are terrified of falling in and dare not look down. You can't overthink it, because it will psyche you out.

Think about how your child will leap across that chasm. I know your first thought is likely, "I'll build her a bridge!" The problem is she's got to do this on her own. And if you do the building, she'll knock it down. Instead, she'll take several steps backward to get a running start before she leaps and covers her eyes as she soars across.

Visualize every major developmental stage or challenge as a chasm our children worry about crossing. Don't be surprised when they take several steps backward before their next attempt to move forward. And expect them to sometimes leap with blinders on. They have to stop thinking, suppress their fears, and jump! No wonder a 10-year-old about to start a new middle school or a ninth grader about to enter high school seems cranky, irrational, and occasionally thoughtless before these required leaps. Before we rush to judgment, we must understand it is difficult for even the most emotionally intelligent adults to be so in touch with their emotions that they can be clearly articulated, especially in times of change or crisis.

Rather, adults, too, come up with the rationales that allow them to move blindly forward, sometimes against their instinctual desire to hold onto familiarity.

Why don't our children come to us and ask us to help them build that bridge across the chasm? We have the experience and are more than eager to share it! They actually do engage our help but just not directly. They sometimes seek our attention in ways that anger or frustrate us but manage to get our attention. Don't let being pushed away make you believe your child needs you less during major transitions. The challenge is giving enough support that he feels secure while also clearly communicating with your relative hands-off demeanor that you trust he can cross on his own. Hovering only gets you forcibly pushed away or makes your child give in to his fears and perceived incompetence. Kids pushing parents away when they need us most does not start in adolescence. Remember the moment your child took those first steps? Rocking on his legs and wiggling his butt in the air just before he pulled himself up to stand? What happened after those first steps? He fell, and you ran over. He may have wanted to say, "Gee, thanks. I sure appreciate your support, but I need to assert my independence right now." Instead, he swatted you away.

Remember when she was 2 years old and would jabber along with those 2-word sentences? She was frustrated because she had more on her mind than her words could convey. So you helped out by finishing her thoughts. She might have wanted to say, "Gosh, thanks. It's challenging to find the right words, so I am appreciative of your help." Instead, she snorted, "No! Me talk!"

And that first date? What an opportunity to really dive deeply into the subject of morality in the context of sexuality. This is the talk you have been practicing since the first day of preschool when she came home and asked, "What makes a boy a boy? Why don't I have one of those?" She wants to pour her heart out, snuggle up to you, and say, "I'm so scared, Dad. I always thought it would be easy; I was going to marry you." Instead, she comments on how you are always "soooooo awkward," and she knows everything there is to know anyway. She says she learned it in health class. (But secretly, you fear her friends texted her the answers last night.)

We parents want the last year before our children attend college to be memorable. We'll want special "dates" during which we can connect deeply while reassuring ourselves we've passed along all our pearls of wisdom and transmitted all our safety rules. "Does he know not to run with scissors?!" "I have to remind her never to put aluminum foil in the microwave!" Why, then, do our children desperately in need of our wisdom say, "Are you kidding? I have so little time left with my friends." Right before they move out, you'll want them to say, "Thanks so much for everything you've done to prepare me for the world. Can I call you between classes or at least send cute little texts to let you know I am thinking of you?" But realistically they may say, "It's a good thing I'm out of here, because I couldn't stand one more minute in this prison." Why might they say this? Because it's easier than saying, "Do you think you'll miss me as much as I'm already missing you?"

Point 4
They Are Uncomfortable With How Much They Love Us

For your sense of well-being, it is critical to understand why our adolescents sometimes go farther than just finding us awkward or pushing us away; sometimes they seem to hate us! The truth is our children love us so intensely it makes them uncomfortable; therefore, they push those feelings away as forcefully as they can.

They love me too much?! Seriously? Yes, seriously. If you can suspend your disbelief for a moment and listen to your heart, this will ring true. Then your child's adolescence will be far easier because you will find it easier to remain unconditionally loving. You'll still have moments when you are ready to explode and lament that your child does not *deserve* all you have done for him, but you'll be able to catch yourself and restore your loving feelings by remembering, "He loves me so much it hurts."

At puberty, the brain is triggered to prepare a child to become a man or a woman. Adolescence is about getting ready to fly on your own; it is about growing wings. Up until this triggering event, your child has been well cared for and quite content living comfortably in your nest. Why would anybody feel good about leaving a warm and cozy nest? As he begins to understand he will need to fly, the nest begins to feel prickly (think 12- to 14-year-olds). By the time he is ready to launch, the nest must seem absolutely uninhabitable (think second half of senior year). Our kids sometimes act as if they can't stand us because they can't otherwise imagine going. They'll remember again how deeply they feel about us after they realize they can fly on their own. Hopefully, at that point they will return for many landings.

Should I Expect My Teen to Be Trouble? Or to Reject Me?

There is a real danger to preparing a parent for a potentially tumultuous adolescence. While all young people will have their moments, most parents will cherish the adolescent years. Personally, I found it uplifting to watch my girls gain new understandings of the complexities of life, have been endlessly entertained by their more sophisticated senses of humor, and have so enjoyed the glimpses of the adults they are to be.

You must not expect problems because kids will produce the behaviors you expect. Furthermore, if they catch you lamenting the loss of childhood, they will feel rejected as they grow. This will add to the anxiety they already have about getting older.

On the other hand, expect some pushing away. That way, it will be less likely to trigger your anger or frustration, which will only heighten the tension.

You should be well armed with an understanding of adolescent development so you won't be taken by surprise and will be more able to ignore demeaning portrayals of teens you hear around you. If you hear a parent complaining endlessly about her 14-year-old daughter, she is telling a story. It would not be interesting if she were to add, "But most of the time, she's just terrific. Last night, we spent an hour cuddling." That's not a story!

The next time someone tells you, "Uh-oh, she's almost 13; buckle up," nod politely, smile, and say, "I'm looking forward to the ride. There will be some bumps, but I am sure she'll come through just fine. She has already proven what a fine person she is."

The next time your teen says, "I can't stand you!" don't let your buttons get pushed, as that will escalate the matter and leave you feeling awful later. Take a time-out. Walk away. Smile inside and say to yourself, "She hates how much she loves me."

Successful adults never stop learning in the workplace. They see constructive criticism as an opportunity for growth rather than a personal attack. They see intelligence as something built through work and experience; it is not something present or absent.

Successful 35-, 40-, and 50-year-olds are resilient. Rather than lamenting their shortcomings, they seek growth. Rather than cursing the darkness, they seek light. They are not easily defeated; they know how to recover and to use adversity as a means to build their strength.

Of course, success also includes being able to earn a living and attain a good education. I believe all of the points discussed significantly enhance one's ability to do so while finding meaning and satisfaction in what they do.

Morality

Children are a magnificent blend of selfishness and altruism. They are born as pleasure-seeking machines, seeking comfort and happiness precisely when they need it—immediately. They behave as if the world revolves around them, and in a sense it does because they are helpless to meet their own needs. They are described as *egocentric* to capture the me-centeredness of their actions and behaviors. At the same time, an empathy toward other children and living creatures appears as early as the toddler years and is well-grounded by preschool. I will never forget 4-year-old Talia explaining to me why she felt it was important to spend time with Eeyore. "He seems so sad, but I know when he is with me, I can at least make him happy."

Our challenge as parents is to mold our children into the moral beings we hope for them to become. Over time, they will have to learn to control impulses that offer momentary pleasure but put them at risk. We need to help them develop an inner compass that guides them to make decisions and always take into consideration how their actions affect others.

This discussion of morality is not separate from our understanding of success. Morality is certainly tied into one's commitment to repairing the world and lifting others up. It is also tightly linked to social and emotional intelligences and one's collaborative spirit. It is difficult to be genuinely collaborative if you don't have authentic respect toward others.

66 When it comes to things that could hurt other people, you should step in with a loving hand to teach your children right from wrong. 99

—14-year-old female, Maine

Holding our kids to high moral standards will also be a critical element in striking the balance between protecting our children and letting them learn from life's lessons. Central to finding the right balance is putting into place appropriate monitoring and boundaries that assure safety and morality issues never go beyond our designated outer limits. Then, however, we must allow kids to determine their behaviors within those boundaries. For our children to be able to do this wisely, we need them to have a clear-cut set of values and reasonable decision-making skills.

When morality is preached and not lived, even young children sense our hypocrisy. To paraphrase Ralph Waldo Emerson, our actions can speak so loudly that children cannot hear the words we say. Our role is to be the stable moral compass on the shoreline, the lighthouse, from which they can measure their behaviors. Children listen to what we say about our neighbors. If they hear us talk about inclusion but don't see us practicing it, our words will ring hollow. If they hear us warn of the perils of drugs but see us escape our feelings primarily through drinking, it is not our words that will be heeded.

> **❝** We're going to question you with everything, because that's just how we are. Instead of shutting us down with, "Because I said so," which I know sometimes is necessary, explain why and your reasoning behind it and not in a patronizing way…. **❞**
>
> —16-year-old female, New Jersey

What's Love Got to Do With It?

Let's take a moment to recap some of the key elements a person needs to be successful and lead a moral life. Successful adults are generous of spirit, compassionate, and empathetic. They have the moral imperative to improve the lot of others and consistently take into consideration how their actions affect others. Children raised with unconditional love feel secure enough to look outside of themselves and safe enough to take the chance and consider others' needs. On the other hand, when young people perceive the love they receive is dependent on their performance or behavior, it becomes difficult for them to see outside their own efforts and feel worthy. They will have earned the right to be selfish or to see only in the moment.

> 66 I think there is a good way to balance support and direction. You can lovingly give your children guidance. Unconditional love should be absolute. Expectations should be expected to vary as the child grows. 99
>
> —17-year-old female, Pennsylvania

When it comes to being a good person—considerate, respectful, honest, fair, generous, responsible—your standards should be uncompromisingly high. You have earned the right to hold your child to high expectations in a way that nobody else could. It is your knowledge of who your child *really* is that will get him through the worst of times. It is our living and active memory of how very special our children are that will restore them to their better selves during those moments when their behavior is unacceptable.

> 66 Accept kids for who they are and not focus on their faults. We make mistakes too. 99
>
> —13-year-old male, Washington

I am blessed with 2 wonderful daughters. They're 18 years old now. By definition, we've had our *moments*. It is during those moments my unwavering awareness of the beauty inside of them paid off. Sure, they might have had an attitude momentarily. They might have been disrespect-ful, acted thoughtlessly, or said something hurtful enough that it easily could have pushed my buttons and thrown me into a tirade of emotions and recriminations. Precisely because of how much I cared, I would have been set up to explode. If I didn't care, my emotions would not reside so close to the surface.

During those tenuous moments, I saw my girls for who they were, not how they behaved. Only my wife and I can thoroughly understand what compassionate, sensitive young ladies they are. They are the little girls who used to run to me as I got off the train, screaming, "Abbi's home! Abbi's home!" Talia is the girl who was deeply devastated at the age of 4 when she first understood where meat came from. "Did you know some people are eating real chickens when they eat chicken? Why would they do that? Don't they like chickens?" Ilana is the girl who spent all of her birthday money to buy me a special pillow, and she gave it to me saying, "If you sleep better, it will change your *whooooole* life." They are the girls who wouldn't let us kill bugs. They hated us turning off the lights in the summertime, because they didn't want the hovering moths to get lost. They made us guide them out of our house with flashlights so they could rejoin their moth grandmas. Funny, funny little girls. Adventurous. They had laughs that could fill any silence and hearts the size of Montana. Even now, I don't know anybody who wants to protect their friends from unwise decisions more than they do. They are loyal, concerned, sensitive young people.

When we had our momentary lapses into dysfunction, as all families do, I needed only to reconnect with how passionately I cherished them. In moments of anger, I needed only to visualize the little girls inside the young women. I needed only to reframe their anger into passion, their volatility into sensitivity. It took some deep breaths sometimes and even some self-talk to calm myself to the point that I could set aside my own frustration and focus instead on remembering their overwhelming strengths. Once I was there, my demeanor changed instantly. The energy I was transmitting changed from frustration to adoration. Maybe it showed through a glint in my eye. Maybe it became apparent on some deeper level that words don't have the capacity to describe. But it was a palpable change, at least to my daughters. Negativity would subside. I could then become part of the solution, in sharp contrast to further escalating whatever underlying issue first stirred the emotions.

This is what I really mean by high expectations. Children need at least one person (more is better) who is absolutely, exuberantly, and irrationally in love with them. This love is not really irrational because it is rooted in a child's essential goodness, the core of her being that only her parents fully understand.

This is especially critical during adolescence. Teens receive plenty of messages saying they are lazy, argumentative, thoughtless, self-centered, or unstable. Kids sense these low expectations. "Why," they figure, "should I be any different?" Remember, the fundamental question of adolescence is, "Who am I?" Young people care as deeply about its related question, "Am I normal?" They hunt for clues of what normal is and mimic those portrayals. We must not allow our children to answer these critical life-shaping ques- tions by filling in the blanks with others' low expectations. If you are a parent of a minority child, this point may be of particular importance to you. Tragically, we live in a world where minority youth are disproportionately showered with messages of low expectations.

We have to fight all of these messages as a society. We have to reframe teenagers as our greatest hope: idealistic, passionate people who are committed to justice, have a righteous indignation against inexplicable realities, and are formulating a vision filled with better possibilities.

This starts in each of our homes.

Our children are programmed to get all of the resources—time, love, attention—they can get from us. They learn what gets attention from us and repeat that behavior often. When your child was 2 years old, you quickly grasped how to elicit good behavior: catch him being good; redirect him when he's not. The same principle applies throughout childhood and during adolescence. Nevertheless, as our kids grow we tend to increasingly focus on what they are doing wrong. We falsely believe this will reap the highest yield of our limited time. This strategy backfires because our kids quickly adjust their behaviors to maximize our attention. They ratchet those attention-getting behaviors up a notch or so. Let's return to what we knew when they were toddlers as a tried-and-true approach to encouraging desired behaviors. Let's remember the core goodness we know exists and expect to see that. Rather than placing negative labels on our children's character ("you're lazy," "you're selfish"), let's remind them of how we know they *can* do better ("I know you'll help your sister out because I remember how generous you were with your time when your brother really needed you").

I found a series of reminders over the years to be really helpful. I celebrated milestones in my girls' lives with memory boxes or letters. In each, I recalled those stories I thought best defined who they were. The boxes and letters were filled with funny stories, but the overriding motivation was to document my girls' growing character development. I captured those instances that demonstrated how deep their values have always been. My sense was they genuinely benefitted from being aware of how much I was noticing. I believe it reinforced those behaviors I cared most about. I hope they save these collections of letters, boxes, and booklets as reminders throughout their lives of who they have always been.

Families are complicated. I don't want to paint a simplistic picture of "just expect the best; you'll get it." You'll still have your ups and downs, your good times and disappointments. They are necessary for kids to figure out who they are. They have to assert their autonomy and fervently prove they are different from you. They need to make mistakes to learn how to recover. Nothing I am suggesting will avoid these complexities altogether, but hopefully it will ground you in the normalcy of high expectations you will return to after these inevitable rough patches.

More Thoughts From Teens

First and foremost, parents should ALWAYS love their child(ren) unconditionally! The same belief applies to expectations; parents should ALWAYS have high expectations for their child(ren)! In order to balance the 2, parents should be clear and open with how they feel and what they think. They should share with their child(ren) how much they love them and how nothing in the world could ever change this unconditional love. In the same conversation, parents should then proceed to explain the high expectations that they hold for their child(ren) and why they have these expectations. I will proceed to explain the "why" factor in the following sentences: Parents want their children to be successful. Parents want their children to be happy. Parents want their children to lead better lives than their own.
—17-year-old male, Arizona

It was shocking and incomprehensible when we heard some kids say, "My dad is going to give me $20 for every A I get on my report card." I continue to hear my peers say such things to this day, and I will be a senior in high school this fall. Never in my life have I ever felt deprived because I didn't receive a reward for my grades. My parents have raised my siblings and me to strive toward excellence. We have been taught to work hard for what we want, and we don't work hard just so we can receive some type of validation.
—17-year-old female, Maryland

My parents both have very high expectations for me, but they don't say that; instead, they tell me to set my own expectations, come up with my own plan to achieve it, and stick with it. They only interfere when they don't think I'm doing my best, but they don't get mad or anything; they just give me a gentle reminder that it is my obligation to try and do my best. I think I feel more obliged to reach my own goals this way, while at the same time I'm aiming high without damaging my relationship with my parents.
—Unknown age, female, Taiwan

Unconditional love should be just that—UNconditional.... Never tell your teen that they are a bad person.... Since parents are the biggest thing in a kid's life, by telling us you're very, very disappointed in us and that you just can't believe you raised a child like us, you're defining how we value ourselves. Instead, say, "You know, son, I'm very disappointed in YOUR ACTIONS. You have not only disobeyed me, but you have not helped yourself. I LOVE YOU, and FOR THAT REASON I have to give you these consequences. You will be grounded for 2 weeks because IN YOUR FUTURE AS AN ADULT, which is coming up very soon, you're going to need discipline. Son, I'M LOOKING OUT FOR YOUR FUTURE, so please take this seriously. Try to LEARN that you have to respect authority." Remember to remind us that you have our best intentions in mind! Don't ever assume that we know anything.… Lay everything out on the line.

—14-year-old female, Michigan

For us, it's hard to remember what you may have said a week ago when we know you're upset, so even if it's repetitive, even if we say, "Okay, I get it, you've said that a million times," it is your responsibility, with all respect parents, to tell us, "I'm going to say it to you anyways, maybe ten million more times, because it's really important for you to GROW and BECOME THE PERSON YOU ARE MEANT TO BE." Lastly, don't ever, please, pull the guilt trip. "I have spent so much time teaching you and all you have done is show me that you don't listen, that I have wasted that time." "I have spent your whole life teaching you; I don't deserve for you to disrespect me like that." If you're going to treat us like children, expect us to be like children. If you're going to treat us like adults, expect us to be like adults!

—14-year-old female, Michigan

I think most of the time, parents' disappointment and reprimanding is really all out of love; they just have a very backward way of showing it. They are disappointed when you don't get the grades because they want to see you excel and go as far as you can in life. I honestly think a simple, "I love you," along with an often dismissive, "Good night," can make the world of difference to a child. Usually, on the rare occasion my parents would say just that, I would cry. Not happy tears or truly sad tears; they were more like realization tears. "Oh, they really do just want the best for me. That's why they're so hard on me, and it always feels like nothing is good enough." There needs to be a distinction between "high expectations" and unrealistic expectations. Because if the bar is set too high, kids will never reach it.… And that doesn't lead to security.…

—18-year-old female, Pennsylvania

CHAPTER

5

High Expectations Gone Awry: The Problem With Focusing Mainly on Academic Performance

It is a good thing to expect your child to be committed to schoolwork and learning. We know that young people whose parents care about school perform better academically. Parents who communicate with their children's teachers to stay informed about their children's classroom performance raise kids who are better connected with school, and school connection fosters academic success. Our challenge is to let our kids know we care, without adding so much pressure that we take away the joy of learning.

There is a great deal of cultural anxiety that the best times are behind us. Parents used to have confidence that their children's futures would be better than their own. Whether or not there is any truth to the growing belief that the future is less secure than the past, our children are suffering from the repercussions of these fears. Education is seen as the key to long-term financial security (and it should be), but there is a sense that only the most selective schools offer a real foothold on success (and that is not true).

Perhaps as a result, it has become increasingly competitive to secure one of those top spots. A myth has developed that the SATs/ACTs will determine your fate. If you do well, life will be handed to you on a silver platter. If not, you should expect a life of mediocrity. Because we (mistakenly) believe this test determines our children's future, we also tell them to relax when they take it, without catching the irony. We tell them that to present themselves as reasonable candidates, they have to be good at everything. To show they are bright and willing to "stretch," they should take multiple advanced placement classes in a variety of topics and earn As in all of them. To show creativity, they should play a musical instrument, preferably one that is not too ordinary. The bassoon is perfect. To demonstrate collaborative skills, a varsity sport is nice. We even tell them in order to show leadership, they should try to be captain by senior year and certainly run to be a class officer. Compassion is important to demonstrate as well, so we save up to send them on distant service projects.

Our kids learn it is about what they do, not who they are. And what they do must be very impressive.

It may be true that to get into a "top college," as narrowly defined by *U.S. News and World Report,* students need to present themselves as superhuman. However, this presentation is rarely rooted in reality and therefore forces some students to compromise their integrity to enhance their resumes. My fear, though, is this push toward perfection will undermine the very ingredients needed for success. Let me underscore this point emphatically: the pressure to produce an attractive college candidate at 18 years old may make a less successful adult in the long run.

People are uneven. Highly successful people are great at something, and their desire to explore other areas is what makes them interesting. We harm kids when we suggest that to make it in this world they must be good at absolutely everything. Imagine how teens who aren't perfect at everything (and that's all of them) respond to this kind of pressure. Some will don the mask of indifference. They'll work hard to pretend they don't care precisely because of how much they do; they'll get off the playing field altogether. Others will push themselves toward perfectionism and therefore decrease their chances for real success.

Our society has a real stake in our young people being high achievers, but it is critical to understand the difference between a high achiever and a perfectionist. High achievers run the world; they excel at something but have no fantasy that they must be good at everything. They revel in their accomplishments. They value constructive criticism because they look for opportunities for growth and self-improvement. They see failures as temporary setbacks to be overcome with greater effort. In sharp contrast, perfectionists consider themselves unacceptable unless they meet impossibly high self-imposed standards. They worry about being discovered as imposters and therefore view constructive criticism as an attack. Their creativity and innovative spirit is stifled; they won't think outside of the box because their fear of failure (or a B+ for that matter) is acute. They aren't as resilient because they see even mild setbacks as catastrophes.

> ❝ I would set standards but provide a guide or map on how to get there. Also, figure out ways they can talk to you once a week about where they are struggling. ❞
>
> —19-year-old female, Alaska

Pressure to be good at everything pushes children toward perfectionism. This drive to excel may produce picture-perfect grades and a sterling resume. It may even get teens into that top-ranked college. But at what expense? Fear of failure? Imposter syndrome? Physical symptoms such as belly pain, headaches, and fatigue? Exhaustion? The health of their relationships?

> Set a bar for your kids, but don't make that bar also a symbol of your love. Don't make it that kids need to reach a certain expectation to obtain your love, because that will just end badly.
>
> —16-year-old female, Pennsylvania

We have focused primarily on our high expectations for grades. It is important to note that the words *sports scores*, *art trophies*, or *piano recitals* could have been substituted for the word *grades*. When we specifically focus on results or products, kids feel like their performance is what matters to us, and we risk generating a backlash of self-doubt, anxiety, or perfectionism.

When we hold our kids to these high expectations, our goal is undoubtedly to guide them toward success. And it may work for some young people. The irony is that for others, it may undercut the core ingredients needed for long-term success—creativity, innovative potential, flexibility, and the ability to benefit and grow from constructive criticism. Most importantly, it may undermine kids' love of learning as they too quickly assess their own performance as good versus bad or a win versus a loss. Driven by these narrow assessments, they perform for the grade rather than work for the knowledge. As a result, they may choose predictable paths that lead to that grade or score. Such a choice can limit kids' exposure to challenges that would better contribute to their growth. And growth must remain our goal.

Young people who experience a lot of external pressure may internalize that pressure and push themselves toward very impressive results. But their success might plateau early on because the character traits that fuel long-term success are undermined.

In just a few pages, we'll talk about how to hold your son or daughter to reasonable academic expectations in ways that will be less likely to backfire. Then later we'll talk about how to know whether your expectations may be creating more harm than good. Preview: it's about looking at your child's performance and well-being and talking to her about it.

Take a Breath

So far, I've used the term *top college;* however, it strikes me as destructive. Top by whose standards? By what measures? You want your child to leave your home and have a *top experience.* Because every teen is different, that optimal learning experience can't possibly be determined by a list. It is about the fit between a place and your child. Some kids thrive in a large university setting and are energized by the frenetic pace. Others prefer the nurturance that comes from close relationships with teachers afforded at smaller institutions. Every school has a culture, a feel, and people learn best when they are comfortable and fit in. They will fit in best at a place where they are stimulated, feel appreciated, and feel like they belong. When children are produced or engineered to get into the top-ranking college, they may not believe they belong. The last thing you want is for your child to be initiated into adulthood wondering whether he is an imposter.

College is not for everyone. For others, the top experience may be a vocational or military setting or a school that fosters creativity. For some kids, the top experience after high school will be an extended service project. These years can really help a young person know how much they matter, and youth armed with a sense of meaning are poised to vigorously dive into the next phase of their lives. Remember, high achievers are found in every field and vocation. The only thing I will state definitively is that everybody deserves to continue learning after high school.

Not All "Lazy" Kids Are Lazy

We've talked about how academic pressure can create short-term gains but long-term losses. It can do some tremendous short-term harm as well. Not all pressured kids will reap near-term gains by doing what it takes to become the model student. Some young people who are pushed too hard may choose to feign laziness or indifference, because it is easier to pretend they don't care than to confess how deeply they do. It is easier to get off of the playing field entirely than to share how incapable they feel of meeting impossibly high standards.

> ❝ When parents have too high of expectations, it can ruin a kid. Parents have to make expectations reachable but also make them a challenge for the kid…. There are kids in my class that are really smart, but they just don't try…. You have to push them enough so that they'll achieve but not so much that they want to quit everything. ❞
>
> —16-year-old female, Pennsylvania

When taken to its extreme, the pressure of unattainably high expectations can cause kids to burn out to the point they might turn to alcohol or drugs to self-medicate their stress. They worry so deeply about failure that they pretend they don't care much about anything. It can be hard work to maintain this image, especially if anxiety drove them toward it in the first place. But that risk is far easier to take than putting in a great effort and disappointing everyone (mostly themselves) anyway.

> ❝ Ever since I was little, like kindergarten, my parents had extremely high expectations for me, whether it was in school, in sports, service, you name it. And as time went on, I began putting the pressure on myself. In a way, this could be a good thing, but it ate at me. When I didn't live up to my father's expectations, I not only failed to achieve his approval, but I also failed to achieve my own acceptance. This really devastated my own self-worth and has taken many years to overcome. ❞
>
> —17-year-old female, Pennsylvania

Some young people don't worry incessantly about failure; they have owned it. They may have accepted the judgments of others who have labeled them as somehow inadequate. They accept the inevitability of failure. They do what it takes to seal the failure. They see it as even better if their choice also feels good in the moment. "I can never get in shape, so I am not going to waste my time exercising." "I'm dumb. Everybody knows that. My mom is always saying that I'm nothing like my older brother. He got a scholarship to go to some great college. I don't want to go to college anyway. "

If your son or daughter has gone from performing well in school to becoming an underachiever, don't assume laziness is at the root of the problem. Your child could care too much; her fear of disappointing you, her teachers, or her group of competitive friends is so great that the easiest answer may be to stop trying. Being caring, sensitive, and anxious is not the reputation teenagers savor; instead, they'll become kids who are too cool to care about all of that "lame stuff."

I've had numerous gratifying experiences in my practice when parents who have been arguing with their kids over being lazy realize the truth. It is a powerful, transformative moment when a young person is able to reveal what has really been going on. "It's not that I don't care; it's that I care too much." Some will go on to talk about the pressure in their lives; others will say, "I just couldn't stand always hearing that I wasn't living up to my potential." The starting point is parents changing the lens through which they view their children. When they assume laziness, the children accept the label because it offers an easy way out. However, they also feel ashamed and sometimes become angry that their parents aren't seeing them for who they really are. Instead, parents can say, "I know how much you have always cared. I worry you've given up on yourself. I want to better understand what has made you uncomfortable trying. If it has anything to do with something I've said or done, I'll work with you to make it right. If it is pressure you are feeling, I am here to support you. If you have lost confidence in yourself for any reason, we'll figure out a way to help you rebuild that."

One final point: some learning differences do not present until the middle school years or seventh or eighth grade. Many young people, particularly those who are bright, can compensate well for these differences in elementary school. They may not have insight into their learning differences, including focusing difficulties, and will grow increasingly frustrated as they slip academically. They also may learn to pretend they don't care. They are not lazy; they need an academic assessment.

How Focusing on Academic or Athletic Performance Undercuts Our Relationships

When our children are young, we react to their every antic, celebrating them at play and rejoicing at every developmental milestone. When they get older, we have less time and they *occasionally* seem less cute. Part of the reason they seem less cute and cuddly is they let us know they'd like to spend less time with us. Therefore, we try to maximize the time we have together by focusing on topics such as grades, scores, and results, believing these are the high-yield topics we must use our limited time to address. We use this time to reinforce our high expectations, but by focusing only on their performance we undermine our relationships.

" There was a kid competing who I knew was really good, but when he didn't get first like normal, [his mom] got really mad at him and it made him sad. Any sport should be done for fun, not to please your crazy parent obsessed on winning and your child being the best ever. **"**

—13-year-old female, Massachusetts

We push our children away when we do more with less time. When our limited time together is spent on what they are, or are not, doing, it becomes anxiety provoking rather than enjoyable. When we focus our attention on what our kids produce, they begin to feel like our product. We know how they are performing but not how they are feeling. We know how many points they scored but little of their struggles. We miss out on the opportunity to parent during the moments when we are most needed.

Young people sometimes complain that parents care more about grades, scores, or performance than they do about their children. But when I ask young people how much they share with their parents, they respond, "We pretty much talk about school. My personal life is my business." This cycle harms our relationship. First, we try to maximize our yield by focusing on what we think is the important stuff. Then, our kids think this is our primary concern, so they don't share anything else. Next, we feel badly about how little we know of their lives. The cycle builds on itself. To parent our kids in the active sense of the word, we must know them. We cannot know them unless they reveal themselves.

Young people must know they are largely in control of changing this pattern. If they offer their parents their thoughts, feelings, and worries, their parents will likely come through with a listening ear and needed support. If they only share their grades and scores, they can't reasonably expect their parents to comprehend the rich context of their lives.

While you want to hold your child to high academic standards, perhaps even know your child's grades, it is more critical you know his internal life. Don't worry about sacrificing your child's success. Let me assure you that your unconditional love and meaningful presence are precisely the ingredients that will launch your child toward a successful future.

66 You and your child's version of success are probably completely different. If you already have their entire life planned out for them by the time they are born, you're probably going to be disappointed with the way they end up. You're setting them up for failure. 99

—17-year-old female, Virginia

More Thoughts From Teens

Pressure to do well is so heavy and immense that when a parent adds to it, it feels like the whole world is against you. When I was in high school, I felt like I was competing with every single person I met.… The value you had was in what you could put on your résumé to impress someone or how to get into college with a scholarship. Add your mother asking you, "Why didn't you make first soprano?" or "Why didn't you make an A on your Spanish test?" when you thought that you were good enough, and it really just makes you feel like you're a huge failure in the world and that you have to resort to being a loser. I would say that parents should encourage their children, but make it clear that failure isn't the ending point. That failure doesn't define you. Parents should put just as much emphasis on what you should do if you fail just as much as they do if you pass.

—18-year-old female, Alabama

Personally, as a high-achieving teen, [I feel] my parents' high expectations have affected me negatively. I am a perfectionist in all aspects of my life, and I am strongly affected when I don't achieve what I intend to. I also now have a very strong desire to please, working myself far too hard to gain the praise of others. This affects my home life, school life, and especially any relationships I enter. I wish my parents had accepted my achievements a little more instead of telling me that my best is perfection. They love me unconditionally, but sometimes their demands can overshadow that.

—17-year-old female, Pennsylvania

…I have many friends who don't even think that getting a B is acceptable because their parents will be disappointed with them. Some students even fear getting below average because of consequences at home. Parents need to be aware that forcing their children to get good grades to avoid punishment is not the way to go. A child should not be afraid to fail. Failure is something one learns from, and learning is just as important as remembering. Parents should show high support and enthusiasm for getting good grades, but they should act in just the same way if their child were to come home with a D. They should explain that it is not the student's fault and that they are aware of how hard they tried. There will always be a next time, and next time they are sure their child will do better—not because s/he has to but because s/he wants to.

—17-year-old female, Illinois

I react to high expectations in a complicated way. I know my mother loves me unconditionally, so when she sets a high goal for me to get to, I don't look at it like it's her goal. It becomes my own goal…, but when I start to fall behind and she begins to TELL me to do it, I lose my motivation, and once she is reminding me constantly, then it becomes nothing more than, "OK, I'll do it later," or I'll rush though it just to finish it and get it done, whether it is done correctly or not.

—17-year-old male, Oklahoma

It was hard living up to the standards my older sister set. I was an average student, mediocre at sports, and just a general kid. My sister, on the other hand, was an A+ student and received a full ride to college on a soccer scholarship. I know that my parents love me to death, and only want me to succeed in life, but comparing me to the accomplishments of my sister doesn't motivate me. I think parents should encourage kids in whatever area they are good at and leave sibling accomplishments out of the picture. Setting the bar on someone else's accomplishments only makes my accomplishments seem less grand or important.

—19-year-old female, Texas

I get straight As because I can't stand not getting them. My parents have never made me; it is just a part of me. The only thing I don't like about this is that I work my butt off in school. I study until my brain hurts and am stressed beyond belief. Because of the straight As since I started school, it has morphed into an expectation.

—16-year-old female, New Jersey

It's good to have structure and high expectations, but DO NOT try to live through your child. If you expect them to do something—for example, sports—and they don't want to do it, don't make them. Even if they don't do everything you want them to, love them no matter what, and make sure they know you love them. Remind them daily, and never let them forget.

—14-year-old female, Kansas

CHAPTER

6

Setting Expectations That Promote Success

I hope I have made the point that expecting uniform excellence in performance can backfire by leading to short- and long-term negative consequences. That does not mean I am suggesting you should be satisfied with mediocrity. Your expectations and how you choose to praise and criticize may make a difference in achieving your goal of raising a genuine high achiever. In this chapter, I will focus on 4 points.

1. You have to be thoughtful about where you set the bar.

2. You should celebrate unevenness, so your child can discover her spikes.

3. You should praise and notice effort rather than performance. Similarly, you should focus criticism on effort or a specific behavior, not on character.

4. You should support the development of delayed gratification, tenacity, and grit.

Point 1
How High Should You Set the Bar?

It isn't possible to give a simple answer on how high your expectations should be, primarily because I do not know your child nor do I have the benefit of seeing how you convey expectations. But whether or not he is thriving is a good gauge of the interplay between his makeup and how you are communicating expectations. Your child's overall state of well-being is an excellent clue as to whether he is *experiencing* your expectations as pressure or encouragement. Please note the emphasis on the word *experiencing*. That takes the blame off of you. This is not about whether you are doing something right or wrong; it is about how your child absorbs messages. What one child views as helpful encouragement might be viewed by another as far too much pressure. It may be about your child's baseline level of anxiety but is definitely about the lens through which he looks at his performance.

As you are assessing whether or not your child is thriving, it is critical that your reflexive response is not, "Well, he's doing well in school." Many kids who have anxious dispositions or perfectionistic tendencies do terrifically well in school. However, as we've discussed, that is not always predictive of long-term success. You want to consider his overall state of health and well-being, including school performance. How is he getting along at home and with friends? Is he getting enough sleep? Is he physically well, or does he seem to have stress-related symptoms—such as stomach pain, fatigue, or headaches—that are not explained medically? Does he possess a love of learning, or is his innate curiosity crushed?

How much effort he puts into his work may be highly predictive of future success. Therefore, as we will discuss in greater detail in a few pages, we want to keep our focus on effort rather than product or results. But it also means it is OK to want your kid to "stretch" so he can figure out his limits. Your challenge is to estimate how far his reach can go. You'll need to base this on past performance, aptitude, and teachers' guidance. Then, set the bar within reach but at a point where he can discover new capabilities. If you place it beyond his aptitude, he will feel frustrated, incapable, and perhaps angered. He'll feel like it's not possible to please you. If you place it far below his capabilities, he'll feel belittled.

> 66 Parents have to set a bar for their children to try to get to. The bar has to be high enough that your child can't just easily step over but not too high that it's not a possible bar. 99
>
> —14-year-old male, Illinois

The bar you set is not an even one. People's capabilities vary significantly in different subject areas. The beautiful thing about focusing on effort is the results can't reasonably be expected to be the same. Furthermore, we have discussed a goal of raising a high achiever. I want to clarify that every person can be a high achiever in the area that best matches her aptitude. We are not narrowly speaking of academic high achievement; we are speaking of each person being positioned to contribute to her unique potential.

In a perfect world, we would know when encouragement crosses the line into pressure, high expectations, and impossibly steep standards. If you're not sure about where the line is for your child, or where to set the bar, check in with her teachers and coaches. Most importantly, ask her.

66 Goals should be SMART. If the possibility of failure or disappointment is the problem, then minimize the risk. Make sure your child knows what you expect and that your child can reach your expectations, and provide as much support to help him reach them. 99

—18-year-old female, Texas

If you ever find yourself in a position where your child, or another young person you are close to, seems defeated or hopeless and says something like, "I can't," or "I won't be able to do it," ask her to add the word *yet* to the sentence. *I can't yet. I won't be able to do it yet.* That singular word changes the meaning of the sentence and perhaps the tone of the conversation. Tenacity, hard work, and perhaps a little more time will get your child there. This 3-letter word (*yet*) can help a young person reframe the expectation she sets for herself.

Point 2
People Are Uneven, and When We Celebrate Our Unevenness, We Find Our Strengths and Can Accept Our Limitations

Many parents try to take pressure off of their kids by saying, "Just try your best." The idea is right, but the terms are not specific enough. Kids tell us when they hear their parents say this, they *know* their parents really mean, "If you try your best, I'm sure you'll get the As you deserve." Another reason this common phrase backfires is this generation of young people is so afraid of hearing the *d* word ("I'm so DISAPPOINTED") that even the underlying sweetness of the "just try your best" message creates anxiety.

I suggest something far more specific: tell your kids you expect them to put a good effort into everything they do. Explain the reason you demand effort is so they can learn about themselves. Tell your child, "Only with a reasonable effort will you ever trust the results, and with a good effort you can feel good about yourself no matter the results." The most important thoughts follow: "And I know the results will be different for different subjects and activities. That's fine! That's the way you'll learn about your strengths and limitations. People are uneven; this is the right time to learn about yourself."

66 My dad always tells me, 'Your grades are not for me; they are for you.' What this means is that I'm the one that's putting in an effort and going to school, and it is my future career that is on the line. 99

—19-year-old female, New Mexico

Our goal should be to help our children discover and build their "spikes," areas of excellence from which their unique contributions will flow. Nobody excels at everything. Successful people are particularly good at something and usually can work with other people. They become interesting when they try their hand at things they're not particularly good at but truly enjoy (these things will become their hobbies). Understanding this, we hope to allow our children to reveal their spikes.

66 A parent should expect straight As only if that's the result of the child's best effort. Likewise, a parent should be satisfied with Cs if the child tried his or her best to achieve those grades. However, expecting straight As from a child who tries his or her best and achieves a lower grade will only negatively influence the child's learning experience and morale. 99

—19-year-old male, Pennsylvania

Some kids feel added pressure when we tell them to find their passion, especially if they think they need to understand their life's mission in time to write their college essay. **Finding our passion is a process, not an event.** Many people don't find theirs until later in life, and lucky people find more than one. Instead, we should challenge young people to pay attention to what they are good at, enjoy, and are satisfied doing. Most critically, they need to see what areas drive them to keep learning. Which big questions make them want to strive to answer those that remain unasked?

To support this process of self-discovery, we need to allow downtime and tolerate, even encourage, some "pruning." Young people who have every moment planned lack downtime and moments of reflection and will, therefore, never learn how they would have chosen to fill that time with thoughts or actions. Some parents are disappointed when a child wants to quit an activity. They may say, "I didn't invest all of this time, effort, and money just to have you become a quitter." If you ever feel the impulse to say this, try to reframe how you interpret your child's decision to cut back on activities. If your daughter wants to quit everything, consider that something serious might be going on, such as depression, substance use, or a new crowd's influence. But if she wants to quit lacrosse so she can better focus on schoolwork, theater, or volleyball, congratulate her. Think of it as pruning instead of quitting—thinning extraneous branches so the strongest shoots can grow stronger.

If we want our children to discover, and even take pride in, their spikes, we need to celebrate their unevenness. Tell them that, at this stage of their life, you expect them to put their greatest effort into all their endeavors and pay attention to the inevitably varied results. Reinforce that everyone deserves the satisfaction that comes from a good sweat and that we never trust outcomes—good or bad, successes or failures—if we haven't applied ourselves to our potential. One young man shared with me that his father raised him to know intelligence is a start, but hard work is critical to success. He was told, "If I had to hire a man and had 2 before me, I'd hire the one whose jeans were worn out at the knees from hard work rather than the one whose seat was worn from sitting." When we know we have put in a reasonable effort, we'll celebrate our successes and won't judge ourselves for our unevenness.

> **"** If a kid is staying home every night just to do homework to get the best grades, even on the weekends, then the parent is pushing too much. But when schoolwork is optional and not a priority for the child, then the parent is not pushing hard enough. **"**
>
> —16-year-old female, Pennsylvania

We should reassure our children that later in life they will be able to easily set aside those things that neither interest them nor are a natural fit for their efforts. For now, though, they should take full advantage of the wonderful opportunity they have in school to be exposed to so much.

Explain to your child some key points about unevenness.

- There are some things that will come easily to you and for which you'll be able to get top grades, but you won't find them that interesting. Accept the grades, but learn this is not the career you should choose. You might be tempted to do what comes easily; you might even feel like you're a natural, but you'll get bored if you lack interest and the field doesn't challenge you.

- There are other things you're good at and love doing but that you need to put a decent effort into to get to your peak performance. You'll find when you don't *get* something, that piques your interest more and you'll do what it takes to get to the answer. You've found your career. Careers are about loving what you do and working hard to continue improving so you can make your greatest contribution.

- There are some things you are not very good at but really enjoy. You find them fascinating and are motivated to build your skills and understanding. This may not be your career, but you've found a hobby.

- Finally, there are things you are not good at and that you don't find interesting. You still need to take the necessary steps to learn them, such as getting help from teachers and friends. But don't get down on yourself as long as you know you've put in a reasonable effort. Learn these things well enough to be able to be well-rounded, participate in conversations, and have relationships with a wide variety of people. (For example, you don't want to go to dinner at your new girlfriend's house and ask her father, the engineer, what kind of choo-choo train he drives.)

Let's return for a moment to the point that there are many avenues for success other than academic. Your child's "spikes" may not take him to college. Many factors determine the best way for your child to contribute to the world, including his aptitude and interests. What you don't want is for him to learn to pretend he doesn't care about anything because he doesn't fit into a box of others' creation. What you want is for him to be optimally successful in whatever role he chooses to take in society. This approach of recognizing and celebrating everybody's spikes and unevenness positions all children to enter adulthood feeling good about who they are and how they might contribute.

> A teen will face many obstacles because that is simply the way life works, because nothing is easy to achieve, especially high goals, in life. If a child has really given their all yet still hasn't achieved their goal and can't reach their goal,…support and encourage them to still keep going on with their other dreams, because even if one door closes maybe 15 others will open.
>
> —16-year-old female, Pennsylvania

Point 3
Using Praise and Criticism Wisely

Parents and teachers used to be told they should do whatever they could to build their kids' self-esteem, so we got into the habit of delivering effusive and frequent compliments. A generation was raised to feel "special as a butterfly" and "unique as a snowflake." Kids' art projects were raved about as if they were museum worthy, and every goal was celebrated as if it were an Olympic victory. Kids were told, "Good job!" as they slid down the sliding board, with no credit ever given to gravity.

We should celebrate kids' accomplishments, but overpraising may backfire. The self-esteem movement of the last couple of decades made 2 mistakes. First, it praised so effusively that kids didn't develop real confidence. Authentic, well-earned confidence is what builds lasting self-esteem. Confidence is rooted in a feeling of competence. We build a sense of competence when we offer well-deserved and targeted praise after observing something noteworthy. Second, it hoped to make kids feel good all the time and neglected to prepare them for when they wouldn't. Have you ever had one of those "I'm not as special as a butterfly" moments? When told your whole life that you're a star, the bad feelings that life's challenges inevitably bring might trigger additional discomfort—"I really shouldn't be having these feelings"—or disconnect you from a reasonable range of emotions.

Promoting Growth: Seeing
Your Child as a Developing Person

Dr Carol Dweck is a Stanford University psychologist who studies the effect that praise, and conversely criticism, has on student performance. Her 3 decades of research has heavily influenced the way I think about promoting success. This impressive body of scientific work guides us as we consider how best to hold our children to high expectations in a way that will promote, rather than undermine, their success and emotional well-being. In a book that may shift how you offer feedback, *Mindset: The New Psychology of Success,* she talks about a *growth mind-set* compared to a *fixed mind-set* and explains how these different ways of thinking influence performance and well-being in childhood, adolescence, and adulthood. Of greatest relevance here, she guides parents, teachers, and coaches how to interact with children in a way more likely to create a growth mind-set.

Young people with a growth mind-set (those most likely to become high achievers) believe their intelligence can be built through effort, so they are willing to put in the sustained work needed to accomplish the desired result. When they don't succeed as they had hoped, they don't see themselves as failures but as learners. People with a growth mind-set want to get constructive, reliable feedback on their performance because they know they need these assessments to improve.

Dweck summarized, "The passion for stretching yourself and sticking to it, even (or especially) when it's not going well, is the hallmark of the growth mindset." This is the tenacity and resilience needed to succeed over the long-term.

People with a fixed mind-set (including perfectionists) view things more simply. You're smart or not. They view failure as a sure sign that they're not. And their definition of failure can be astonishingly narrow, such as the B+. They view hard work as a sign that they may not have natural intelligence and therefore may shun those endeavors that would require hard work (another reason to not think outside of the box). Their goal, therefore, becomes to avoid failure, or even a stumble, because they are most comfortable when every circumstance confirms they're smart.

Dweck explains that the person with a fixed mind-set often worries about whether they will win or lose or look intelligent or stupid. Can you imagine the discomfort this thinking generates and how it could stifle the love of learning, especially if school is the environment where one consistently experiences these feelings? Sometimes resilience is about overcoming those voices from within that tell us we are not acceptable *unless* or would be worthwhile *only if* we achieve a particular milestone.

People with a growth mind-set say they feel smart when they grow, and those with fixed mind-sets feel smart when they avoid errors. This undermines the likelihood of success for those with a fixed mind-set because their fear leads them to avoid challenging goals; instead, they take comfort in their achievements with the safe ones. We want our kids to feel comfortable, even joyous, in taking the "stretch" rather than to be satisfied with easy, predictable results.

Praise

Dweck's research offers some clues into how to praise in a manner more likely to promote a growth mind-set. She conducted a series of classic experiments that demonstrated dramatic differences in children's performances based on the type of praise they received. Grade schoolers completed a set of puzzles that were designed so the kids would do fairly well. The group was randomly divided into 2 subgroups. After the first set of puzzles, each kid was individually told his or her scores and given a single line of praise. Some students were recognized for their intelligence and were essentially told, "You must be smart at this"; the others were noted for their effort: "You must have worked really hard."

The pupils were then given a choice of which tests to take for the second round. They could choose a more difficult test that promised greater learning or an easier test similar to the one they completed and for which they had already received praise. Ninety percent of those praised for their *effort* chose the harder set of puzzles, whereas most praised for their *intelligence* chose the easy test. Next, all the students completed a test that was 2 years above their grade level. As expected, it was difficult for most of them, and many were not able to complete the tasks. The students who had been praised for their effort on the first test assumed they simply hadn't worked hard enough. Those praised for their intelligence took their failure as proof they were no longer smart or perhaps never were. Their discomfort was visible, and some had notable anxiety. Then a third round of tests, on the same level as the initial easy test, was given to the students. Those who were initially praised for their intelligence fared worse than their very first attempt, whereas those praised for their effort showed improvement.

If one line of praise made a difference in performance in these young students, can you imagine what difference the style of praise might make in a child's life when consistently given in the home?

These studies suggest we should recognize the process, not the product, and praise effort rather than grades and test scores. Praise and criticism is a way we convey our high expectations. Therefore, these simple points may be the easiest, and most effective, way to hold your child to high expectations while promoting the kind of growth mind-set that leads to success. As importantly, our children will be more likely to avoid the insecurity and self-doubt associated with perfectionism and fear of failure.

Dweck writes about another concerning possibility: children who are incessantly praised might become so worried about losing that praise that they will do what it takes to maintain their position, even if it involves tearing others down. This tells us that how we offer feedback can affect more than our children's success; it can affect their integrity.

Perhaps the concept that best explains the effect of praise and criticism is judgment. Dr Dweck teaches that every interaction can send a message to children and adolescents about how to think about themselves. Are we drawing conclusions about some fixed trait they have such as intelligence, artistic talent, or athletic prowess? (You are so beautiful. You are so smart. You're such a great soccer player/dancer/artist.) When we do, they feel judged and are more likely to think their current state is, or should be, permanent. This may generate anxiety about losing that permanent state they may believe now labels them. Instead, we want to see them as developing people, capable of change, growth, and learning from each experience.

Whenever we focus on what is produced (eg, a piece of art, a score or grade), we reinforce the sense that it is a true reflection of the person's worth. When we instead focus on the creative process it took to produce the work of art, or the effort put in to earn the grade, we emphasize the fluidity and capacity for improvement. In fact, Dweck notes that young people with fixed mind-sets are more likely to give a test the power to define them as smart or not or as good or bad at a particular subject. Bestowing such power on a test will naturally increase their anxiety and likely decrease their performance. When we focus mostly on test results, we reinforce this self-defeating cycle.

Intelligence is traditionally (and incorrectly) measured in a way that assumes it is fixed. Dweck, and many others, would strongly argue that while intelligence may to some degree be inborn, it is capable of being built through exposure and experience. It follows logically that someone with a growth mind-set will position herself to gain the increased exposure and experience that develops her intelligence.

We need our children to feel in control of their lives. Effort is something completely within their control. When they attribute their effort to the outcomes they achieve, they will gain that sense of control. When we notice the work they put into something generates a result, we are supporting their development as a growing human being.

Criticism

Let's apply some of these same principles to criticism. Remember that criticism can be essential for children. If we just praised everything, it would seem sweet at first pass, but how would your child learn to take responsibility? Nor should we give feedback that gives easy excuses. Our goal is for our children to gain a sense of control. Excusing their behavior takes control away from them by denying they were responsible for their choices and therefore ultimately undermining their confidence.

Criticism should be well targeted and specific; it should never be generalized. It should be about something that happened, not something permanent. When we generalize it, it sounds like, "You *are* XXXX." That criticism clearly communicates this is a fixed trait. The child would naturally believe, "Well, I guess if I am XXXX, there is not much of a possibility of change." That child will live down to the judgment you have passed along. If, on the other hand, you said, "You *did* YYYY," the child knows he controlled what happened. To twist the words a bit, his *effort* created YYYY; therefore, if he points his effort in another direction, he might accomplish that as well. Now, pepper in some guidance. "You did YYYY and this is not the kind of behavior I like to see. I know you can do better, because I have also seen you do ZZZZ."

I left the criticisms in the example blank so you could fill in the topics you'd likely complain about in your own home and to point out that I am suggesting a "choreograph" you can generally apply. Now, let's use messiness as an example. "You are a slob!" is a demeaning label that implies a permanent state. More productive and effective feedback would be, "Your room is really messy, and I tripped over your Rollerblades in the living room." It is accurate and clearly demonstrates that the parent is frustrated by a particular action. Then the parent could remind the child he has the power and skills to address the problem. "I know you can keep things neat and organized when you put in the time. Your hockey equipment in the garage is a perfect example. Everything is in its place so you can find exactly what you need when you need it."

This is critical to consider thoughtfully when you are not angry. While angry, we tend to have inaccurate thoughts fueled by rage or disappointment. During these moments, we tend to see a person as mean, selfish, or lazy. In calmer moments, we understand clearly that the person was only *behaving* in that manner. Therefore, this is a skill set that has to be practiced when calm so it can be drawn from when we are angry or stressed.

When we remain targeted in our criticism, it can feel constructive, and our children can develop further. When we generalize our rage, our children feel they are being attacked. Worse still, they might believe us.

Tying It Together

So what does this look like as we talk to our kids? We have to not pass judgment or make the circumstance we evaluate feel permanent. Therefore, you do not want to say, "You are _____ " (emphasis on the word *are*), or, "Your performance was _____," because both thoughts, even if said with the most supportive of intentions, imply acceptance or lack of acceptance/judgment. If I had to encapsulate what you should say in a script, it would look something like, "I'm noticing that you _____ (fill in with some deed or action the child controlled [eg, studied, put your heart into it, practiced] and as a result you _____ (fill in with desired or undesired outcome)." With this approach, a child or adolescent will understand the outcome was fluid and the result was affected by her action.

See Table 6-1 for examples of what to say and what not to say. Note that we are suggesting

- Praising effort, not results.

- Noticing process (what someone did to get there) rather than product (what it looked like when she got there).

- Being specific and well targeted with our praise and criticism rather than overgeneralizing either.

Table 6-1. How to Use Praise and Criticism Wisely

Do Say	Don't Say
What did you learn in school today?	How did you do on your test?
How'd you pick up your game?	How many goals did you score?
Were you proud of your piece in the art exhibition?	Did you get the blue ribbon?
I love watching you think. You work so hard to figure things out.	You're so smart.
Tell me about your picture. It seems to have so much feeling.	You're such a great artist.
I think you did well because you really studied. It paid off.	Math sure comes naturally to you.
I really admire how you'll search for the answers and get help until you feel confident.	I'm so proud of your grades.
I think that you didn't put in as much time studying as you needed, because you spent all last evening surfing on the computer.	You got a C- because you are lazy.

Do Say	Don't Say
You need to get your head in the game. You seem really distracted now. I need you to focus.	The way you let that goal past you makes me feel like you just don't care.
Why do you think you did better on the last exam?	Your grades are slipping. Sometimes I wonder if you even care.
You really let your sister down. She could have used your help with homework tonight. She was so appreciative when you helped her understand her assignment last week.	You can be such a selfish jerk!
I didn't appreciate that you didn't walk the dogs.	You are always thinking about yourself instead of realizing how busy I am.

Parts of this table are excerpted from my book *Building Resilience in Children and Teens: Giving Kids Roots and Wings*.

Point 4
Promote Tenacity, Delayed Gratification, and Grit

As parents, we hope for our children to reach their full potential. The search for the "secret sauce" to get them there continues, but we seem to be gaining insight into at least some of the ingredients.

We long assumed intelligence was the greatest predictor of success. This was a convenient answer because it was relatively easy to measure (albeit with known biases), and we thought we knew how to take advantage of intelligence; we bestowed knowledge. However, it has become increasingly clear that although intelligence is important, tenacity, diligence, and a commitment to hard work and practice may better predict real-world success. Dr Angela Duckworth, at the University of Pennsylvania, studies this extensively and coined the term *grit* to describe this predictor of success.

She describes people with grit as those who view life as a marathon rather than a sprint. They have a passionate desire to reach a goal and stick to a plan to get there. They are willing to work hard, even at the expense of immediate gratification.

Runners can see the finish line when they run a sprint. Marathoners can only imagine the finish line. They find the fortitude to continue, knowing the reward is not immediately tangible but exists nonetheless. Perseverance itself is the accomplishment; beating your own time or surpassing previous limits is the reward.

Let's take this metaphor a step further to begin tying it to the next part of this book, Protection Versus Learning From Life's Lessons. Those who succeed in life's journey learn to recover when they stumble. When a sprinter falls, the race is over. A marathoner can stumble and make a full recovery.

We do not yet know precisely how to make gritty kids, but Dr Duckworth's and others' works hold promise to offer trustworthy suggestions in the not too distant future. Currently, various schools and programs are developing and testing different models of how best to reinforce and develop this intriguing trait.

Let's consider what you might do to develop grit in your child now. Before we dive in, let's remember that good parenting intentions sometimes backfire. We have learned this from our efforts at "growing" kids with self-esteem, as well as from Dr Dweck's research on praise. We don't want grit to become yet another thing we pressure our kids about or add to our list of disappointments. We also don't want to guess at how to instill grit, while solid research is ongoing. We can, however, stick with strategies I *know* will add to your child's resilience and will likely also increase his tenacity, diligence, and love of learning.

Delayed Gratification

Children who can delay gratification will be better able to focus on routine tasks such as studying instead of reaching for the shiny ball enticing them in the moment. However, because this may be linked to temperament, your influence to teach this may be minimal. Nevertheless, you should reinforce patience by helping your child learn the essential life lesson that better things come to those who wait.

Kids arrive in the world as self-centered pleasure machines. They are all about instant gratification. "I want it *NOW!*" They charm us to meet their every need. But we quickly socialize them to learn that not every want can be immediately answered. We may need to attend to another child first. The tapioca comes after the strained peas. Homework is done before watching TV.

Teaching kids patience flies in the face of our impulsive desire to indulge our children. Who doesn't love to see our children giggle in delight when we give them exactly what they wanted? Personally, I like chocolate pudding better than I like broccoli. I really do. But I eat my broccoli first.

It may help you restrain from being overly indulgent when you imagine how some adults you know may have been parented. People who were overly indulged as children without also being taught the importance of patience and sharing can act selfishly as adults. They may refuse to wait in lines, leave work for coworkers to complete after they go home, and seem unconcerned about others' experiences.

The key to helping children learn delayed gratification may be reinforcing another benefit they receive from the process. If putting off pleasure always feels like giving something up, we should expect resistance. But if children and teens could experience pride by controlling their impulses, they would end up gaining something. Drs Eran Magen and James Gross have tested and supported this concept by exploring how willpower helps people resist temptation.[2] People who were more successful in avoiding temptation could consider how much strength it took to overcome their impulses. For example,

"I'd really like that ice cream," transformed into, "It amazes me how well I can wait until I've done my work before I get my snack. I seriously don't think I could have done this last year."

There are daily activities you can do with your children that will convey the messages about delayed gratification without stooping to a heavy-handed lecture. Help children learn how to save money, or cook with them. They'll appreciate the new skates when they know they saved for them or earned them through doing extra chores. Every master chef learns that meals seasoned by patience taste better. Raw cookie dough might taste good but not as much as a warm cookie oozing melted chocolate chunks. Children learn this best through modeling. Find yourself talking out loud occasionally when you forgo immediate pleasure to reap a greater reward later.

Many things that feel good for a moment can get in the way of both success and our well-being. When we're stressed, we may look for feel-good solutions that end up hurting us in the near-term and long run. Children and adolescents who are able to make wise decisions, even in the face of stress, learn to trust their ability to control their own lives. They don't feel powerless because they have seen how good decisions can make them feel better and benefit them in the long-term.

Parents who are committed to raising resilient children know that learning to delay gratification is a critical part of a child's developing self-control. The word *developing* is critical because we would be unfair to our younger children if we expected them to have well-developed impulse control.

---

[2]Magen Eran, Gross JJ. Harnessing the need for immediate gratification: cognitive reconstrual modulates the reward value of temptations. *Emotion.* 2007;2(7):415–428. Dr Magen is a psychologist who is currently research director of counseling and psychological services at the University of Pennsylvania. Dr Gross is a professor in the Department of Psychology at Stanford University.

We also have to be forgiving of our human impulses. We don't want our kids to feel guilty for allowing themselves pleasure. This is another case when your unwavering love is critical to your child's well-being. When our love is unconditional, it allows our children to be forgiving of themselves, even as they face their human shortcomings.

If Children Love Learning, It Won't Seem Like Work, and Their Tenacious Devotion to Learning Will Be a Source of Pleasure

Children love learning when it is stimulating and associated with something they care about. Children are programmed to be intrigued by new surroundings and excited by adventure. If you want your child to love reading, have her associate it from a very young age with being with you and having your full attention. If you want a child who is amazed by the mysteries that surround us (ie, a lover of science), take walks and notice everything! Look under lichen-covered bark of a fallen tree and find a new universe of insects and fungi. Lie in a field and watch the birds flock. Then go home and learn about migration and weather patterns.

Dr Dweck's work also helps us understand how to maintain rather than stifle a love of learning. Let's not focus on what learning produces (test scores, grades). Let's instead savor watching our kids explore new horizons and celebrate the diligence they display in their searches. Her work also describes how to help children view constructive criticism as learning opportunities rather than destructive comments to be avoided at all costs. Children with grit should long for constructive criticism and feedback as necessary fuel to improve their work, learn "on the job," and grow to be successful.

Stumbling and Recovering

Perhaps more than anything, children learn tenacity when they learn how to recover after failure. They will find that their second and third (or maybe 14th) attempt can produce immeasurable improvements over the first. They need to learn to fail, sometimes gracefully and sometimes lacking grace entirely, so they also learn to get back up. They need to understand their limitations, so they can develop their work-arounds, those skill sets that compensate for their shortcomings. They need to celebrate their unevenness so they can hone those "spikes" to their full potential. We cannot raise our kids with the belief that the stakes are too high to fail. In fact, the stakes are so high that we must allow childhood and adolescence to be the time to learn how to fail. If young people do not learn their own unevenness, and how to compensate for their human limitations, they will make all of their mistakes in adulthood when the consequences may be too great.

In Part 2, Protection Versus Learning From Life's Lessons, we will have a fuller discussion exploring when to protect our children from failure and when to let them learn from life's lessons.

66 Effort is all we can give, and hard work is a very admirable quality in a society filled with many lazy people. Effort, or hard work, when valued over the outcome, teaches us that the process is more important than the outcome and teaches us to value every moment of our lives. This creates a happier individual and makes the teen years more bearable. 99

—15-year-old male, Maryland

More Thoughts From Teens

Let the child try out as many different things as possible until he or she really latches onto something or has a great ability at it. It's then the parents' job to push that kid to reach their potential. However, the child is still just a child and whatever it is—sports, music—it isn't their entire life. Parents should push children but not to the point where they are missing out on birthday parties or not getting home until 9:00 at night on a school night, etc. If the child also feels like he doesn't want to play music or sports anymore, then let it be. If the kid really enjoys the activity, then he or she will come back to it without a doubt. Sometimes it is just a kid's way of saying they need a break when they want to "quit."

—18-year-old male, Pennsylvania

…One year my load felt especially unbearable. Two clubs that I was involved in but wasn't really enjoying were debate and after-school jazz band. I was already involved with the regular band and a number of school athletic teams and programs, but my mother felt debate was especially important for the sake of my high school applications. Despite her perspective on this, she was willing to allow me to drop both debate and after-school jazz band because she knew that I was struggling. She actually cared about whether or not I thought it was worth it. In another instance, there was a church play happening that I'd agreed to be a part of. At the last minute, I decided that I didn't want to be a part of it anymore because I just didn't feel like attending the practice. In that instance, my mom forced me to participate anyway because I'd made a promise. People were dependent on me. It was a matter of making me suffer in the short-term to let me learn a lesson about how to conduct myself in life from then on. At the time, I was upset…. Looking back, I realize my mom was right to force me.

—14-year-old female, Georgia

The use of more flexible words would allow the coexistence of high standards and unconditional support. By showing your affection, you can give your child security and set high standards. You should voice your expectations clearly and with emphasis on their importance, but don't overdo it…. Use words like *want, should, best if, ideally,* etc, rather than *need, must, have to,* etc.

—16-year-old male, Illinois

When I was in about the fourth grade, I brought home a math test that I had a failing grade on. My mom was really disappointed and told me that I couldn't go to dance practice that night because I needed to do corrections on the test. I was really mad at her and started screaming about how they always told us, me and my brother, "to do our best," but now I was in trouble for something that I couldn't help. My mom took the paper and started asking questions straight off it, all multiplication, and I answered 4 or 5 correctly and she handed me the paper back. She told me that if I could do those problems now, then there was no reason I couldn't have done them the day before on the test. Through this experience, she made it clear to me that if I truly hadn't known the problems, then I wouldn't have been punished, but the fact that I knew them, and was most likely in a rush to be the first one done, was the actual reason I was in trouble. She showed me that not knowing the answers is fine, that you can work on that in order to get better grades and a better understanding of the subject, but being careless was not OK. She made it clear that she expected me to do my best; it wasn't that she didn't love me or was angry that I hadn't but rather that we both knew that I could do better, and that's what she expected. [**Author's Note:** The mother here did not allow for the possibility that the child went "blank" from anxiety. Were that the case, this approach may have backfired.]

—15-year-old female, Texas

Help your child during classes and sports so that you can learn their limitations…. If expectations are set at, around, or above your child's limits, it will inspire growth and learning. When your child doesn't reach expectations, don't be too fast to discipline. If you know that the expectations you set should have been easily attainable, let it be known and give discipline. If the goal you set was slightly beyond their limits and they fell short, celebrate their attempt and help them achieve that goal next time.

—19-year-old male, "military brat" who has lived in multiple states and countries

… Parents can shift the focus of achievement from themselves to their kids. For example, I took all online classes for my freshman year of high school and was at risk of failing because I had only completed half a semester's worth of work by February. It was a terrible experience for all of us, but my mother made it clear that she wasn't upset because I had failed her in some way. Rather, she was angry because I had failed myself, and she was concerned that if I didn't learn better work habits, my whole academic future would be at risk, which was true. Because of the way she handled the situation, it was immediately evident to me that the problem wasn't about parental love; it was about how her love for me made her concerned that I was going to ruin my chances for a better life. This distinction made it easier for me overall to recover from my mistakes and eventually graduate from high school in the top 10% of my class. High expectations should always be about the child, not the parent, and if both parties understand that, there shouldn't be any confusion regarding the parent's unconditional love for the child.

—18-year-old male, North Carolina

My parents have high expectations for the means, not the end. For example, my final physics exam would determine whether or not I got an A or an A- in the class. I'd struggled with physics all year, and I'd made it my goal to have an A by the end of the year. The only problem? I needed a perfect score on the final to get an A. So for a week, I studied for physics, and on the day before the exam I even spent 6 hours in the dean's office studying with my teacher for the final. All the work paid off. I called my mom on the last day of school to tell her that I'd gotten a 100. She was excited for me, just as excited as I was about the A, but she told me the thing she was most proud of me for was the amount of work I'd put in before the test.

—16-year-old female, Georgia

Your expectations should be set up from an early age—that your child commits, tries hard, and is honest. Set these up when they're young to create a strong moral compass. After that has been created, let them make mistakes, and correct them, but let them make MISTAKES. It's one thing if they screw up accidentally and quite another if they purposefully screw you over. Learn the difference.

— 17-year-old male, Illinois

Parents should remember to create realistic expectations. Not for themselves but for their children. For example, Dan is doing bad in school; he's failing multiple classes. Instead of Dan's parents telling him his grades are unacceptable and that he needs to get an A, they should sit down and work with him. Figure out why he's failing classes. Then work with him. Ask him what grade he thinks he is capable of achieving. After both, perhaps Dan and his parents can agree that he can manage a C+. Give Dan the tools he needs in order to achieve his realistic expectation. This shows Dan that you are not disappointed in him. It sends a message to Dan that everyone, including Dan, knows he can do better and gives him room for necessary improvement.

—17-year-old female, Pennsylvania

A parent might say, "It's OK that you got a D on that test, honey; everyone gets a bad grade once in awhile, but to make up those missed points, how about you do Mr Jones's extra credit assignment? I'm not mad at you, but I do want you to try to make up those points and to allot a few more minutes for studying next time, OK?" In this example, the parent shows their unconditional love by showing the child their acceptance of the situation while holding their child to high expectations by suggesting the extra credit to repair any damage inflicted by the situation.

—14-year-old male, California

CHAPTER

7

Setting Clear Expectations
About Risky Behaviors

It is our responsibility to hold our kids to the highest of expectations when it comes to risky behaviors. *The bottom line: if it compromises safety or morality, you can't do it.* On the other hand, there is a certain degree of riskiness necessary in childhood and adolescence; we can't outlaw something that seems to be programmed in so many kids. As always, our challenge is striking the right balance. In this case, it is going to be allowing our children to stretch their wings and experience some risk while protecting them from long-term harm. (Part 2, Protection Versus Learning From Life's Lessons, explores this balancing act in depth, but it is important to briefly touch on this subject now, while we are discussing the expectations we set for our kids.)

I know I am suggesting you go against your instinctual need to have your child avoid all risks, but the suggestion is made for you to best support child development. Young people are programmed to take the greatest risk of their lifetime toward the end of adolescence. They are preparing themselves to leave a comfortable home where they are well cared for and protected to strike out in the world on their own. If you think about it, that step toward independence seems like a crazy choice. It takes a lot of practice over the years with smaller risks before being able to take that unimaginable risk. Letting them practice is good. Allowing them to compromise safety while practicing is not acceptable.

66 …HAVE RULES. CHILDREN NEED RULES. We all know that one kid who never hears no. Don't have that child. 99

—16-year-old female, Illinois

To understand your critical role in supporting healthy development, it is important to recall that adolescence is about trying to answer a fundamental question, "Who am I?" I want you to visualize your teen's efforts to answer this question as if he needs to put together a jigsaw puzzle of 10,000 pieces to create the full picture of who he is. He feels he has to complete it on his own, so he rarely, if ever, asks for help. In fact, instead of knowing we all work on figuring out who we are over our entire lifespan, he mistakenly believes it has to be completed before he leaves home. He even feels pressure to figure it all out in time to write his "who I am" college essay.

How does he begin assembling the puzzle? He begins with the corners and moves to the edges. What does he do next? He groups the like pieces and continually refers back to the picture on the box. Then he experiments with the pieces in the middle. Sometimes he gets the right fit, but it usually takes several attempts. Often he pushes and shoves some pieces together, convincing himself if he believes hard enough that they should fit, they somehow will. He later discovers there was another piece that fit more nicely without the forced effort.

When we monitor our children appropriately and know how to discipline effectively, we clarify the edges of the puzzle. When we show our children what stable, secure, consistent adults look like, we are the pictures on the box to which they can refer. Young people with clear boundaries and loving, functional role models are nicely positioned to complete their puzzles with relative ease.

How does this metaphor help us understand our behavioral expectations? First, it reinforces that we have to live and model the expectations we set. Second, it tells us we should set clear edges or boundaries beyond which we should not allow our children to stray. Kids feel more secure when they know someone has set clear behavioral limits. But if something is within those clearly defined borders, it is for them to experiment how those inner pieces might join together.

You can count on me not to let you crash against the rocks, but you'll learn to ride the waves yourself.

66 Respect is what every parent wants from their child and should have. Parents should have a deal of trust with their kids and that comes with setting a good example. I'm not staying that parents have to be perfect, but in my opinion I usually don't trust and respect someone who constantly makes bad decisions. 99

—14-year-old female, Illinois

More Thoughts From Teens

You can't always control your achievements or other activities that you do, and you may not always be good at everything that you do. But behavior is something that you can always control yourself, and I think that parents need to be very clear with behavior. My mom wants me to be on my best behavior at all times so that I can grow into a kind, understanding, polite, honest, and admirable young man. She gave me these values. Basically, I hold myself to high standards, even more than I normally would, when I see other teens not holding themselves to high standards.

—16-year-old male, Pennsylvania

Let them know that you have high expectations, but also let them know that you know they are humans, and they're going to make mistakes, and that's OK with you. Then, when they do make those mistakes, stay calm. Remember they're just teenagers and it's not the end of the world. Let them make these mistakes, because all they can do is learn from them. I think it only makes situations worse when parents go off on their kids and yell at them. The mistake has been made, the child feels bad, and yelling at them isn't going to change what happened, so why do it? All it's going to do is make things worse. Make sure you listen to their opinion, and take it into consideration. They're people, too, and they want to be respected just as much as you do. If they feel like you aren't respecting them, then they'll wonder why they should respect you. Obviously, make it clear what you expect out of them and what is acceptable and what's not and that there will be consequences when certain rules are not followed.

—17-year-old female, Virginia

Moments for Personal Reflection
or Serious Discussion

The real work of parenting doesn't happen while reading a book; it happens in the everyday interactions with your child. And those interactions often involve more than just the 2 of you. Some of the toughest moments are experienced with the dynamic tension you feel as you co-parent with other caring adults.

But the most challenging moments may be when you sit with yourself and reflect on why you do what you do. *How did my mother's words come out of my mouth? Why did that make me feel so angry? Why do I feel so defeated when my son doesn't listen to me about that one particular topic?*

It is during those personal moments you can gain awareness of the patterns you are repeating or insights into the pain for which you may be overcorrecting. Then you can consider if the words you say, and the messages you convey, are offering both the unconditional, unwavering love and the high expectations you know will benefit your child.

Equipped with this self-knowledge and clarification of your real goals, you are freed to adjust your approach. Now you are ready for a real conversation with your child during which you can discuss how you can be a guide toward the direction you both agree will lead to a safe, happy, moral, successful future.

Following are some of the questions to consider and perhaps discuss with your partner:

- Do you give love unconditionally? Do you speak of that love? How do you show it? Does your child know how crazy you are about him?

- Is it possible you are putting conditions on that love by linking it somehow to performance?

- Was love given to you unconditionally while growing up? If it was withheld, or kept close to the chest by someone very important to you, how might that have affected you?

- Are you striking the right balance between closeness and the healthy distance that fosters self-reliance?

- Does the thought of your child growing up excite you? Intimidate you? Sadden you?

- What messages did you receive growing up about success?

- Do you consider yourself successful? Why or why not?

- Until reading this book, how would you have defined success for your child? Was it about grades? Talent? Performance?

- Now that you are reading this book, how would you define success for your child?

- How were you praised when you were young? How were you criticized?

- Do you tend to ask only about results or to pay more attention to the effort?

- How do you criticize? Would your child say that you are specific in your criticism or might he sometimes feel attacked?

- Would you think of yourself as having a fixed mind-set or a growth mind-set? How do you think you might have developed that way of thinking?

- Do you compare your child's achievements to those of a sibling? A neighbor? Do you assign labels to your children? For example, *He will be a doctor. She's more like an artist.*

- Do you consider downtime a waste of time? Do you appreciate that your child needs time to reboot?

- Are you able to delay gratification?

- Do you help your child understand the benefits of how hard work and patience can pay off later?

- Are you clear about what you consider the boundaries of appropriate behavior?

- Do you feel like approaching parenting a bit differently would be a sign of weakness and inconsistency, or do you see possible change as an act of thoughtful parenting? Assuming that you see flexibility or change as a bad thing, where might you have learned that?

Now, look at the list of things to say and not to say to your child in Table 6-1. Talk with your partner about what kind of scenarios you encounter with your child during which you might find yourself praising or criticizing. Practice feedback in ways that will support your child's healthy and successful development.

PART

2

Protection Versus Learning From Life's Lessons

How do I protect my child while also letting her learn life's lessons?

There is no role more fundamental to parenting than to protect our children. However, we also know that overprotection can harm young people because they won't learn to navigate the world unless they are exposed to real challenges.

Our instinctual need to protect our children seems to be in direct opposition with our logical understanding of the need to prepare them. How can we balance these seemingly contradictory imperatives?

What You Will Learn

I hope to build the case that you can *both* protect your child from life's dangers and prepare him for life's challenges. It is about knowing where to place your protective boundaries, how to convey self-protective skills, and when to get out of the way—or at least watch from a distance. My daughters and I invite you to consider the balancing act we suggest and to draw your own conclusions after discussion with your partner, relatives, friends, and children.

Here is a preview of the points I will make over the next few chapters.

- Our duty is to protect our children. It is a matter of survival. But as they develop, their survival depends on us less.

- In many ways, as they grow older, and their needs are more complex, they need us more. But if they sense that we are overprotecting them, they will believe we consider them incapable.

- Our challenge is to temper our protective instincts so we can offer the needed balance of protection and guidance while allowing life to be an effective teacher.

- When safety is at immediate risk, our job is to jump in with full protective force.

- When morality is in question, our role is to offer full clarity about acceptable and unacceptable behaviors.

- You do not come unprepared in striking the balance between safety and protection. You can draw from what you've learned as a parent as early as the toddler years.

- Kids need to experience failure while they are still under their parents' watchful eyes. If we treat the stakes as too high for error, they will suffer their failures later—often with far greater consequences. Mistakes help people learn their limitations, as well as develop the skill sets that will compensate for their unevenness.

- Your job as a parent is to set clear boundaries and then (mostly) get out of the way.

- You'll find it far easier to get out of the way after you have imparted the needed skills to manage life's complexities.
  - We must offer our children a repertoire of self-care strategies so they know that their efficiency, focus, and well-being will be enhanced when they consistently make the time to eat well, exercise, sleep, and take a few moments to relax.
  - We hope that no matter how career focused our children may be, their work and home life will remain balanced so that family will be prioritized and health and wellness never sacrificed.
  - The only way our children can meet the goal of being both successful and balanced is for them to master efficiency. Therefore, they deserve exposure to the kind of organizational strategies that will allow them, if necessary, to accomplish more in less time.
  - We should prepare our children with the skills to accurately see another person's viewpoint, to assess the person's intentions, and to develop the self-advocacy skills to present their perspective.
  - Peer interactions are practice for future romantic and collegial relationships. Therefore, our kids need to learn how to navigate

peer life on their own, but we can equip them with strategies that will help them remain within safe boundaries as they do so.

- Everything risky you fear your child might do can be driven by stress. When our children are prepared to respond to stress in positive ways, they will be protected far into the future; they will repeatedly draw from these healthy adaptive strategies as they navigate an increasingly demanding world.

■ We want to set limits in a way that actually enhances our children's freedom. Limits are restrictive when given with the goal of controlling rather than protecting. They are smothering when they prevent someone from trying something she is perfectly capable of handling. They are disorienting when inconsistent. They offer security when they are clear markers for what is in- and out-of-bounds.

- While some boundaries can be established as firm, permanent rules, most are in place only until our kids gain more experience or demonstrate the responsibility that shows they need less supervision.
- Parents who balance monitoring with love and warmth and who are responsive to their children's needs raise kids who engage in fewer risky behaviors, perform better in school, and have a greater sense of well-being when entering adulthood.
- Setting boundaries is only the first step toward assuring safety; limits only have meaning if we also monitor that they are followed.
- Until recently, we were told it was our job to ask a lot of questions. The who, when, where, what, and whys of monitoring defined actively involved parents. But it is not what we *ask*; it is what we *know*. When we ask a lot of questions, the answers are not always truthful. To effectively monitor our children, we want to be the kind of parents to whom kids choose to disclose what is going on in their lives.

■ As we focus on independence, we must never forget that our real goal should be lifelong *inter*dependence. We *can* create the intergenerational relationships in which we all will flourish when our teens leave our house knowing that we supported, even celebrated, their growing independence. If, however, we install "control buttons," we may undermine our teens' desire to maintain a close connection with us.

CHAPTER

8

Protection Versus Preparation

Our duty is to protect our children. They are born as vulnerable and defenseless beings. We are hardwired to meet their every need from the instant we are given the honor to care for them.

Development is a process whereby our children's survival depends on us less and less. First they learn to grasp an item and bring it to their mouths. Then they can walk, and soon after they can talk. With each new skill, they move closer to the day when they could survive without us.

But surviving and thriving are 2 different things. In some ways, as our children grow older they need us more. Their needs become far more complex than survival. They must learn to find their place in an increasingly complicated world.

Our challenge is to temper our protective instincts so we can offer our children the balance they need of protection and guidance. Hardest of all, we need to learn when a hands-off approach allows life to be an effective teacher.

My Challenge

As the 3 of us sat down and discussed this chapter, my daughters warned me that the idea that you shouldn't protect your children from everything (and couldn't) is very well-known, so devoting an entire chapter to it might feel condescending. I countered that although people may rationally understand how important it is to get out of the way, it is directly in opposition to our parental instincts.

It may be that my girls can't fully relate yet to the inner conflict we parents feel because they haven't yet undergone the shock that hits when you realize you are responsible for another life. If my girls don't fully understand the internal conflict my wife and I go through as we struggle with the line between protection and overprotection, I'll bet that your children may not either.

Even if we intellectually understand that our kids need to walk through life's puddles, that does not mean our emotions are in sync with our minds. I suspect that is why many parents are overprotective, even as they catch themselves being so. I have 2 challenges in this part of the book to make the case that protection is critical, but overprotection is harmful. The first is to strengthen your intellectual understanding of the benefits children gain by learning to ride the waves themselves. The second, and far more difficult, is to bring your feelings and your intellect together so that you can rationally and intuitively know your child will gain strength from discovering the competencies within her. Only when you deeply believe the best way of protecting your child is to prepare her for an unpredictable world will you comfortably make the decision to guide from a safe distance.

In the next few chapters, we hope to give you the tools that will enable you to comfortably strike the balance between protection and preparation.

> ❝The world is a scary place, but parents have to realize they cannot hold their child's hand through everything.… Children may find themselves facing the challenges their parents once dealt with when they were their age…but everyone needs to experience them on their own to get through them. ❞
>
> —16-year-old female, Pennsylvania

Life Isn't Easy, Neither Are the Answers

Let's look at the following scenarios and consider how in each parents must balance the need to protect their child with letting him benefit from learning a life lesson.

Scenario 1: Fifteen-year-old Sara has always been at the top of her class. She is a fine gymnast and plays the violin in the community orchestra. One day she runs into the house and declares to her mother that she has had "the worst day EVER!" She begins ranting about how she got a B- on her biology lab. "…It's not fair because I did all the work on it, and my lab partners did nothing, and now my GPA is ruined and I am never getting into college. It's Charly's fault because he was supposed to graph up the results and he did a terrible job. Ms Diamond doesn't care what happens to me anyway. She didn't teach us anything; we had to learn it all from the book. She's lazy and hates teaching!" Should Sara's mother call the principal to discuss reprimanding Ms Diamond over her poor teaching skills? Should she call Ms Diamond to make sure she understands that Sara's group let her down?

Scenario 2: Eleven-year-old Elisheva got into a screaming fight after school with her oldest and closest friend, Neha. She is sure their friendship is over but doesn't care because she never wants to speak to her again anyway. Should Elisheva's mother invite Neha's mother over for tea so they can figure out a way to get their girls talking again? Or should she give Elisheva's a big reassuring hug and tell her that she should feel relieved because Neha had become a bad influence on her?

Scenario 3: Sixteen-year-old Max is brought home by the police an hour after curfew on Saturday night. They caught him in the park with a large group of kids who were smoking marijuana. He has to appear in court, where he might get a significant fine and is likely to lose his driver's permit. What should his father do?

Scenario 4: Nine-year-old Victor really wants to make the travel soccer team. His coach told him he would have a good chance if he could pick up his passing game. He has a great shot but tends to go for the goal instead of setting up his teammates. As he prepares, his father is proud that he learns to dribble, stabilize the ball, and pass. However, in the tryouts, Victor takes shot after shot. Victor is angry when Paolo misses an easy goal and tells him, "We'll never win with you on the team!" Victor does not make the team because the coach says he has a lot to learn about being a team player. What, if anything, should his father say to the coach? To Victor? Would your thoughts be different if Victor were age 7, 11, or 15?

Scenario 5: Fourteen-year-old Terrel went to a party over the weekend and slept late Sunday morning. He is not ready to turn in his homework on Monday. His score drops a full grade for every day the work is late. What should his parents do?

Scenario 6: Seventeen-year-old Courtney shouts, "See ya!" as she runs down the steps, knowing she is going to be picked up soon by her friends. Her parents look out the window as a car pulls up. First they see smoke coming out of the windows. Then they notice the kids in the back seat are all drinking beer. The driver is an old friend of the family. He lowers the window and shouts, "Ride's here, Courtney! Hurry up!" But his voice sounds different; he seems to be slurring. What should Courtney's parents do? Should they call the driver's parents? Stop Courtney from getting into the car?

In the situations described, the parents do not have easy decisions to make. Like in real life, there are reasonable people who could differ on the best course of action. I, though an "expert," cannot offer definitive answers because I do not know Sara, Elisheva, Max, Victor, Terrel, and Courtney. There might be something about their temperament or previous experiences which would make me modify what would otherwise be pretty clear directives.

With that said, here are some general guidelines.

- When safety is at immediate risk, there is no wiggle room. A parent's job is to intervene when necessary. It is *not* too controlling when you prevent your child from getting into a dangerous situation, such as a car with a drunk driver as in Courtney's situation. Her situation leaves no room for error. Her parents should refuse to allow her to leave the house.

- When morality is in question, there is no ambiguity. A parent's role is to be crystal clear about acceptable and unacceptable behaviors.

- When young people are caught with their behavior outside of an acceptable boundary, they need to bear the consequences. We can stand beside our children and help them process the experience. We must let them know unequivocally that our love is unwavering. We can even advocate for our child by letting the person in authority (eg, a teacher, coach, or police officer) know that our child is a wonderful person. We can assure the authority figure that we will monitor and give appropriate consequences at home, making it clear that we are taking the situation seriously and sharing the responsibility that a lesson will be driven home. We can advocate for restorative justice, which gives the child the ability to apologize and make amends to a person who was hurt by his actions, rather than punishment. But ultimately, the child must learn that not everything is fixable. In the real world, parents cannot step in and prevent consequences. It is better that your child learns some of these very serious lessons while still a minor. Finally, it is imperative that young people understand the serious consequences of behavioral choices; it could save their life or prevent them from descending down a slippery slope.

66 Kids make mistakes. It's better to make mistakes as a kid and not have it on your permanent record. If you are an adult, you could go to jail and have trouble finding a job. Make a mistake when you are young; you'll learn from it and not pay as severe consequences. With that said, don't let your kid rule the free world. Use good judgment that is common sense. Some creepy party in a sketchy part of town? I think not. Dating? It's a natural process. **99**

—15-year-old female, Vermont

- When a young person is not prepared with a school assignment, she needs to live with the consequences. In the workplace, there are few second chances.

- When your child thinks a teacher or coach is being unfair, it is reasonable to conduct your own assessments. However, your child will be best served if he learns self-advocacy skills. When children become adults, parents cannot call to yell at or persuade their boss to rethink a decision. Self-advocacy is a developmental process and a skill that builds over time and only with experience. On the other hand, only you know your child's unique developmental needs and special circumstances that could be influencing his mood, behavior, or performance. It is reasonable to pass along your insights because child professionals, such as teachers or coaches, should want this information.

- Parents should not interfere with personal relationships. The skills learned in childhood and adolescence teach how to interact with others throughout life. We absolutely can serve as guides when asked; being a sounding board is our best strategy.

- We must allow our children to perform unevenly, even if it means failure. Childhood and adolescence is the time when a person develops her "spikes," becomes aware of her unevenness, and develops strategies to work around her limitations. Parents should support children to reach their potential, even in those areas of limitations, but should not compensate for them or collude in hiding them.

You Are Better Prepared Than You Think

You have been practicing the balancing act between safety and allowing healthy, creative development from the moment your infant began creeping on the floor. You know the only way children learn is to test and manipulate their environment. You even allowed some accidents to happen to let your child learn not to repeat them. In the early years, you knew that your toddler's security in how far she could "stretch" had everything to do with her consistently checking back with you. She made sure you were visible and exuding that confidence from which she was drawing her own. You were a lighthouse even then—the stable, solid presence that allowed her to measure her own security. You kept an eye on the waves to make sure they were safe to venture into.

Many of the challenges you witness as your child grows will not be new to you. However, the fact that the waves are not always within your sight will naturally create more anxiety for you. The dangers are not as concrete. It is not as simple as making sure your 2-year-old does not toddle into traffic. Now dangers are about risk behaviors, moral choices, and long-term success. Uncertainty, nearly by definition, creates more anxiety for parents. Take comfort, however, in the experience you do have.

You knew to get down on your knees as you childproofed your home. You understood that if you did not see the world from your 16-month-old's view, you would likely never understand potential dangers. Adults don't think of sticking forks in electric sockets, let alone licking the outlets. They are not mysteries right in our view. We wouldn't consider swatting a hot steaming pot off of the stove. A toddler only sees puffs of steam and views the pot handle as a ready-made lever to pull. *Never stop trying to see the world from your child or adolescent's viewpoint.*

You didn't let your child put her hands on the stove. You didn't let her run into the street. You didn't let her walk onto a lake with a fresh coating of thin ice. *Never stop sensing when something poses an absolute danger with no room for error.*

You let your child build block towers even though you knew they would fall down. You let her take a bubble bath even though the floor would end up soaking wet. You let her knock over a few things so she could learn that items could break. You even let her paint on the walls. *Never stop letting your child make an occasional mess so that she can stretch her limits and learn how to clean up.*

You saw your 2-year-old trip and fall many times. You learned that if you ran over screaming and picked him up immediately, he was terrified and kept crying. You grew to understand that after a brief assessment, making sure he was OK, you'd give the knowing nod that said it all: "You're OK, little man." Same injury. Same event. But then he'd smile, chortle, get up, and run away. *Never stop letting your child know that you trust in his ability to pick himself up and move on.*

You taught your child so much. You took him to the playground every day and even had an art corner in your living room. You wanted him to benefit from a real teacher and to learn from playmates as well. You walked into the preschool together. You weren't sure if he held your hand tightly or if you weren't able to let go. He screamed for you not to leave. The teacher came over and gently walked him away. You peered through the window a few moments later and saw him jump from the teacher's comforting lap and begin running in circles with some other kids. *Never stop letting your child stretch his horizons, even when it is scary (for both of you). It may be the best way he can build his confidence and even his intelligence.*

Your 3-year-old got in squabbles in the sandbox. You wanted to reprimand that "evil" toddler who insisted on using the same yellow shovel. You nearly leapt off the bench to demand his mother teach him a thing or 2 about waiting his turn. But you took a deep breath and watched. Then you beamed with pride as your child gave the yellow shovel to the small boy and walked a few steps to pick up the blue one. *Never stop trusting in your child's innate flexibility and need to learn compromise, patience, and fairness.*

Never Stop Being Protective, but Don't Be Overprotective

Protection

The word *protection* evokes such positive feelings. It makes us think of holding our babies in warm blankets. It suggests we have the ability to keep our loved ones content, safe, and secure. Likely among our best moments of parenting are those when we were trusted to offer comfort in a way that only we knew how.

I believe the most meaningful, if not momentous, instant in my life was when I knew—really knew—that I filled the role of protector and comforter for my girls. I remember the exact spot in the girls' room as I laid on their carpet and the precise look on 7-month-old Talia's face. She was crying hysterically. I was pretty adept at rocking, strolling, and playing; I could even elicit giggles and change my girls' moods easily. But when they were ravenously hungry or out-of-control irritable, only my wife Celia could calm them. Tali was beyond the point of no return, and Celia was gone. My regular tricks were not working. Then, perhaps out of pity, Tali looked at me with a furrowed brow and spoke to me with her eyes: "Thanks for trying so hard. In fact, I think you'll do." She then placed her head on my chest, kept staring into my eyes, and allowed me to soothe her. I believe that moment was the single most masculine instant of my life. It was when I became a real father. Ilana blessed me with a nearly identical experience within a few days.

Trust

I think part of the reason it feels so good to protect somebody you love so deeply is you know you are wholly trusted. Unconditional love is a protective force because it makes safety and security guaranteed. Your unwavering love does not diminish as your child grows. Though it will be tested, I think you'll find it increases every day.

As our children grow, many of us struggle with dialing down our protective instincts. The problem becomes when our efforts to shield our children from harm cross the line into *overprotection*. Overprotection sends the clear message of, "I don't trust you." It implies that you do not find your child capable or competent. Your child may experience this as a shattering message that you lack confidence in her. Recall from earlier that your toddler's security, especially in testing how far she could "stretch," had everything to do with her checking back to see that you were exuding that confidence from which she was drawing her own. In the case of overprotection, our children don't draw strength from our confidence; they are undermined by our anxiety. You worry because you care. I couldn't possibly ask you to stop worrying; rather, my hope is to offer you strategies in Chapters 10 and 11 that you can use to prepare your child so you can comfortably trust you have less to worry about.

Protection and Trust

Protection and trust go together. It is protective to our children when we trust them. When we overprotect them, our mistrust undercuts their growth. Our love is most effective when we can appropriately shift our protective instincts toward preparing them to thrive in the real world. They will flourish outside of our homes, not because we protected them by never trusting them to venture forth but because they gained the confidence to do so through the protective force of our deeply rooted love.

Taking Off the Training Wheels

Childhood and adolescence is the time to make and learn from mistakes. It is the time to rebound from our errors and grow from our challenges. In truth, we are much safer to make mistakes as children because we remain under our parents' protective gaze. If we do not experience these errors, we won't test our limitations and therefore won't benefit from learning how to optimize our strengths in the face of those limitations. We won't fully know when to seek support. If we don't have the opportunity for this growth as a child, we are destined to make mistakes in adulthood when the stakes are much higher.

Our challenge as parents is to let our children experience the natural consequences from their actions while protecting them from those circumstances that could cause irreparable harm or threaten their safety.

Our pulse raced when we took off the training wheels. We took a deep breath and removed them nonetheless, because we reassured ourselves that we had taught our children how to ride. The wheels were on long enough. They were prepared.

If we are to raise our children to thrive through good *and* bad times, we must strike the balance between protection and overprotection. To find that proper balance, we must rationally and emotionally trust that the best way to protect them is to prepare them for the future.

More Thoughts From Teens

We need our parents less than we did earlier in our lives; at the same time, we require them even more. The most difficult part for a parent is knowing when a child needs you to step in and when the best course of action would be to stand back and let them find their way. Disregarding topics such as suicide, sexual abuse, and substance abuse, a child needs to learn how to find their way through the world so that they can stand on their own 2 feet and face the world around them. Unless the child directly asks for advice, which in a healthy parent-child relationship will happen, the parent should at most offer subtle advice without shoving the child toward any one choice.

—15-year-old male, Maryland

Parents should start by putting their child on a metaphorical "leash." The leash should be long enough to let their child see a small bit of the world and short enough that the child is still quite protected by his/her parents. As time goes on, the leash should slowly start to get longer, and longer, until it reaches a point where the leash is long enough to let the child see some of the good and bad of the world and be able to learn from it. The longer the leash gets, the more likely the child is to get tangled around one of life's obstacles, so the parents still need to be there to help untangle their child, just in case. As time goes on, the child will get used to the longer leash and learn how not to get it tangled around something. Eventually, when the time is right, the parents will have to let go of the leash and trust that their child knows his/her way back.

—14-year-old male, California

If you know, in your very core of being, that your youth has a stable head on their shoulders and has done hardly anything to show you otherwise, please trust them. I also think it is important for youth to remind their parents that they acknowledge this may be hard for them. The youth must also reinforce this idea of being stable and responsible. Yes, we will have our slipups either way, whether you protect us or not. But as long as we know in our hearts what is right and wrong, we will continue to learn.… Parents, you may know that your kid will likely face disappointment, but by not allowing your youth to pursue this "soon-to-be life lesson," you impede your youth's ability to say that they tried and that's the best they could do. And also give them the peace of mind that they went for what they thought was right; therefore, they will never regret not knowing what could have been.

—19-year-old female, Texas

(Counter Point) Parents really need to be here for their children no matter what. For example, if a child has put off their school project to the last minute, the stress of having to get it done on time is often enough to teach them a lesson to work ahead next time. I don't think a parent should let their child fail, and they should always help in getting the project finished, without doing it entirely. Honestly, it is embarrassing enough for a child to be in the situation, so their parents being there and helping them get through it means a lot and helps build a positive relationship between parent and child that will mean so much as the child grows older and is faced with new challenges. I also think that parents should try to protect their children from whatever they can…. I have learned from my situation that children today do not need to experience everything to learn a lesson. There are enough people that surround them in school and other places that one can learn from their peers.

—18-year-old female, Pennsylvania

My friend's parents are extremely protective. And this causes her to take every opportunity she gets to rebel. It's almost painful to be around them because every time she can do something to upset or anger them, she will. Another friend of mine has helicopter parents. She actually doesn't leave her house at all for fear of upsetting her family. She doesn't want to disappoint her father. She doesn't do anything, not because she worries something might happen to her but rather how her dad would react to what happened to her. All of this causes her to have really bad anxiety.

—18-year-old female, Pennsylvania

My parents only intervene when I enter into situations in which I violate their trust, ie, drugs, sex, drinking, etc. However, my parents also understand that if they keep me under an iron grip, then I will not experience life's lessons and experiences. So they do trust me but only after I've earned that trust through my actions and not only my words.

—16-year-old male, New Jersey

My parents are so overprotective they won't even let me sleep at my best friend's house for some reason. They must think that I am doing some type of bad activity. Parents should not jump to any conclusion of what their child is doing without good evidence. Parents should allow their children to learn from life's lessons, which is the best way because you just saying no encourages them to do it.

—16-year-old male, Pennsylvania

CHAPTER

9

The Upside of Failure

"And why do we fall, Bruce? So we can learn to pick ourselves up."

—Thomas Wayne, *Batman Begins*

Our kids need to experience some failure during childhood and adolescence, while they are still under our watchful eyes. If we treat the stakes as too high now, they will suffer their failures later when the consequences are much greater. When young people learn their limitations, they learn the compensations and work-arounds they'll need throughout their lifetimes.

It is critical to consider this as we try to shift from protection to preparation. Overprotection now plainly sets our children up for failure later in their adult lives.

Failure?

Failure is such a harsh word. It is full of judgment. It has an unforgiving, finite tone. I use it here intentionally to desensitize you to the concept. In truth, though, more appropriate words would be *mistakes, missteps, misadventures,* or *misfortunes*—all of which suggest a more palatable temporary state.

A first step to becoming comfortable with the concept of allowing failure in your children's lives is to see it as a passing event. It is sometimes a wake-up call, occasionally devastating, but always an opportunity for growth.

Let's consider the different areas in which our mistakes, missteps, misadventures, or misfortunes—indeed, even our failures—as children, build our strengths.

66 It may be hard to let them [teens] make those mistakes, and they may get hurt in the process, but that's all it is, a process. Teens will be hurt by something one day and over it the next. They will learn what happens when they make stupid mistakes, and they won't make them again. 99

—17-year-old female, Pennsylvania

Stretch

As long as we set our goals within easy reach, we can pretty much guarantee that we'll avoid failure altogether. It is not very difficult to succeed if your definition of success is halfhearted. But is that success? Will you experience pride if at the end of the day you conclude, "I was good enough?" Will you reach contentment or feel fulfilled if you report, "I did what I could?"

We discussed earlier that one of my greatest concerns for kids who are externally driven, meaning they perform because of pressure or emphasis on performance, is they work hard to win or make the grade. They place less emphasis on real success than on a guaranteed outcome. They'll get good grades in school but won't think outside of the box. They will stifle their creative energies out of fear of failure and therefore will limit their innovative potential.

Some businesses that care about innovation measure their triumphs *and* disappointments. You might think their hope is to highlight their many accomplishments while noting few, if any, failures. To the contrary, they want their "failure index" to reveal a reasonable proportion of failures. If everyone were operating in the safe zone, they would have plenty of successes but would never know their achievements reached close to their potential. When there are also failures, they can assume they considered and tested a wide breadth of possibilities beyond the confines of "the box." This leaves them reassured that their achievements were maximized given their current capabilities. They trust that with time, experience, further study, and commitment, the contributions they will be able to deliver will come because their innovators will continue to test the limits and learn from each error.

Experience!

"There is no passion to be found playing small—in settling for a life that is less than the one you are capable of living."

—Nelson Mandela

The concept of a "failure index" could be applied to our own lives. When we live within the confines of a box of our own making, we may never learn what exists just outside of its walls. When our fear of failure prevents us from testing our limits and therefore fully experiencing life, we are diminished.

When we fear our children's missteps, believing the stakes are too high, our children will incorporate our discomfort into their being. When we are overprotective, it might push them toward rebellion, in which case they might unwisely test their limits. Or our overprotection might have them internalize a sense of fragility, forever limiting their potential to experience life for fear of breaking.

" Expression and experimentation are a big part of a teen's life. Trying new things allows us to truly decide who we are and what our likes and dislikes are. Unless your teen is in a completely harmful situation that is either life or death, let them go through it; simply guide them when asked. **"**

—17-year-old female, Pennsylvania

Stick to It

Tenacity and grit are core character ingredients of a person destined for success. By its very definition, tenacity is about maintaining determination, even amidst disappointment, failure, or recrimination. While some people may be born with more resolve, this is something that is learned through experience. If one fears failure, one easily gives up with even a whiff of it. People with a fixed mind-set, to use Carol Dweck's framework, may change directions or abandon their thoughts or plans as soon as they feel that uncomfortable sense of approaching the possibility of not succeeding.

It is our job to celebrate our children when they test their limits and go beyond them. We must support them through their disappointments and encourage them to regroup and try again. We can help them learn that they will find the solution only after testing many paths or devoting time to practice.

We cannot instill this life lesson without failure as our ally. We must be as open to using our children's missteps as teaching tools as we are to seeking their successes. When we notice failures, we can encourage our children to view them as signals to try harder or change direction. Failures are not events to be avoided at all costs or signals to retreat. To drive the lessons home, we ask our children to retrace the path that led to a misstep and consider how another choice would have led to a different result. The key is for them to know a failure is not a disaster, nor is it a random event. They have the opportunity to learn from it and try again and again, if necessary, until they get the results they desire.

Think

Knowledge is not innate; it must be gained through study and experience. Intelligence may be genetically endowed, but it can also be developed. Therefore, how we think and what we know is largely influenced by what we do.

What kids *do* seems to be at least partly related to how we respond to their actions. When we focus on results or their performance, they tend to fear not producing. They are more likely to have the fixed mind-set or perfectionistic tendencies that stifle their creativity and desire to "stretch." Less stretching, less learning. On the other hand, when we focus on kids' efforts and the process by which they learn, they are more likely to go to their limits and beyond. Perhaps most relevant is that effort allows for mistakes; indeed, maximum effort almost expects stumbles. The challenge is in recovery and improvement.

When thinking outside of the box is encouraged, you can expect that many particularly innovative thoughts will be missteps. They will have to be reconsidered and modified, which requires more planning and thought. Furthermore, most people will not easily understand even those creative ideas that are destined for ultimate success. The innovator, therefore, has to think about how to distill his or her creative ideas into strategies that allow others to utilize them. It will likely take several attempts before the idea is reframed well enough for others to understand it.

Feel

When my family and I traveled to the US Virgin Islands, a gentleman, who was clearly a philosopher as well as master chef of fruit concoctions, served us smoothies.

The man took my daughters aside, having no idea of my interests, and said, "You know girls, life is like an EKG. Do you know what an EKG is, like on the doctors' shows on TV? It goes up and it goes down; that is life! Truth be told, when it stops going up and down, that is death. Life is good; the ups and downs are what make life worth living." I should mention I have found this concept on the Web used by many people and apologize for not being able to attribute its original source. But our source was a wonderful person who knew that every opportunity with young people presents a moment for shaping their perspectives. Youth should be about absorbing wisdom. Unfortunately, in our fast-paced world, not many adults take time to share their thoughts with young people.

It is life's ups and downs that build our compassion, empathy, and emotional resilience. Could you truly experience life's joys to the fullest without also knowing some of its misfortunes?

I occasionally share with youth audiences how my toughest moments largely shaped who I am. I suffered severe depression when I was 17 years old. Few knew it because I masked it with humor. But it was the lowest point in my life. I learned during that episode what helped and what didn't. I learned that shame and stigma could prevent people from seeking needed attention. I learned the importance of family, as I relied on my brother as I never had before. I learned about recovery and that even the worst feelings would pass. I believe the experience sensitized me to others' feelings and instilled deeply rooted empathy. On reflection, this period of 6 or 7 months as a late adolescent offered me the motivation and passion to spend my life lifting adolescents up and the capacity to serve them without judgment.

That was 35 years ago. I have the best life of anybody I know. I hope to never feel that way again, but if I do, I know it, too, shall pass. But the point I want to underscore most fervently is that the lowest time in my life paved my life path.

For those of you who have sensitive, sad, or anxious children, be prepared: their adolescence might be harder than most. It can hurt to feel; it is tough to care. But what a blessing sensitivity is. Do not suggest that your child "just get past it" or "stop making such a big deal of it." Rather, be with him. Your unwavering love is the consistent force he needs. Let him express his emotions to you, and, in turn, let him know you are grateful for his sharing with you who he *really* is.

> It is vital that a child be subjected to both highs and lows. If children do not learn how to deal with lows when they are young, how are they expected to cope when they are older?
>
> —17-year-old male, Pennsylvania

Sometimes we are not enough. Security rooted from a strong connection with parents is the key to resilience. But even if we have the strongest connection, our kids still have limits that can be exceeded when life gets too tough to manage. Resilience does not mean invulnerability. All people can reach their limits. It is not a sign of weakness on our children's part, nor a sign of poor parenting on ours, when our children reach their personal limits.

When young people reach their limits of resilience, they have to deal with their own sense of inadequacy; therefore, it's important they do not also have to worry about letting us down. If you want to ensure this never happens, let go of the fantasy that your child can handle everything as long as you parent well. When we view our children's problems as a reflection on us, we won't be poised to help them through the toughest times because we'll be working through our own feelings of inadequacy.

The first step is to reinforce that your supportive presence remains guaranteed. Listen, be a sounding board, offer advice only when prompted, and give hugs. Share that you are sorry for your child's current pain but happy to have a kid who feels deeply. When your child needs more than that, it is time to turn to professional help.

Many parents need to work through their own disappointment that their child needs more than they can offer. Think of your decision to seek further help as an act of love, not failure. You care so deeply that you will get whatever help your child needs to thrive. Furthermore, know that sometimes it is precisely your child's love for you that is the reason she needs to go to someone else for help. Sometimes because of the fear of disappointing or worrying us, adolescents will shield us from their painful realities. They need someone whose emotions they do not have to consider as they unload theirs.

It may be a challenge to guide a teenager to agree to seek professional guidance. Some feel ashamed that they can't handle their problems independently and worry that going for help confirms they are weak or "crazy." If you have ambivalent thoughts about professional support, try to overcome them *before* talking to your child. She will sense your mixed emotions easily, become more ashamed, and therefore be even more resistant. If you truly believe seeking help is a positive step forward, your adolescent is far more likely to see it that way.

Here are a few key points to communicate about help-seeking.

- You are thankful for the depth of your child's sensitivity and emotions. You know these traits will benefit her later, but she may need help learning how to manage all of those feelings now.

- Emotional distress is treatable, and professionals know how to support people to feel better.

- Seeking help is an act of strength. Strong people know they are capable of feeling better and deserve to feel better, and they will take the steps to feel better.

- Professionals do not pity the youth they serve; they serve because they want to.

- Professionals honor privacy and care for people without judgment.

- Professionals do not offer solutions or solve problems entirely but instead try to find strengths and build on them. People will solve their own problems and will have the support to do so. They will use these new skills to live a fuller life and to help other people.

Bounce

Resilience is about being able to recover from adversity, bouncing back even when life brings you down. There is no doubt the core ingredient necessary to build a resilient young person is a deeply rooted connection to someone who believes in him wholeheartedly and unconditionally. But there is so much more needed to prepare our children to thrive through good and bad times. Borrowing heavily from the positive youth development model and the framework first proposed by Rick Little, Richard Lerner, and colleagues, I have proposed The Seven Cs Model of Resilience. It is thoroughly detailed in my book *Building Resilience in Children and Teens: Giving Kids Roots and Wings*. The book describes how to support the development of these 7 key attributes children need to flourish through both stable and challenging times.

1. *Confidence* in their ability to master life's circumstances

2. A sense of *competence* that is earned from their developing mastery

3. A deeply rooted sense of *connection* to family, school, friends, and community

4. A strong *character* that demonstrates their integrity, knowledge of right from wrong, and tenacity

5. The knowledge that they matter, which comes from understanding *contributions* they can make

6. The possession of a wide repertoire of positive *coping* strategies, so that when life presents challenges they will reach for healthy solutions to manage their stress rather than quick easy fixes that may bring them harm

7. A sense of *control* based on the understanding that decisions they make and actions they take make a difference to their circumstances

Resilience is not an inborn trait; it is developed in response to life circumstances. Our support during trying times makes all the difference. If we are to help our children develop the resilience that will carry them forth throughout their lives, we need to allow exposure to some trials during their childhood. As desperately as we wish we could encase them in Bubble Wrap, we cannot protect them from the ups and downs of life. When we view these problems as disasters to be avoided at all costs, we limit our children's opportunities to build resilience. When we welcome these circumstances as temporary setbacks from which they can grow, we frame them as opportunities. Modeling how to view the circumstances is more important than any words we might say.

66 Hand-holding your child through every obstacle is not going to set them up to be successful. In fact, quite the opposite. 99

—16-year-old male, Pennsylvania

Relate

We hope our children will ultimately find a partner with whom they have lifelong loving and healthy relationships, and we dream they will build a home in which their own children flourish. We want them to also have fulfilling relationships with friends and community members. Finally, we hope they will find their interactions in the workplace collaborative and productive.

We would be lying to ourselves, and to them, if we said that relationships are easy. In fact, those relationships most important to us are likely the most difficult because of our emotional investment in them.

Childhood squabbles are about learning to negotiate and self-advocate. Early ones are about learning that others have a point of view. Later ones are about learning compromise and forgiveness. Some disagreements offer us the opportunity to learn that no matter how hard we try to understand another's perspective, our minds will never meet. But we can still have a peaceful resolution if we respectfully listen and agree to disagree. Sometimes we even learn that conflict avoidance altogether is the best plan.

As much as it is painful to watch our children be unhappy, when we jump in to fix their social mishaps we deprive them of the opportunity to gain critical interpersonal knowledge. As much as it can be infuriating to watch our children be treated unfairly by teachers or coaches, we rob them of the chance to develop self-advocacy skills when we aggressively charge to fix the problem. We also take away the opportunity for them to grasp that an action on their part may have initiated a cycle of misunderstandings.

Succeed

We want our kids to make their mark in the world. For them to be able to accomplish and contribute to their potential, they have to learn how to focus their energies. They have to lead with their strengths and not allow limitations to hold them back. By necessity, they have to learn, therefore, to distinguish between their strengths and limitations; they have to understand their unevenness. Their "spikes" have to be evident. The only way for them to arrive at this level of insight is to try out many things. In most endeavors they will not excel, and in some they will fail miserably. Protecting them from the self-awareness of their very real strong points and weaknesses prevents them from achieving success.

Next, let's return to those traits we said we wanted our children to develop so they will be successful 35-, 40-, and 50-year-olds. We'll briefly review how mistakes, missteps, mishaps, and misadventures, even failures, contribute to the development of these characteristics.

Happy

Happiness in adulthood is about contentment. Contentment comes from feeling like you are making your contribution and living your life to the fullest. It is about experiencing life with all of its abundant pleasures, as well as its disappointments and tragedies. Also, to know happiness, we have to have some familiarity with its opposite.

Compassionate, Empathetic, and Generous of Spirit

As we discussed developing the capacity to feel, we spoke of the experiences that build sensitivity. These moments that create our greatest distress are also those that motivate us to care for others. As we are lifted up in our moments of need, we are driven to share our strengths with others in their moments of vulnerability.

Hardworking, Tenacious, and Gritty

The only way to learn tenacity and grit is to know struggle and to experience how to overcome challenges.

Flexible, Creative, and Innovative

The people endowed with these traits may be those who ensure our society's survival. They have to come up with the big ideas not yet imagined. They may meet with more failures along the way than the rest of us precisely because they think outside of the box. Therefore, we hope they will be able to tolerate a very high "failure index." We need them to learn from each misstep and come up with creative solutions to overcome the challenges.

Collaborative and Appreciative of Constructive Criticism

Great collaborators accept others' failures sometimes precisely so they can also draw from the outer reaches of their potential. People who make it in the workplace grow on the job. The only way to grow on the job is to learn from others' wisdom and experience. More experienced colleagues teach us best by forcing us to reshape our approaches and consider better strategies. When we view this as a personal attack, or validation that we are incapable, we will stagnate in our careers. When we see their critiques as opportunities for growth, our capacity to contribute will continually be enhanced.

Resilient

We develop a resilient mind-set when we gain the experience of rebounding from life's challenges. We think in a resilient way when we can distinguish a "real tiger" from a "paper tiger," knowing the difference between something that threatens our lives versus something that just feels scary. Mistakes do not challenge our survival. Missteps allow us to correct our path.

Limits of Failure

By now you might think I am enamored by all of the benefits of failure. Not quite so. I am not suggesting a hands-off approach to parenting. I believe there are times you should step in. There is no lesson learned like learning it yourself through experience. But we can still help our children experience growth when we help them avert a catastrophe, as long as we simultaneously help them understand where their choices or actions are leading.

So when do you step in? The themes will become increasingly familiar. If it involves safety, you do not allow a mistake. If it treads on immorality, you do not allow misadventure. If it could cause irreparable harm, you work to prevent permanent damage. These last 2 categories leave room for your judgment, because only an assessment of specific circumstances can determine when a situation is immoral or could lead to long-standing harm.

❝ My mom always tells me that sometimes she lets me win some battles but never the war. Never lose the war with your kids, because that's when failures become damaging. **❞**

—16-year-old female, New Jersey

This leads nicely to our forthcoming discussion on boundaries and monitoring in Chapters 12 and 13. We need to set those limits beyond which our children cannot stray because the risks of physical danger, irreparable harm, or immoral behavior are simply too great.

More Thoughts From Teens

Parents need to remind their kids to do their homework and do the best that they can in all of their classes. Sometimes, though, kids have to learn some lessons for themselves. A hard lesson I have learned is not to procrastinate; after a couple of nights of working on projects until midnight, now I always finish them early. My parents had warned me not to procrastinate, but that was a lesson I had to learn the hard way.

—14-year-old female, Maine

… A situation where protection is needed is mental health. As a person who has struggled with depression and anxiety, I would not be where I am without the support of my parents. I do not think any kid can deal with depression without a strong support group. This is probably the worst situation to allow a kid to deal with by themselves. So watch your kids and make sure they are healthy. It can be tough to detect but not impossible.

—16-year-old male, Pennsylvania

… I find it much easier to learn life lessons from actual experiences instead of a punishment or a grounding for an attempted act that is unsafe or not wise. For example, if a teen was trespassing, or was doing something unwise or unlawful, it would typically be best for them to learn the lesson on their own. Getting caught and chased off a property can be scary and might lead to fear of doing that same unwise act. This also applies to social and economic things as well; if a child wants to spend their money on something expensive and most likely not useful or "worth it," let them. It is best to learn your lesson the hard way than to get scolded for attempting it. I was once set on building a go-kart out of PVC pipe, which was not a good material to use given its weak structure. My parents were aware of this and did not stop me. I ended up spending over $900 of my own money on what eventually became a mound of scrap. I learned many good life lessons from that experience.

—13-year-old male, Illinois

The lessons you learn about the real world are from the mistakes and decisions that you make, not from what your parents tell you. Some parents try to protect their teens too much (as mine did) and in the end it does more harm than good. It makes kids want to do whatever you told them they couldn't do even more. They are more likely to sneak out, more likely to lie, and less likely to tell you anything. Because of how overprotective my parents were, I never told them anything about what was going on in my life, academically or personally.

—19-year-old female, Texas

My friend's mom is insanely overprotective, despite the fact that my friend is the most pure and levelheaded person. Her mom doesn't let her drive the car, even though she has had her license for nearly a year. Her mom wouldn't let her date a good guy at 17 because she "wasn't old enough to date." At some point, parents need to accept the fact that their children are growing up and are old enough to make decisions for themselves. If you let your daughter date and she gets her heart broken, she'll learn to stay away from inappropriate dates. If you let her drive and she gets a ticket, she'll learn to drive more carefully.

—17-year-old female, New Jersey

Parents should let teens learn the same way they did—from experience! The times when they should step in are life-altering or life-threatening times. Other than that, let them learn by themselves. Yes, you want to help us and we do care what you think, but holding us back from something because it didn't work out for you when you were our age is just gonna make us rebel against you. Yes, you know how it will turn out, but you did it, and you're just fine now and you're brighter for experiencing it. So you should let them do the same. It will make them value what you tried to keep them from even more, and it will really stick with them.

—17-year-old female, Louisiana

Children have to sink or swim. If a parent doesn't allow their child to get hurt or make a huge mistake and keeps them restricted their whole childhood, then the outcome could be disastrous. All children are young, stupid, and going to make mistakes. If I make a huge mistake and can come back to a safe environment, I will learn from it and not do it when I am an adult and it really counts. But if I am kept away from all my curiosities during childhood, then I am going to make all these mistakes as an adult. This is potentially much more dangerous.

—Anonymous

I fell into a very deep depression that no one saw or cared about. [My mother] assumed that I would just adapt, but I went over the deep end, even contemplating death. When a kid asks for help, you should really help them. It's hard enough for them to come to you to begin with. No one is eager to go running to mommy, so when it comes to the point where we feel we really do need to come to you, it's something that we feel we just can't handle ourselves, that is when we need you.

—14-year-old female, Georgia

My parents, while heavily involved in the academic, athletic, and other extracurricular aspects of my life, weren't really around for the social or emotional experiences. Everyday, I wish it were the other way around. I could have played just as well at my basketball games without my mom sitting in the stands; I regret not being able to reach out to her to talk about boys or the latest idea plaguing my mind. Because of this detachment, I learned most of my "life lessons" from other people I encountered, usually the hard way, and the mountain of books and movies in my room. These lessons definitely stuck with me more, and made me stronger, but the struggle was constantly all too real for me. I know I'll learn something better by doing it for myself, but it would be nice if, after the fact, I could talk with my mom or dad about it. A single word of encouragement during a rough patch would have been worth more than a thousand words of praise after a perfect test score. The advice I'd give to parents is to simply ask, "Do you want to talk about it?" or "How are you really feeling about it?" Sometimes (most times) that's enough to get me to let down my walls—the walls I've constructed throughout the years as I've fallen and found it too hard to get up on my own….

—16-year-old female, Georgia

CHAPTER

10

Navigational Strategies

I t's not easy to quiet our instinctual inner alarm that tells us we need to protect our kids. It becomes far more palatable when we make the transition from the mind-set of protection to that of preparation. A further step to calming our automatic jump-in reflex is to understand that failures bring growth. Once at this point, we can (at least intellectually) understand that our job as parents is to set clear boundaries and then (mostly) get out of the way. We watch from the sidelines because we know that our kids need to learn to deal with life's complexities. We recognize this as *their* work and, with varying moments of reluctance, let them find their way through. We can, however, have a role in helping them know how to approach that work. After all, people bring tools to the workplace, right?

The overriding truth is you'll find it far easier to get out of the way when you know your child is equipped with the needed skills to manage his life. This chapter is about strategies to navigate the world, and the next is about managing life's inevitable stressors in healthy ways. These chapters provide the toolkit you hope your child will possess as he learns to be more independent and enters unchartered waters. It brings no guarantees whatsoever but may offer you peace of mind that your child is better prepared or at least that you've done your part to offer proactive guidance.

What's in the Toolkit?

For our kids to be able to handle life's ups and downs and to optimally handle interpersonal relationships, we hope they can

- Learn to take care of themselves, so they can remain healthy and achieve optimal life-work-family balance.

- Incorporate organizational strategies that will lead to success and efficiency that will enable them to have healthy life-work-family balance.

- Interact well with people no matter where they meet them.

- Learn self-advocacy skills, so they can present their cases without alienating or inflaming someone with whom they disagree.

- Have healthy friendships while not being unduly influenced by peer pressure.

Self-care Strategies

No matter what life brings, we handle it better when we first care for ourselves. Despite this widely accepted "grandma's wisdom," the first things to go when we get overwhelmed are precisely those self-care strategies that offer us the best chance of maintaining the stamina needed to dig ourselves out from under the pile. People say they are too busy to eat well, exercise, take a few moments to relax, or sleep. Kids tell us they don't have time to exercise or sit down for a decent meal. "Relaxation? Are you nuts?! And sleep?! How can I sleep when I'll fail this test tomorrow if I don't study?" We need to help them understand they do not have the time *not* to eat well, exercise, sleep, and take a few moments to relax.

Efficiency is the secret to success and life balance. There is always going to be too much to do if you can't concentrate. People focus better and are more alert when they eat foods that infuse their brain with a steady supply of nutrients. Exercise will keep them more attentive and will relieve the anxiety that is preventing them from absorbing new information. Relaxation, even for a few minutes, will reboot their brain and allow them to refocus. It is proven that people absorb more information when they have an occasional complete shift in focus. Play, meditation, or a brief escape into a book can successfully serve as that "refresh button."

Sleep is not expendable. High school kids may believe their homework is so voluminous that they have to stay up into the wee hours of the morning. They may be correct in saying they have been assigned too much work. That is all the more reason not to enter the cycle of sleeplessness and fatigue. When they stay up too late, they won't be able to focus the next day in school. Therefore, they won't absorb information and they'll just have more work to bring home the next night. But when they get home, they'll be exhausted, so they'll be inefficient in reviewing what their fatigue caused them to miss during the day, and their new homework will be attacked with impaired concentration and efficiency. Short naps might help, but long ones interrupt sleep-wake patterns and diminish restful, restorative sleep. The cycle feeds on itself.

These topics are covered in greater detail in Chapter 11, Preparing Your Child for a Stressful World. I want to underscore here that self-care is central to stress management, but it is also critical for success.

I'm sure you believe me; the problem is your kid won't believe you. Time pressures demand an instant response, such as getting right to work, staying up late, or grabbing the donut and coffee. It takes life experience to learn how important a healthy body is to concentration, efficiency, and stamina. The first step is to model the right behaviors so your words don't seem hypocritical. Second, have a full discussion on the matter so your child is well-informed. Try to have this conversation prior to high school, so your child can incorporate it into his lifestyle before having to deal with pressing demands.

In my experience working with families, it is challenging to get time-pressured adolescents to believe there is a yield when investing time in anything other than work or sport. They need to learn it themselves. Try challenging your child to follow your suggestions for a few days while keeping a diary of the effects. Ask her to incorporate one lifestyle switch at a time, so she is able to more effectively monitor "the experiment."

Nutrition and sleep will pay off instantly in enhanced concentration and stamina. But not all lifestyle changes will offer immediate, convincing benefits. Kids may need to experience a few days of enhanced sleep to see how much more efficient they will be at learning and completing homework. Soon they'll find their need to stay up late diminishes. Relaxation pays off pretty quickly, as long as your child doesn't choose a technique that requires skill development. For immediate results, suggest games or reading a book. Then, once your child sees that relaxation breaks work, invite her to explore the benefits of mindfulness or meditation. Exercise offers immediate results for anxiety reduction, but the full benefits may take a while to enjoy. Athletic children already know how exercise clears their brains, restores their calm, and builds their energy. They may only need your permission to act on their existing wisdom. If your child is unconditioned, she may need a longer trial, allowing exercise to be added slowly to maximize the benefits while minimizing the early discomfort. I tell kids if they follow my advice on exercise, the first few days they'll be saying, "I hate Dr Ken, I hate Dr Ken, I hate Dr Ken." After those first several days, they will look forward it.

Don't be too rigid in demanding your child follows your wellness rules. This is something he needs to learn himself after he is well informed by you. Even an adolescent well practiced in self-care strategies will need to make exceptions for himself. All high school students will have projects that require some late nights. Rare exceptions are OK, and you should not choose to fight battles on the night when your teen needs to focus on completing a big assignment. You'll lose anyway. However, make sure your children know cramming for tests late into the night is likely to decrease their performance and therefore is almost always a bad idea. This ties in nicely to the organizational skills that allow more time for ongoing learning.

Organizational Skills

We hope our children will grow to be both successful and well-balanced. We dream they will have satisfying careers that allow them to make meaningful contributions, as well as reinforce for them that they matter. That is likely going to take some hard work; ideally, it will feel less like work if it remains aligned with their sense of purpose. We also hope that no matter how career focused our children may become, their work and home life will remain balanced so that family will be prioritized and their health and wellness never sacrificed. The only way our children can meet the goal of being both successful and balanced is for them to master efficiency. Learning to be efficient takes an investment of time, but efficiency frees up time.

Many young people in this generation are spread so thin that they see multitasking as the only possible solution. Multitasking is rarely the best way to maximize accomplishment; focus is the best strategy. However, when done in a way that prioritizes different tasks and still works toward producing well-thought-out, quality products, working on different tasks simultaneously can be reasonable. The key is that our children learn that being busy is not the same as accomplishing something. In addition, technology is now such a large part of their lives that many consider it normal to conduct several conversations (via text or social media) while doing work. This is never a good idea.

Another reason multitasking may harm our children is it contributes to a frenetic pace of life that makes taking the time for self-care seem like a luxury. Their lack of firsthand experience of the efficiency gained through proper exercise, relaxation, nutrition, and sleep makes it harder for them to believe us as we try to teach them about self-care. For this reason, we must model self-care. However, even if we do this, young people may ignore our spoken advice and choose not to copy our modeled behaviors because they feel compelled to do what they believe they have to do to get their work done or participate in their activities.

If your child rejects your input on organizational strategies because she does not believe you understand all she has to handle, consider turning to the Internet. Search for "organizational strategies" for children or adolescents and you will find a wealth of advice to which you can direct your child. If you feel your child would benefit from involving a professional, consider exploring the resources offered by the National Association of Professional Organizers (www.napo.net).

Remember that even if your child rejects your input one day, he might be receptive to it the next. In addition to ideas you may pick up on the Internet, here are a variety of ideas that have helped my patients increase their organizational skills. If your child travels between homes, that alone can be disruptive to his ability to stay organized. It is particularly important, therefore, that each of the following strategies are replicated in each setting. It may also be useful to use electronics rather than paper to create tools that easily travel.

Study Space

Have your child designate and stick to a space as a study area. It should be well lit and well supplied with study materials. Just as the bed should only be used for sleeping (never as a study area!), the study space should be a place where your child trains herself to know, "If I am here, I should be working." Study breaks should be elsewhere. Exceptions can be those 3- to 4-minute brain-rebooting breaks, such as a quick computer or phone game. The key is to play time-limited games, not the ones that can consume an endless amount of time by drawing you in as you advance levels. Those breaks allow the brain a quick change of attention that will allow further focus later. This is not a space to use social media because that can become a time sink with no end point.

External File Cabinets

Some kids seem to be born organized, but most need to learn how to prioritize their plans. People naturally shift their attention to the most interesting or fun project, but the "shiny ball" is not always the most important task. We all can benefit from an external file cabinet to help learn internal organizational strategies. A starting point is to organize paper flow, so we spend less time looking for lost items and can visually see what is done and what is left to do. Young people might have a binder or desk trays that organize items into "homework to do" and "homework done" for each of their class subjects.

A daily planner can help them track a list of tasks needing completion. The list should be comprehensive, including all that needs to be done, but constructed in a way that assures progress but simultaneously avoids the frustration that comes with feeling nothing ever gets accomplished. The list needs to clarify which items are priorities. Otherwise, all items can appear equal and one naturally will fill in as many boxes as possible by finishing the easy (but not very important) tasks. But sometimes those priority boxes represent large projects that take extended time to complete. To avoid the sense that nothing is getting done, it is helpful to take those big tasks (the "mountains") and break them into their component parts (the "hills") so your child can feel good about the progress he is making. Nothing feels better than watching boxes get filled. Also, we need to encourage youth to put things on their list that will give them pleasure or help them relax. Putting these items on a task list will reinforce these are vital items to do every day, no matter how burdensome your child's list of accomplishments seems to be. We want our children to start a lifelong habit of scheduling time for themselves and to be shared with loved ones.

Also, help your child know that ideas always come into and out of our minds, and it is maddening to lose good ideas. Your child should have a strategy to capture those fleeting flashes of brilliance (eg, Post-it notes, an app on an electronic phone or tablet, or a small pad of paper). The key, however, is to consolidate those ideas at the end of the day onto the central list to avoid the frustration of having written down the ideas only to have them vanish.

The organizational strategies just described are prime examples of something you inform your child about and then get out of the way. Learning the usefulness of these critical tools is their work. Bite your lip if you even consider giving an, "I told you so." Instead, try, "Any ideas on how you could have done better here?"

Presentation Skills

In this age of cyber-communication, the basics of face-to-face communication may be something kids have less experience with or find awkward. The ease by which communication now flows electronically offers many advantages, but the workplace (and home!) still require old-fashioned human connections, and we mustn't let these skills lapse. I strongly advise that you try to have your children be comfortable with regular communication before they enter the world of communication through texting or typing. Once they enter that world, face-to-face talking becomes a relative rarity, and handling oneself by phone becomes even rarer.

The bottom line is you want your child to have the social skills later on to look an employer in the eye, firmly and appropriately shake his or her hand, and say, "I'm the person for the job." You also want your child to know how to put others at ease or present herself in a way that makes others feel she is well mannered, respectful, and perhaps someone they would like to get to know. People who are naturally introverted or shy need to learn how to bring themselves out and to mask their discomfort. Those who, on the other hand, are naturally extroverted or gregarious may need to learn to tone themselves down to give others a chance to warm up.

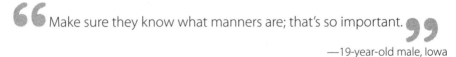

" Make sure they know what manners are; that's so important. **"**

—19-year-old male, Iowa

So, just as you taught your 2-year-old to say please and thank you, you want to make sure your kid knows how to

- Gain someone's attention politely.

- Respectfully and professionally introduce himself.

- Shake someone's hand.

- Maintain eye contact (when culturally appropriate).

- Briefly explain his need(s).

- Display confidence in his abilities, without seeming arrogant.

- Be appropriately humble, without being self-defeating.

- Thank someone for his or her time and attention.

Self-advocacy Skills

When we hear our kid's point of view, it is easy to believe the adults in her life—teachers, coaches, even parents!—are "soooooooooo unfair." She may be right. People throughout their lives will be unreasonable and unfair. However, we won't be able to protect our children then; therefore, the best thing we can do now is to prepare them with the skills to accurately see another person's viewpoint, assess the person's intentions, and develop the self-advocacy skills to present their perspective.

If you believe your child is genuinely being treated unjustly by a teacher or coach, you should strongly advocate on your child's behalf, particularly if your child is in the early years of high school or younger. But as an experienced adult, you know you have to assess the situation objectively. If you go into attack mode, all you will receive is defensiveness and force the other person to dig his or her heels in. Instead, give the involved adult the benefit of the doubt that as a child professional, he or she cares about kids and is trying to do what is right. Give the person an "A for effort." This strengths-based start allows you to acknowledge the common desire for your child to thrive, and then both of you can mutually determine the best path forward.

This approach turns down the volume on any potential disagreement. You assumed a misunderstanding, expected you were speaking to a reasonable caring person, and were open minded to hear another perspective. This likely will allow you to more effectively come to a solution. It may be, however, that you occasionally find the person's viewpoint completely unacceptable. By this point, you have gained a fair assessment and can take your advocacy to the next level by speaking to a supervisor. You have learned all of this from experience.

Let's be honest, though. Sometimes we behave badly. Something rises within us when we think our children are emotionally wounded. Our instinctual "momma tiger" or "papa bear" protective rage comes out and all we know about human relationships flies out the window. Hopefully, our irrationality passes first, allowing us to enter the discussion in a state of calm, prepared to give that presumptive A. When we control our anger and are thoughtful and strategic in our approach as we advocate for our children, we model for them how to handle themselves in the future when they will stand up for themselves.

Kids do not always assume the best of their teachers or coaches. They might jump to the assumption they are being treated unfairly. Our kids will develop interaction skills that serve them far into the future when we help them consider others' intentions. Teach them to give that A and to consider how the adult may have been trying to do the right thing. You might say, "I know Coach Roberts upset you, but I know she cares about you. Why do you think she might have had you sit out the second half of the game?" Your child may indignantly respond, "Why are you taking her side?!" Explain that, on the contrary, you are completely on your child's side. But we get the most out of our coaches and educators when we learn from them, and sometimes their lessons don't feel good but teach us non-etheless. Further, it is important to teach your child how to stand up for herself and that the first step toward self-advocacy is to avoid conflict and learn how to partner with someone to collaboratively arrive at solutions.

Self-advocacy 101: The "I" Statement

The first step to learning self-advocacy is knowing how to present your viewpoint in a way that is less likely to make someone else defensive. The "I" statement is a lifelong skill for teaching youth to use with others and for you to use in your household to discuss meaningful issues. When any of us, young person or adult, is angry, frustrated, or worried, we tend to blame the other person for causing a problem. When people are blamed, they feel judged and become defensive. This makes them hold their position more rigidly or even become hostile.

Many arguments start with people telling others precisely what they are doing wrong. These statements often begin with "you." The natural response to, "You did this," is a defensive-offensive, "I did not; you caused it!" Instead, using "I" statements like, "I feel this way when…" or, "This makes me think…" may encourage the other person to problem-solve, or even feel empathy, because the natural response then becomes, "How can I help you feel better?" or "How can we solve this?"

For example, if your child is frustrated with his coach, he may say, "You are being so unfair! You know I deserved to start the game. Why are you punishing me?" Instead, suggest he say, "I tried hard to train for this game and felt really disappointed to get so little playing time. Can you help me understand what I can do to start the next game?"

Or if your child is angry with her teacher, she might feel like saying, "You know I deserved a B on that paper. You are totally unfair. You give the kids you like better grades!" Instead, suggest she say, "I was really disappointed that I got a C on my paper. I thought I did a good job. Can you help me understand why you thought I deserved a lower grade?"

On extraordinarily rare occasions, your child may even feel like you are not being fair. No, really, it is possible. She might want to shout, "You are totally unfair! You are always punishing me for being born, and you obviously like my sister/brother better than me." That might make you feel defensive. Instead, she should say, "I really feel like I wasn't treated fairly, and it makes me sad and frustrated. Sometimes, I even feel like I am not as loved as other people around here."

I would be a bit shocked if that didn't draw out your love and lead you to explore why she feels that way.

Other Strategies to Advocate, Deescalate, and Negotiate

- Always come prepared to any self-advocacy session with a concrete concern and potential solution. Ideally, the solution involves steps both parties can take.

- Always come prepared to any discussion with facts to back up your assertion. Also, be prepared to present a clear request.

- Everybody needs to learn how to take a time-out. A rational presentation is more likely to meet with success.

- Take the time to calmly explain why something upsets you.

- Allow the other person time to fully explain himself. He will be less likely to react angrily or reject your views if he feels genuinely heard.

- Don't bring up things from the past; focus on the current issue.

- Never tell anybody that any feeling they have is wrong, so you ensure thoughts and feelings are shared. Without thoughts and feelings on the table, conflicts often don't get settled.

- On the other hand, you don't have to share *all* of your feelings. Just those that are relevant to moving forward.

- If you've made a mistake, apologies go a long way!

Peer Relation Skills

In your dreams, your sweet innocent child would be confronted with peer pressure and would adamantly respond, "I will not participate in this behavior because it conflicts with my ethical, moral, and spiritual standards. I do not have to go along with the crowd, because I stand tall as my own person." Back to reality. Your teenager is trying to figure out whether or not she is normal and is using peers as a benchmark. Peer pressure is not what we see on made-for-TV movies. It rarely is about one young person saying to another, "Smoke this or die." Instead, it is about kids doing what they think they have to do to fit in.

As we will discuss in Chapter 13, Effective Monitoring, your kid will likely not want you to discuss his relationships with peers because they reside in clear personal territory. Furthermore, peer interactions are practice for future romantic or collegial relationships. Our kids need to learn how to navigate peer life on their own, but we can equip them with strategies that will help them remain within safe boundaries as they do so.

There are 3 categories of peer interaction skills you can help your child learn.

- Learning to say no

- Recognizing manipulation and responding to it

- Shifting the blame to save face

The Unique Power of No

It is unrealistic to expect young people to defy their friends and say, "No, I won't do that. It's against my moral values." It is difficult because the word *no* has become so weakened.

It is important for your child to learn how powerful the word *no* can be. Many kids grow up hearing flexible nos. They learn if they wear us down, they will turn our initial no into a "well, maybe" and finally a yes. They also learn that no can mean, "I'm really tired; ask me later."

If parents reserve the word *no* for when we mean it, it adds weight to the word. This will make it easier for preteens and teens to understand how to use it themselves. We parents need to learn to say, "Maybe," or, "I'll have to think about it," instead of spontaneous nos, when we don't mean it. Our spoken accuracy counts here, because we want our kids to learn to be very clear with their nos, yeses, and maybes.

Equivocal nos lead to conflicting double messages, which can be particularly hazardous in sexual circumstances. Although gender roles are shifting and girls pursue boys more aggressively than in past generations, the following scenario remains common:

A boy comes on to a girl, charms her, and eventually asks her to have sex. She thinks he's cute and doesn't want to say no because that sounds so mean and final, and she doesn't want to push him away. So she says no coyly, with a smile or giggle. He doesn't hear no; he hears, "Maybe. Keep flirting; there's a real possibility here." He may even hear, "Yes." Mixed signals can potentially lead to date rape. Kids need to say no like they mean it. Similar scenarios could be played out with drugs. "No" is not mean; it is honest and clear. It doesn't hurt feelings; it spares them.

How do you teach this lesson? Start, as always, by modeling. In this case, that means judiciously and effectively using the word as previously described. This is also one of those areas where you can teach best by pulling off a stealth role play. Watch TV together and wait for one of those scenes that makes you want to jump out of your seat and scream, "Idiot! Don't you know what he's trying to do?! Can't you see through this line?!" But instead, look at your daughter and say, "OMG, what do you think she should say?" I can almost guarantee she'll find your question "awkward" (which ties with "annoying" for my favorite new words, because apparently they describe all of my friends and me so well). The moment of embarrassment will make her answer with a shy smile while she says, "Stop it; I would say no." That's when you say that her no, when accompanied by a smile, was not convincing. If your son is sitting next to you and you witness a similar episode, explain that the word *no* means no, regardless of how it is said.

Dealing With Manipulation

We tend to believe that peer pressure comes from an aggressive, sinister child or teen who threatens or manipulates our naïve and vulnerable child. Peer pressure is subtler and often does not involve words. Much of it is internally driven. Kids want to be normal; they look around and choose to do what others do to make sure they fit in. Or they want to enter a new peer group and will prove they deserve to be there by choosing similar behaviors.

"If I just smoke this cigarette, the sixth graders will notice I'm cool enough to hang out with."

"I am not going to hang out with Liza, because Jason won't think I'm in the right crowd, and he'll never ask me out."

There's no guaranteed way to prepare kids to manage this internally driven peer pressure. All we can do is help them develop strong character and always be available to listen to them when they need a sounding board.

Although most peer pressure is internally driven, young people still manipulate their peers. Some of these messages come from groupthink; others come directly from individuals. Kids tend to know which groups they fit into, which they don't, and which they wish they did. Much of peer culture is about telling kids (verbally or nonverbally, subtly or blatantly) why they are out and what they need to do to get in. "I really like hanging out with you, and going back to your house was fun when we were kids, but it's just that now after practice, the rest of us go out to the field and slam back a few beers. Check it out." It's helpful to have more than one circle of friends. That way, when a group moves into behaviors beyond your child's comfort zone, he won't be left isolated. If being an outcast is the only option, few kids can withstand the pressure. You want your child to be able to turn to other friends.

Kids also have to be prepared to recognize and handle manipulative messages. They are rarely delivered in a rude or confrontational manner; rather, they are couched in friendship, even love. "C'mon, haven't I proven to you that you should trust me?" The messages include lines like, "I really love you and need to show you," or, "I want to hang with you, man. I just really want to get high too." With younger kids, it sounds like, "I'm your best friend, aren't I? C'mon, I just really want to _____, and it won't be much fun without you."

It had long been taught that the best way to deal with these manipulative lines was to first recognize a line and then respond by reversing the pressure toward the other person. For instance, "I really love you and I need to show you," would be answered with, "If you loved me, you would wait," or, "C'mon, everyone gets high; we're best friends and do everything together," would be countered by, "I'm not everyone, and I don't have to be your friend."

This back-in-your face approach is flawed because it ignores that kids, especially preteens and teens, urgently want to feel loved and accepted. So while they listen to us when we suggest they reverse the pressure, and might even practice the technique in classrooms, they may not use it. We may want our children to defy, even abandon, peers with riskier behaviors, but we may be asking more than what kids will do. Therefore, we have to prepare them with a skill set that is less satisfying to us but more practical for them.

We can teach kids to handle this kind of pressure while allowing them to keep their friends and still control their own actions. This strategy has 3 stages.

- First, they need to be able to recognize a line. Even young children can recognize manipulation when we point it out on television, in the neighborhood, or in our own lives. "He sounds like he is doing me a favor, but I know he really wants me to…" "Why do you think they give out those toys with the special meals?"

- Second, young people need to be prepared to state their positions clearly, without leaving room for argument or negotiation. They have to be direct but not argumentative, accusatory, judgmental, or self-righteous, or else they risk losing their friends. "I'm just not ready for sex." "I'm not going to do drugs." "I won't steal that." "I can't cut school." "I'm not going to cheat."

- Third, they need to have the knowledge and comfort to quickly come up with an alternative response or action that maintains, even enhances, the friendship on their terms. "We can hang at my house instead. I've got a new game we can play, or we can go down to the skate park." "I am glad you love me because I love you too. I still want to be with you, and we'll figure out what we're both comfortable with sexually." "I won't smoke weed, but if you aren't too wasted, text me and we'll shoot hoops later." "I won't cheat, but I'm not bad at math, so I'll definitely help you study."

The best way to teach these strategies is through role playing. But be careful, because role play can make everyone feel uncomfortable. Don't talk about any specific friend, because you enter that personal territory where you are not allowed to venture. Look for external situations to teach these skills. Keep your sensors up when you watch television together or notice a group of kids behaving badly when you drive past them together. Most importantly, remind your child that the goal of discussing these strategies is so you can comfortably get out of the way, knowing he is prepared.

Code Words

We can further strengthen our children's ability to control their behaviors if we prepare them with strategies to reject unwanted behaviors and get out of difficult situations without losing face. This is particularly important for teenagers, because if their decisions don't match those of their friends, they can experience embarrassment and rejection. Given the choice of doing what they know to be right versus avoiding humiliation or being ostracized, many kids choose not to listen to their own moral compass. We don't want our kids to be put in that position; we want them to be able to both do what is right and avoid peer conflict.

Of all I have written over the years, it is the following strategy that has brought me the most concrete feedback. Parents' letters or e-mails often begin with, "Code word saved my child's life." Here's how it works. You and your child select a code word or phrase to be used only in a difficult situation and never to be shared with friends. Try not to restrict its use to an emergency, because that will lessen its power to help your child escape any risky situation. You don't want him to ask himself, "Is this serious enough to get my parent involved?" You want to have an understanding that says, "Use me when you need me!"

Code words should be agreed on during a neutral time. If you wait until the big party or the first date, that will convey you expect trouble. Just calmly agree that any time your child is uncomfortable or unsafe, he just needs to call or text you and drop the word into the conversation. If it is unusual for your child to call you from a party, you can make it easier by asking the questions that would allow him to respond using the word or phrase.

For example, 14-year-old Mike is at a friend's home when other kids show up with cases of beer and some marijuana. Mike has never tried alcohol or marijuana and feels uncomfortable. He thinks if he turns it down, his friends will think he's judging them or he's scared. This group of friends is important to him, and he doesn't know what to do.

> ❝ Keep both yourself and your teen educated about risks and benefits of each decision. For example, if they want to go to a party, who is it with and what is their reputation? Make sure you have some plan in case the risks develop into an unacceptable situation…. Make sure they know that they can contact you in case of an emergency or another situation, and be available for them. ❞
>
> —16-year-old male, Colorado

> " You can't change the fact that your children will be exposed to these situations; you can only change how they will handle these situations through open conversation and a strong foundation of trust. "
>
> —17-year-old male, Pennsylvania

If he and his parents have agreed on a code word and practiced how to use it, Mike can get out of the situation. He complains to his friends that he has to call home or his father will get very angry. He warns them to be quiet so his father doesn't figure out he's at a party. Then he phones home in front of them, intentionally allowing them to hear his end of the conversation.

"Hey, Dad. I'm over at Caleb's. We're studying. I'll be home pretty late. But I didn't have time to walk Spotty. Can you take him out for me?"

Spotty is their code word. When Dad hears it, he knows his son is in a difficult situation, so he raises his voice loudly enough to be heard by Mike's friends, "You're already late! I told you to be home by 8:00! You can study on your own. Get home now!"

If Mike has a way to get home and thinks he can leave immediately and still save face with his friends, he can say, "OK. I'm leaving now," slam down the phone, and grumble to his friends, "I have to go or he'll ground me." If he can't get home easily, he can heighten the urgency by instigating an argument.

"Don't tell me what to do. I'm staying!" That's the signal to his father that Mike needs to be rescued. So his father yells—again, loudly enough for the friends to hear—"What's Caleb's address? I'm coming right now. You'd better be at the door when I get there." Then he whispers, "If your friends need a ride, have them ready too!" (If the conversation occurs by text, be careful not to insert side comments because your kid may want to show his friends the whole thread as proof of your tyrannical streak.)

Mike can complain to his friends about how annoying and controlling his father is, all while getting himself out of a risky situation without losing face or being embarrassed. His friends will sympathize with him. It is critical that when kids use this strategy, they are rewarded for their good sense and never punished for the difficult situation they found themselves in. It is, of course, a great opportunity for discussion. Finally, refresh the code word by replacing it with a new one so that friends do not catch on.

A code word can also be used to help children gain confidence in approaching a challenging or potentially uncomfortable social situation because they know they have an escape plan if needed. An introverted child, for example, may find going to your office party or a school social overwhelming. To increase her comfort at taking the "stretch," you could say, "You know, all you have to do is use a code word to tell me that you want to leave or be picked up." Rollercoaster friendships are an uncomfortable and anxiety-provoking reality of mid-adolescence, particularly among girls. A code word can give your child the confidence to face a friend, thereby averting the increased awkwardness that builds with the passage of time. For example, your daughter can more easily take the risk of going to a sleepover knowing she has an escape strategy, if needed.

A code word would be a valuable addition to the Contract for Life (www.sadd.org/contract.htm) created by Students Against Destructive Decisions (SADD). In this potentially lifesaving agreement, the teen promises to call for a safe ride if any substance or situation might decrease the driver's focus. We hope our teens will call us because they are familiar with the contract and value their safety so highly. But it is still not easy to face a crowd and say, "I'm calling my mother." When a code word is added to the contract, it makes it easier to follow through.

Shifting the Blame

A code word is a formal way of allowing your child to shift the blame to the parent. But she can do this without always needing to be rescued. Let your children know that it is fine for them to blame you for any choice that helps them stay away from risky behaviors or situations. They don't need to call you, just publicly register their complaints about you.

"My parents are so controlling; they ground me when I don't get home on time."

"My mother said that if I ever get caught speeding, she won't let me drive for a year."

"I can't smoke weed with you because she sniffs me and stares into my eyes when I get home."

"They'll send me to another school if I get caught cutting classes again."

"They'll make me quit the team if I don't keep a B average, so I have to study."

The list is endless, and it's not just parents who have to take the blame. Your child can suggest that any other responsible adult is holding her accountable, such as a principal or guidance counselor who is giving "one last chance" or a doctor who warns that her asthma will land her in the hospital if she doesn't quit smoking.

To make it more natural for your child to blame your monitoring as the reason she is forced to do the right thing, never give up the good-night routine. Think about how wonderful it was to put your small child to bed. You bathed, cuddled, and read to her. You heard her prayers and listened to her day's adventures. Nice, wasn't it? Well, you don't have to give your teen baths anymore, but you should never stop hearing her life's adventures. Teens often go to bed later than us and even arrive home after we are asleep. No matter what, they should end their day with a "check-in rule," even if it wakes you. It is a generally positive thing that will position you to be there when needed, as kids may need our support the most after a night out. But it also prevents your child from sneaking in. It makes, "She smells me!" a reality. Your child will naturally use that she touches base with you before bed, no matter what, as a way to police herself.

Peer culture can be tough to navigate for any young person. Face-saving maneuvers allow young people to follow through on sound decisions. These techniques also reinforce you as a person your child can always rely on.

Reinforcing Thought

When your child is equipped with navigational skills, you can take a bit of a breath and trust he is more likely to succeed as well as deal with challenges. When you have imparted these skills, you can feel good that your job is (largely) done. Sometimes our children will not use these skills until challenged. Those challenges, even if originally met with failure, are precisely what serve as the reminders that these skills are needed. Always stay open to helping your child build them, and offer continued guidance or troubleshooting, when asked.

> **"** Being a teenager means crossing the bridge into adulthood. As it is the first major bridge you cross in your life, it is helpful to have some guidance as to where and where not to step on this bridge. **"**
>
> —16-year-old female, Florida

More Thoughts From Teens

There are dangers in life that parents cannot and will not be able to protect their children from. That being said, I feel that parents often forget to remind their children about having healthy relationships. Regardless of whether it's with a friend, teacher, or romantic interest, the importance of a healthy relationship is often overlooked. The physical safety aspects are almost always taken care of in parental teachings, yet they almost always seem to forget that during our teenage years, our emotional health is just as important. I feel that parents need to protect their children from unhealthy relationships. What I mean by this is that the lines of communication MUST stay open (about the little things, too, because the little things almost always are gateways to the larger things), and parents need to be open about what one should or should not expect from a relationship.

—Anonymous

Parents need to realistically inform their children about the lessons they will face. I am disappointed by some of the choices I made in my first relationship because my parents implied that I should hold myself to abstinence from nearly everything. They never gave me a realistic representation of what a relationship would be, and as a result, I made mistakes that should have been avoided. However, parents should not shield their children from lessons, because their children will face these lessons at one time or another....

—17-year-old female, Pennsylvania

When a child is trying something for the first time, like getting their license or going to a big dance, the parents should give them the necessary education to be cautious about what they might encounter in those situations. But then once the child knows the situation clearly and the boundaries that the parents have set, they should let the child enter the situation. And if something does happen, make sure they are alright and then talk to them about what they can learn from making that choice and how they can improve if they are in the same situation in the future.

—16-year-old female, Pennsylvania

CHAPTER

11

Preparing Your Child for a Stressful World

Let's return to the question we are wrestling with, "How do I protect my child while letting her learn life's lessons?" Thus far, we have tried to bring your heart (which says protect at all costs) and mind (which says my child must learn life's lessons) into alignment by demonstrating that your child profits when she prepares for and confronts challenges. Although you can't protect your child from all stressors, no matter what you do, lighthouse parenting means you will intentionally allow your child to ride some waves so she can gain experience managing turbulence. But we can't casually approach this decision because adversities generate stress, and, in turn, stress can lead to many worrisome behaviors. This means your child must simultaneously be equipped to manage the repercussions of stress in healthy ways. When our children are prepared to respond to stress in positive ways, they will be protected far into the future, as they will repeatedly draw from these healthy adaptive strategies to navigate an increasingly demanding world.

We will discuss positive coping strategies briefly here. They are covered in great detail for parents and kids in my book *Building Resilience in Children and Teens: Giving Your Kids Roots and Wings*. They are also presented in our multimedia textbook for professionals *Reaching Teens: Strength-based Communication Strategies to Build Resilience and Support Healthy Adolescent Development*. Both comprehensive works offer written examples and films of action-based strategies. The discussion that follows is excerpted and edited from those works.

Stress 101

Adults deal with ongoing stress in various ways—exercise, meditation, long walks, turning down overtime or weekend work, painkillers, smoking, or another glass of wine. How do kids deal with stress? Depending on their ages and temperaments, some choose healthy, positive strategies such as play, exercise, creative expression, or talking, but others withdraw, sulk, or zone out. Still, others may act aggressively, talk back, and have tantrums. Older children may turn to the coping mechanisms they see peers using—smoking, drugs, fighting, sexual activity, eating disorders, self-mutilation, and delinquency. Adults usually view these activities as behavioral problems. In actuality, these negative behaviors are often attempts to counter stress in the vain hope of making it all go away.

When kids are stressed, they usually don't think rationally about the best way to make themselves feel better. They find relief by acting impulsively or following the paths most readily available to them, the ones they see other kids (or you) taking. Many don't know healthier and more effective alternatives. Unless we guide them toward positive ways to relieve and reduce stress, they choose the negative behaviors of peers or the culture they absorb from the media. They can become caught up in a cycle of negative coping methods, risky behaviors, and even addictions.

We do not have the option of eliminating stress from their lives. But we can help them avoid entrance into negative cycles of coping strategies. We won't be effective by just ranting about the evils or dangers of those coping strategies we fear. We have to start by understanding that most of these behaviors are actually effective, in the short-term, at relieving stress. The child who's hassled on the school bus lets off steam by punching the kid who's bothering him. A teen girl who feels that she has little control over her life and how she is treated may seize control of what she can, such as how to manage her body size and shape. By denying herself food, she takes some control, which temporarily decreases her stress, but the long-range result can lead to an eating disorder. A teen who is anxious about living up to expectations of parents or teachers may turn to drugs for relief. His feelings of inadequacy or fear of failure are diminished in that haze of marijuana. The feelings resurface after the high wears off, so he may use drugs more frequently to keep his stress at bay.

These negative strategies are quick fixes that may relieve stress, but they have consequences that are harmful to individual children, families, and society. Our job is to guide young people to understand that although stress is part of life, healthy ways of coping with it can ultimately be protective, productive, and satisfying.

Can Stress Be a Good Thing?

It is too simplistic to see stress only in a negative light. In fact, stress can be a lifesaver. In times of danger, stress gets our adrenaline going so we can move quickly to escape a harmful threat. An appropriate level of stress may be a driving influence that leads us to positive achievements. A little stress pumps us up to perform well for a presentation at work. Just enough stress energizes a child to play an instrument at a recital or train for a race. Problems arise, however, when stress becomes chronic or we don't manage it well enough to perform the tasks and responsibilities before us. Then stress can become a destructive force that harms our bodies, paralyzes our efforts, or drives us toward dangerous behaviors.

Stress as a Lifesaver

The human body can transform quickly to meet multiple needs. Intricate connections between nerves, hormones, and cells allow for rapid changes to occur based on the emotions, thoughts, pleasures, and fears our brains experience. Our bodies are finely tuned machines whose functions differ depending on our surroundings and states of relaxation, vigilance, arousal, or fear.

But our bodies were not designed to survive 21st-century lifestyles. Our bodies were designed to survive in the jungle when, at any moment, a tiger might leap out of the brush. In the moment of a tiger attack, our brain would register terror before the danger was even brought to consciousness. Our nervous system would immediately begin firing, and hormones would surge throughout our body. Some hormones, such as adrenaline, give the needed initial burst of energy to run, while others spark a cascade to mobilize the body's immediate needs (increased blood pressure and a release of sugar for energy) and prepare for some of its longer-term requirements (replenishing water and sugar).

Without the stress reaction, our ancestors would not have survived. But stress has helped us do more than run from tigers. It keeps us alert and prepared. It takes only one experience with a tiger to become attuned to the sounds of rustling brush. That same heightened vigilance, caused by low stress levels, can be helpful. It's what helps us finish reports and our children study in anticipation of a test.

Few of us need to race from tigers today, but crises—such as violence, war, natural disasters, and major illnesses—require intense efforts for survival. But most of the events that cause stress are not immediately life-threatening—a fight with a spouse, pressure at work, economic worries, or the ongoing challenge of balancing our many roles. These events are undoubtedly stressful, but they do not challenge our safety; therefore, I refer to them as "paper tigers." Our bodies are not designed to react to stress day after day. In an actual sprint for survival, we use up every hormone and our bodies return to their normal resting states. In the modern world of paper tigers, those same stress hormones remain in our bodies because we don't react as fully to our hormonal bursts. We don't sprint away. Instead, our stress hormones remain unused, continue to circulate, and cause us damage.

We have more subtle varieties of hormones than those generated during a carnivorous attack. The body's intricate wiring allows us to meet a broad variety of needs. Blood pressure, for example, ranges widely during the day. During sleep, it can be low. It rises rapidly in times of crisis or maximum exertion. When we're functioning in the midst of a hectic day, blood pressure is somewhere in the middle range. Factors that control blood pressure—heart rate, constriction of the blood vessels, salt and water intake—are in a constant dance to meet the body's needs. That dance is carried out through the movements and fluctuations of nerves and hormones, all magically choreographed by the brain. The brain is not an objective choreographer, however. It is heavily influenced by emotion and passion. Sometimes blood pressure goes up because of a real need, such as the need to run or even to stand after lying down. At other times, it goes up because of an intense emotion or remains high in a state of vigilance for a coming crisis.

Summary

- Stress is nothing new. We'll always have some degree of stress in our lives.

- Stress is an important tool that can aid our survival.

- The body's reaction to stress is mediated through a complex interplay of sensory input—sights, smells, and sounds—as well as the brain and nervous system, hormones, and the body's cells and organs.

- Emotions play an important role in how we experience stress because the brain is the conductor of this system. The way we think about stress and what we choose to do about it affects the impact a stressful event has on us.

With these points as a backdrop, let's return to the discussion of parenting. Despite our desire to shelter our kids, we cannot completely eliminate stress from their lives. But we can play a vital role in helping them learn to respond to stress in the most beneficial ways. A first step is helping them understand how to distinguish a real crisis from a bump in the road.

When a young person blows a mild stressor way out of proportion (such as cramming for a test she is overly worried about), she will be unable to prepare well because she will lose her ability to focus. She'll run from that tiger and be incapable of concentrating on anything but escape. In situations like these, parents' subtle (or not so subtle) messages can determine how children define *crisis* and how their stress hormones mobilize. Do you want your child to perceive a B- or messy room as a major crisis?

I don't want to mislead you. I do not think parents control their children's worlds and determine entirely how they define crises. Parents can't control poverty, racism, and all the other -isms that plague humanity. Parents can't control the weather, disease, random violence, or war. But we can prepare children to navigate a range of crises by helping them realistically assess the immediacy of a threat, develop strategies to deal with and address problems, and have counterbalancing relaxation tools that help them modify the effects of stress throughout their lives. Perhaps most importantly, we can *model* for them how to handle stress in healthy ways.

How Do I Know if My Child Is Too Stressed, and What Can I Do?

Too often, adults believe our kids have nothing to worry about because they don't have a job or a family to support. To the contrary, there are few things more stressful than trying to figure out how you fit into the world. All young people have stress, however; they show it in a myriad of ways. Remember that a bit of stress is energizing. A bit more is manageable and teaches us life lessons, including ideally how to remain comfortable and focused even during stressful times. Look for the signs that your child's current level of stress may be more than he can comfortably handle.

Do not expect your child to make it easy for you by saying, "I am stressed beyond my comfort zone or outside of the range my current skill set allows me to reasonably manage!" It is more likely he will grow irritable, less patient, and less understanding of others. Sometimes you'll see red-hot outrage. You will likely feel that irritability more strongly than other adults in your child's life. The security your relationship offers creates a safe setting to release pent-up frustration and anger.

Kids may or may not be conscious of the connection between their behavior and stress in their lives. So asking about it may not be effective. Be present. Maintain your calm demeanor by reminding yourself that the rage may not be about you. Please keep in mind, it's normal for children to have occasional tantrums and for teenagers to be moody; you are looking for something that appears out of the ordinary. When in doubt, turn to a child professional, such as a teacher, to get an objective opinion.

Nearly all people have physical symptoms related to stress. It makes us terribly uncomfortable. We feel nervous, unsafe, insecure, and ungrounded. We can't think clearly. We become restless and ultimately exhausted from our diminished sleep. Our muscles ache, our bellies feel bloated, and our hearts throb. Frequent patterns of headache, belly pain, and fatigue tend to point to the possibility that stress is driving those uncomfortable feelings. This is especially true when there is no medical explanation. Tell your child's health care professional if you've noticed that physical symptoms seem to be tied to stressful events. The professional will still consider medical concerns but will be better able to get to the bottom of stress-related symptoms.

Similar to the behavioral symptoms of stress, your child may or may not have a conscious awareness of the connection between his mood and his body's reaction. A health care professional can reduce stress by offering reassurance that the body is healthy, and it is part of the human condition to have physical symptoms related to stress. Your child's pain and discomfort is absolutely real. He is not faking or crazy.

Our assessment about whether or not stress is overwhelming our kids includes considering their behavioral and physical symptoms, as well as looking at their overall functioning. School performance holding steady is a good sign, but it should not be used to erase concerns. Some kids cope by diving into school, making grades a poor measure of overall well-being. Or they may have so much anxiety about school performance that their grades remain high, even while other indicators of healthy functioning falter. Therefore, you must consider the whole picture—their mood, their physical state, school performance, social life, home relationships, good nutrition, and adequate sleep.

The stress-reduction strategies that follow are useful in helping children and teens manage existing stress. These strategies are also designed to be preventive. We hope children who are well equipped to deal with stress will experience less of it in the first place. But if you're worried about your child's ability to cope or know that she has been under recent stress, please use her teacher, counselor, pediatrician, or clergy to help you decide the level of support she needs. A starting point is to check in with your child directly. If you are worried, please refer to those points made in Chapter 9, The Upside of Failure, about how to guide your child to seek professional guidance while helping her understand that help-seeking is an act of strength.

Dealing With Stress

We hate discomfort, whether it's emotional or physical. To avoid it, we figure out some way to make ourselves feel comfortable again. Anything that can banish those disquieting feelings will make us feel more settled, at least for the moment.

There are positive and negative ways of coping. It's not that positive ways always work and negative ones always fail. On the contrary, some negative ways offer immediate relief. The difference is that positive coping strategies enhance well-being and lead to at least partial relief. Negative strategies might offer short-term quick relief, but in the long run they end up causing harm to the individual or community, and they perpetuate and intensify the cycle of stress.

I can't guarantee your child will never try a worrisome behavior. Even if he is emotionally intelligent and equipped with good coping strategies, some of those feared behaviors are fun or feel good. A young teen may try drugs to test his limits, rebel, or have fun with friends. We hope he will move beyond this phase quickly. But a young person who seeks solace through drugs, who uses an altered state of consciousness to mask his feelings, may be destined for addiction. Children with safer, healthier means of coping with stress don't need to blur their consciousness with drugs.

Virtually all the behaviors we fear in children and teenagers are mis-guided attempts to diminish their stress. Procrastination, feigned laziness, and boredom are methods of dealing with school-related stress. They temporarily push stress out of sight and mind for a while. Bullying, smoking, drugs, gangs, sex, disordered eating, and self-mutilation are also efforts to deal with stress. Our challenge is to raise children who have a variety of pos-itive coping strategies that will enhance their strengths. We can help children and teens avoid dangerous behaviors by equipping them with a wide range of alternative, effective, and safe coping strategies.

The ability to cope with life's stressors in a positive way is key to remaining physically and emotionally healthy (Figure 11-1).

Everyone has an individual style in response to challenge. Research has looked at which styles help different people cope most effectively. Some people cope by tackling a problem head-on and trying to fix it. Others focus more on the emotions those problems create; they tend to do what makes them feel better to decrease their discomfort. Both styles, *problem focused* and *emotion focused,* engage the problem. Some people choose to avoid the problem through *denial* or *withdrawal.*

People who choose to engage a problem actively tend to choose 1 of 2 approaches; they try to change the stressor itself to make themselves feel more comfortable, or they change themselves just enough to adapt to the stressor.

For example, Sage feels overwhelmed by homework. She uses a problem-focused strategy by breaking her assignments into segments she can handle one at a time. When Jake's friends challenge him to smoke cigarettes and he talks with his best friend about why he doesn't want to smoke, he attacks the problem.

Coping Styles and Stress Management

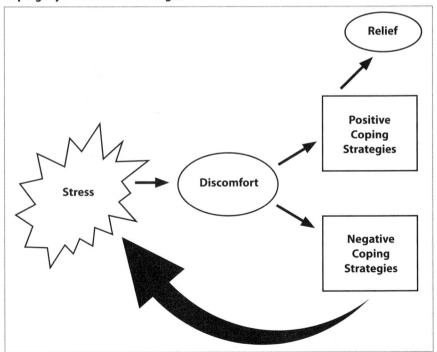

Figure 11-1. Stress can lead to positive responses, potential growth, or more stress.

Some people who use emotion-focused strategies want to escape stressful feelings and may choose to deny the problem exists. What works for them? Negative approaches include drinking alcohol to cloud their awareness of the problem or bullying others to feel in control. But not all emotion-focused styles are negative. Many can be positive if they help deal with feelings in healthy ways such as exercise and meditation or by releasing pent-up stress through strategies such as journaling, crying, or laughing.

> Figure out a way for the child to choose good decisions instead of forcing them or yelling at them. When my mom yells, I feel like I'm more likely to do things out of spite of what she says. When she shows me how to choose good decisions, I try to do the right thing.
>
> —19-year-old female, Alaska

Changing Coping Skills as Your Child Grows

Coping skills evolve over time. Even infants experience stress and have their own strategies to address it. They cry to get an adult to meet their needs. A parent's presence is enough to return them to a calm state. This is also true for small children who can calm themselves with snuggles and draw their sense of security from parents. Other children carry a security blanket or toy everywhere to comfort them in a world full of unfamiliar objects and strangers. Preschool-aged children develop fantasies to soothe upsetting emotions and reassure themselves.

Another common coping strategy for young children is avoidance: don't see it, run away from it, and the problem ceases to exist. As children reach school age, they grasp how stress affects their emotions and become better able to calm those emotions. They problem-solve and take active steps to address their concerns as they get older. They learn to relax without thinking about a fantasy figure to solve their problems. They reassure themselves that parents will become available if they are not present at the moment. They learn to reframe situations and soothe their emotions with positive self-talk. As children approach adolescence, their coping strategies become increasingly sophisticated.

My point here is not to make you obsess about which strategies your child uses at different ages but to help you realize that your child's repertoire evolves over time. If you directly discuss coping with a younger child, you may only add to his worries by making him wonder whether he is doing a good-enough job in dealing with his fears. Focus your energies instead on modeling appropriate coping strategies. Help preschool-aged and older children know that most of their worries represent a problem, and they can take steps to address that problem. Expose them to the kind of things they'll be able to draw from later as they widen their available options. Adolescents, in particular, need to see you make wise coping decisions. They will reject your words if they seem hypocritical.

Getting Into the Right Mind-set

It's important to first think about how much weight we give to a stressor. Sometimes stress comes from a real and present danger, in which case we should mount a full response. But in most cases, how stressed we are has a lot to do with our perception. There is no better coping strategy than using our thinking skills to accurately assess a stressor and, when appropriate, downplay its meaning in our lives.

Whenever a challenge arises, we need to ask ourselves 3 questions to help us use the appropriate lens.

1. Is this a "real tiger" or "paper tiger"?
   Our stress responses instantly transform our bodies into a fight-or-flight mode. In these survival modes, there is little room for rational discussion or focused study. You are not supposed to say to a tiger, "You seem rather upset, but is there any way we can work this out, because I really have to focus on my trigonometry homework right now?" People cannot solve problems in crisis mode. Because so few adversities represent imminent danger, a first step is to calm your thinking by reminding yourself, "I am not under attack."

2. How will I feel next week about this thing that is bothering me so much right now? Or tomorrow? Or next year?
   My grandmother, Belle Moore, prepared me to reassure myself with the inwardly spoken words, "This, too, shall pass." She said no matter how much something was hurting in the moment, it would always feel better with the passage of time. Dr Martin Seligman, in *The Optimistic Child,* mirrors this point when he writes about the adaptive benefit of viewing problems as temporary and surmountable.

3. Is this good situation permanent?
   Sometimes we become anxious or worried even when, or especially when, good things happen to us. Will we lose this opportunity? Did we

deserve it in the first place? Does this luck seem out of the ordinary? Will it be fleeting? Stop! This is a perfect time to catch those self-defeating thoughts and just appreciate the good fortune. Perhaps you earned it.

A Comprehensive Stress Management Plan for Children and Adolescents (and for Us to Model!)

A comprehensive stress-reduction plan should include a wide array of strategies that prepare youth to

- Accurately assess the stressor.
- Effectively problem-solve.
- Maintain a state of health optimal for managing stress.
- Manage emotions in a healthy way.
- Use safe, healthy strategies to avoid other problems.

A stress management plan needs to be presented quite differently for different ages because coping strategies change across the life span, and children's cognitive capacity to implement a plan varies substantially by developmental stage.

- **Children** should be offered opportunities to learn how to feel emotionally healthy and physically strong. They will learn they feel better after exercise and happier after they have expressed themselves creatively. Blowing bubbles can teach them about controlled and relaxing breathing. Even the youngest child can learn how much better it feels to talk if she is consistently offered a lap and a listening ear. She can learn about escape through play, fantasy, and reading.

- **Preadolescents and early adolescents** will listen attentively as they are taught stress reduction strategies. They will appreciate parental guidance and an acknowledgement that their lives are becoming more complex. They should be offered opportunities to practice what they have learned.

- **Mid- and late adolescents** likely will not want to hear about stress reduction from parents but may still be responsive to professionals. They will attack what they perceive as hypocrisy from adults who tell them what they should do but do not appropriately model healthy behaviors. They can learn from written or Web-based materials and should be given opportunities to design their own plans.

All children and adolescents learn from what their parents model. This is a good time to remind yourself that taking care of you is not a selfish act. Your children are watching, learning, and imitating.

A Stress Management Plan for Children and Teens

It is important that young people learn to assess the stressor as a first step of coping. You will note that the plan fleshed out below includes problem-focused and emotion-focused engagement strategies, as well as healthy disengagement strategies. It also includes basic wellness strategies that build a strong body capable of enduring stress (exercise, relaxation, nutrition, and proper sleep).

The plan has 4 broad categories and 10 points. It is not a 10-step plan; there is no right order in which to approach stress. Rather, you will see a wide variety of options to draw from at appropriate times. For example, some strategies that involve thinking make no sense during extreme stress. Then, it is better to exercise to use up the stress hormones before attempting to thoughtfully resolve an issue.

Each of the points includes a variety of activities and actions to handle stress. No one should feel pressure to use all techniques. In other words, don't stress about the stress plan. Rather, your child should pick 1 or 2 items from each point to see which best meets his needs at the moment. The best-fit strategies change with circumstances and over time.

The stress management plan includes 4 categories.

1. Tackling the problem
2. Taking care of my body
3. Dealing with emotions
4. Making the world better

Category 1: Tackling the Problem

- **Point 1: Identify and then address the problem.** (This point offers problem-focused engagement strategies.) Any action that addresses the problem diminishes the source of stress. A key to using this strategy is to clarify the problem and divide it into smaller pieces, committing to work on only one piece at a time. This decreases the sense of being overwhelmed and therefore increases a person's sense of control. Strategies to implement this point include making lists and timelines followed by a plan to address each component of the problem. Metaphorically, this is about helping teens revisualize problems from being mountains that are too high to be scaled into hills situated on top of each other that can be easily climbed. As they stand atop each hill, the summit appears more attainable.

- **Point 2: Avoid stress when possible.** (This point is a problem-focused strategy that leads to thoughtful disengagement). This avoidance strategy teaches all young people to consider their triggers to stress and realize that some can be avoided entirely. Young people need to learn that avoiding trouble is an act of strength. Thoughtfully avoiding people, places, or things that set off our stress can open the door to healthier ways of coping.

- **Point 3: Let some things go.** (This is another thoughtful, problem-focused, disengagement strategy.) While it can be useful to try to fix some problems, people who waste energy worrying about things they can't change don't have enough energy conserved to address problems they can fix. The serenity prayer summarizes this point.

  "Grant me the serenity to accept the things I cannot change, the courage to change the things I can, and the wisdom to know the difference."

Category 2: Taking Care of My Body

- **Point 4: The power of exercise.** Exercise is the starting point for someone whose stress hormones prevent him from addressing any other problem or having insight into how to address a crisis. When a stressed person does not exercise, his body is left feeling as if he hasn't run from the "tiger." Therefore, the "tiger" is still lurking and he remains nervous. His chronic stress hormones keep his blood pressure raised in preparation for the need to leap at any moment. It is not surprising, therefore, that exercise is tightly linked to increased health and has been shown to contribute to emotional well-being and positively affect stress, anxiety, depression, and attention-deficit/hyperactivity disorder. Young people can be taught
  - "When you are stressed, your body is saying, 'Run!' So do it."
  - "You may think you don't have time to exercise when you are most stressed, but that is exactly when you need it most."
  - "You will be able to think better after you have used up those stress hormones."

- **Point 5: Active relaxation.** There are 2 parallel nervous systems in the body; one operates when we are in a relaxed state, and the other reacts to emergencies. Although these interact somewhat, they do not run simultaneously. Therefore, a key to relaxation is to stimulate the relaxed system, making the emergency system shut down. A great way of doing this is deep methodical breathing. This is a mainstay of Eastern medicine techniques, yoga, and meditation, and it is even used to gain focus in the martial arts. Young people can be taught
  - "You can flip the switch from being stressed to relaxed if you know how to turn on the relaxed system." One technique is called 4 to 8 breathing: "Breathe deeply and slowly. Try to take a full breath. First fill your stomach and then fill your chest while counting to 4. Hold that breath as long as it feels comfortable; let the breath out while counting to 8. This requires your full concentration. If your mind wanders, as it will, remind yourself to refocus on your counting and breathing. Over time, your mind will be more able to stay focused on how you are feeling now rather than on past or future worries."
  - Mindfulness is a powerful technique that achieves a state of relaxation by living fully in the present while actively reminding us to let go of worries from the past and fears of the future. Breathing is the portal to a state of mindfulness. It is beyond the scope of this book to teach it, but I recommend Dr Dzung Vo's book *The Mindful Teen: Powerful Mindfulness Skills to Help You Handle Stress One Moment at a Time.*

- **Point 6: Eating well.** Proper nutrition is essential to a healthy body and clear mind. Young people can be taught
  - "Everyone knows good nutrition makes you healthier. Only some people realize it also keeps you alert through the day and your mood steady. People who eat mostly junk food have highs and lows in their energy level, which harms their ability to reduce stress. Eating more fruits, vegetables, whole grains, and lean proteins can keep you focused for a longer time."

- **Point 7: Sleeping well.** Proper sleep is key to stress management. Some people do not sleep well because of poor sleep hygiene, including having too much stimulation in their bedrooms and keeping irregular hours. Another source of lost sleep is stress itself; people use the bed as a place to resolve their problems. The basics of sleep hygiene include
  - "Go to sleep about the same time every night."

- "Exercise 4 to 6 hours before bedtime. Your body falls asleep most easily when it has cooled down. If you exercise right before bed, you will be overheated and won't sleep well."
- "A hot shower 1 hour before bedtime also helps your body relax to fall asleep."
- "About half of an hour before bed, go somewhere other than your bed and do something to set your worries aside (see Point 9). Do this in dim light. If you are the kind of person who thinks about all the stuff you have to do tomorrow, make a list before you go to bed and set it aside (see Point 1). If you wake up in the middle of the night thinking, move to another spot to do your worrying. You'll get tired soon; then go back to bed."
- "If you have trouble falling asleep, try 4 to 8 breathing (see Point 5)."

Category 3: Dealing With Emotions

- **Point 8: Take instant vacations.** (This point offers healthy disengagement strategies.) Sometimes the best way to de-stress is to take your mind away to a more relaxing place. Take advantage of your imagination and focus on other interests. Take breaks from stress by using
  - **Visualization:** "Have a favorite place where you can imagine yourself relaxing."
  - **Enjoyable interests or hobbies:** "Get into whatever you enjoy doing that is fun and creative." (This might include playing an instrument, drawing, or writing—activities that focus and use a more creative part of your brain.)
  - **A change in venue:** "Take a walk outside."
  - **Reading:** "Read a good book, even one you have read before." (It may be that reading is the best diversion because it utilizes all of the senses; one has to imagine the sounds, sights, and smells. A reader also experiences emotions, and that can prevent real worries from flooding in.)
  - **Music:** "Listening to music can be a great break from stress and can reset emotions."

- **Point 9: Release emotional tension.** (This point offers emotion-focused engagement strategies.) A person needs to be able to express emotions rather than letting them build inside. The ideas in this category include connecting to others and letting go of feelings with verbal, written, nonverbal, and creative expressions. There are a wide variety of options available to meet someone's temperament and talents.

- **Talking to someone who is worthy of your trust:** "Talking to a good friend, parent, teacher, or professional—such as a doctor, nurse, or counselor—can really help you get worries off your mind. Find an adult who will listen and whom you can ask for advice."
- **Creativity:** "Activities such as art, music, poetry, song, dance, and rap are powerful ways to let your feelings out."
- **Journaling:** "Write it out!"
- **Prayer or meditation:** "Some people find that prayer or meditation alone or with family or friends can ease their problems."
- **Crying or laughing**: "Some people feel so much better inside after a good cry. Laughing can also reboot your mood."

Category 4: Making the World Better

- **Point 10: Contribute.** Children and adolescents who consider how to serve their family, community, school, and nation will feel good about themselves, have a sense of purpose, and benefit from making a difference in other people's lives. First, they will learn it feels good to serve and that may reduce their sense of shame or stigma when they need to reach out for help themselves. Second, children and adolescents who serve others become surrounded by gratitude, which can be a powerful reinforcement to continued positive behaviors. It is particularly important to adolescents who often are the recipient of low expectations. Finally, people who serve others may be better able to put their own problems into perspective.

Pulling It Together

Protecting young people from everything is not an option. It is not even an attractive choice, because we need to prepare them for future stresses when we may not be around. Nobody can control the stresses we need to face. We can only control our reactions to them and how we choose to make ourselves feel better.

CHAPTER

12

Loving Boundaries

Lessons learned through experience have more staying power than those absorbed through words alone. Real-life experiences protect and prepare your child in a way that your wisdom alone can't necessarily do. But the world is far too unpredictable a place to set our children free to let them randomly encounter its teachings. That is where boundaries come in.

Your role is to set limits in a way that they actually enhance your child's freedom. Limits are restrictive when they are given with the goal of controlling rather than protecting. They are smothering when they prevent someone from trying something he is perfectly capable of handling. Limits are disorienting when they are not consistent. On the other hand, they offer security when there are clear markers for what is in- and out-of-bounds.

If boundaries appear to be random, they will be resented and ignored. It is a gift to give a child as few nos as possible, because it allows her to explore her world more fully. Those rare nos will then be heeded because kids intuitively understand the nos must be meaningful. Just as importantly, kids can approach challenges with less apprehension and greater confidence because they know their safety is being monitored. Within purposeful, secure boundaries, they can take advantage of all of the yeses in their lives.

We should help our children understand that we have rules in place because we love them deeply and care for their safety. We do not set random rules and don't place limits to control them. In fact, we celebrate their increasing independence and honor their growing skills and competencies. While some boundaries are *always* or *never* rules, most are in place only until our children gain more experience or demonstrate the responsibility that shows they need less supervision. "*Always* wear a seat belt; *never* drive under the influence of any substance." "You may not drive in bad weather until you've had more experience driving under normal conditions."

Out of Bounds

The theme recurs: if it might compromise safety, it is not allowed. Period. If it threatens morality, it is not acceptable. Nonnegotiable. If it has long-term negative implications, it is unwise. Not forbidden, just not a good choice. We need to come up with an alternative; let's work out a better path.

Back to the Box

Remember that puzzle called "Who Am I?" your child is constructing? Its 10,000 pieces are seemingly random. But they are not a haphazard collection, because hidden among them are the pieces that will form the edges. The first step of constructing the puzzle is to find and assemble the borders. After the puzzle's frame is in place, one looks at the picture on the box to imagine how the inside pieces might go together.

We make it easier for our children to put together the puzzle when we offer clear boundaries. The edges are apparent; they may not stray beyond the limits we set on safety and morality. When we are reliable role models, the picture is in sharp focus.

Now their job is to twist and turn those inner pieces, to shove them together until they fit nicely. Occasionally, they'll take the middle pieces apart again when they realize they had forced some together that didn't quite fit. But they can attack those interior pieces with the curiosity and drive they deserve. Your love throughout the process is unwavering; it fuels them to continue working on that puzzle even when their own confidence is faltering.

Let's pull it together. First, offer clear boundaries beyond which your child cannot stray. Second, stay mostly out of the stuff in the middle; that is their work. Third, be a role model they can consistently measure themselves against as they consider what they'd like to look like.

How Controlling Should We Be?

If we hope for our children to be able to manage their own lives, we must not rigidly control their thoughts, choices, or actions. Young people learn inner control by making decisions and facing the consequences. Inner control, in turn, gradually makes them more capable of denying their impulses. Young people who make the connection between their actions and consequences learn to own personal responsibility rather than blame others for problems and failures. They won't think things passively happen to them; they will view themselves properly as decision-makers and problem-solvers. They may even learn that delaying immediate gratification can lead to greater success.

Lighthouse parents aren't hands-off. Rather, because their goal is for their children to develop inner control, they choose not to manage their kids' every action. Instead, they observe, offer a steady hand, and are generous with their guidance when it is requested.

Parenting Style

When we speak of parenting style, we refer to 4 approaches to parenting that describe the interplay between warmth and control. The 4 styles were first described by Diana Baumrind[1] and further clarified by Eleanor Maccoby and John Martin.[2] Many researchers have studied parenting styles over the years, and notable among them are Laurence Steinberg and colleagues.[3]

Table 12-1 shows how the different combinations of warmth and control play out. Warmth describes how loving, affectionate, and responsive we are with our children. Responsiveness is about our ability to be flexible to meet their changing needs. Control is about how we set rules and monitor their behavior. The relationship between these forces allows us to describe 4 parenting styles.

1. **Authoritarian** parents do not express a lot of warmth, but they set firm rules. This is not to say they are uncaring or don't love their children very dearly, but it may be unclear to their children that they do.

2. **Permissive (or indulgent)** parents are very warm but not as committed to setting boundaries.

3. **Uninvolved (or disengaged)** parents neither express warmth nor set rules.

4. **Authoritative (or balanced)** parents are warm and responsive, and they set appropriate rules.

You may have guessed I hope to see you achieving balance in your parenting style. We know children do best when they gain security that comes from a loving eye.

---

[1] Diana Baumrind is a clinical and developmental psychologist at the Institute of Human Development, University of California, Berkeley.

[2] Eleanor Maccoby focused on the social development of the child at Stanford University. Maccoby and John Martin added to Baumrind's conceptualization of parenting styles in Maccoby EE, Martin JA. Socialization in the context of the family: parent-child interaction. In: Mussen P, Hetherington EM, eds. *Handbook of Child Psychology: Volume IV; Socialization, Personality, and Social Development.* New York: Wiley;1983:1–101.

[3] Laurence Steinberg is a developmental psychologist at Temple University.

Table 12-1. The 4 Parenting Styles

Low warmth	High warmth
High control	Low control
(Authoritarian)	(Permissive or indulgent)
High warmth	Low warmth
Appropriate control	Low control
(Balanced or authoritative)	(Disengaged or uninvolved)

Reflecting on Your Parenting Style

A first step toward becoming more balanced in your style is to reflect on your starting point. Of the 4 styles of parenting, which best describes you? Don't be surprised if you might behave differently on different days. Read about the different parenting styles and consider which seems most like you or your partner. To help you think this through, look at the quotations following the description and consider which sounds like something you might say.

Authoritarian

These parents set high expectations and make a lot of rules but don't usually feel the need to explain them. They expect compliance to their commands. Authoritarian parents may be highly involved and view control as the expression of parental love. They are less likely to communicate warmth or caring.

"Do as I say. Why? Because I said so! Don't question my authority. Until you're 18, I'm the boss in this house!"

Permissive

These parents may teach values and freely give support and love. They rarely set or monitor appropriate boundaries, instead relying heavily on trust. Permissive parents often treat a child like a friend and fear the child won't love them if they clash. Therefore, they avoid discomfort or conflict. Permissive parents hope their children will do the right thing because they have good values and do not want to disappoint them.

"I trust you; you'd never let me down." "We're like best friends, and I am so glad you tell me everything."

Disengaged

This parent will usually take care of a child's basic needs but does not monitor activities closely or set limits unless the child is in trouble or imminent danger. In some cases, a parent's lack of involvement is because of overwhelming demands and distractions in other areas of his or her life. Uninvolved parents don't believe they have much influence anyway. However, when major problems occur, they may come down hard. This leads to inconsistency and mixed messages.

This parent engages rarely or says, "Do what you want." They justify this parenting approach by saying, "Kids will be kids. I figured it out; he will too."

Authoritative or Balanced

This parent sets reasonable limits, expects good behavior, offers a lot of love, and has clearly stated boundaries. These parents are flexible and responsive; they listen to their teen's viewpoint and encourage her to make choices and solve problems. However, when safety or morality is involved, they have clear rules.

"I love you. I'm not your friend; I'm your daddy. That's better because you only get one of me. I'm going to trust you to learn most things on your own. You'll get freedoms when you earn them. But for things that really matter, or might get in the way of safety or morality, you'll do what I know is best."

Why We Want to Achieve Balance

Children raised with authoritarian parents are obedient to a certain point but then may rebel when they are no longer in their parents' house. After all, they may have heard, "While you're under my roof!" and have been looking forward to the day when they weren't. Others reject their parents' authority in mid-adolescence. Some of those who remain obedient may become unwilling or unable to make their own decisions and instead seek authority figures to control them even into adulthood. They also tend to be less happy and have lower social skills.

Children raised with permissive parents feel cherished but sometimes crave boundaries. Because their parents don't set rules, it may be the children's conscience (guilt) that sets boundaries. The thought of disappointing their parents can overwhelm them with anxiety or may influence them to distort the truth.

Those with disengaged parents do the worst because there are few things more painful than not being noticed. They sometimes push their behavior to the extreme just so their parents will react.

If your parenting style leans toward the authoritarian, permissive, or disengaged models, consider what steps you might take to move toward a more balanced approach. There is a great deal of research that finds that children raised with authoritative parents are less likely to have worrisome behaviors and more likely to be academically successful. This parenting style has been shown to delay first sexual contact, lower rates of drug use, improve school performance, and decrease delinquency. Research I was involved in at the Center for Injury Research and Prevention of The Children's Hospital of Philadelphia demonstrated that teens who describe their parents as caring and supportive, and also reported that their parents monitored them and had clear rules and boundaries, were half as likely to be in a car crash, twice as likely to wear a seat belt, and 70% less likely to drink and drive. We also know that parents with a balanced style know the most about what is going on in their kids' lives. Finally, adults who were raised by authoritative parents report greater psychological well-being and fewer depressive symptoms.

It is hard work to shift parenting styles. A good starting point is to think about how you were parented, because you'll better know what you are copying or reacting against. How did you feel about the way you were parented? Did you feel secure? Did you feel controlled? How did you react or feel about your parents' parenting styles? Did you comply with their rules and expectations? Did you rebel?

Did both parents have the same style? If not, how did their conflicting styles affect you? Did you ever manipulate them precisely because their parenting styles didn't match? When did you first learn that if you split them apart, you could usually get what you wanted?

The reason to think this through is so that rather than reacting according to your own childhood experiences, you can arrive at a parenting style that's best for your children. Even with the best of intentions, don't be shocked when your child or teen acts out, you feel angry or out of control, and the very words you vowed never to use, because of how much you resented them when your father or mother spoke them, come out of your mouth. Give yourself a break. This is a process. Kids are pretty resilient, and no single misspeak will destroy them. I promise.

You'll find your style may not always align with your partner's approach. When this is the case, your kids will not know the rules or may manipulate them, setting your family up for problems. It is not possible for you and your partner, or especially your ex-partner, to agree all of the time. But for the sake of the kids and function of your household, your disagreements should be worked out privately so your children receive a consistent message about their boundaries.

Overcoming Your Authoritarian Side

Many of us were raised with authoritarian parents. Even if hearing, "You'll do what I say while you're under my roof," made us dream of the day we would be out of the house, we turned out OK. Why change the rules? The respectful memories of our parents urge us to raise our children the same way.

Furthermore, popular lore showers us with messages that children are becoming spoiled, self-centered, ill-mannered, and out of control. To add to the sense of urgency, some people in the older generation are telling us, "You're letting your kids walk all over you." All of this makes us wonder if we should return to stricter styles of discipline.

Some people suggest a return to physical punishment is the answer despite ample evidence that such discipline is harmful to children. If nothing else, it makes kids feel like victims and instills fear. Children who have been spanked or hit have been punished, but they have not been truly disciplined. Remember that the word *discipline* comes from the same root as *disciple*. True discipline is about guidance and teaching; it is not about control and most certainly does not involve harm. Our goal with discipline must be to guide lovingly.

We ultimately want to help our kids learn self-discipline and control. They should hear us say something like, "My goal is for you to be independent and wise enough to handle the world. But my job is to keep you safe. You'll earn privileges and independence by demonstrating responsibility. If you do something that shows you are not ready for a privilege, you'll return to the freedoms you proved you could handle." It has been said best by Thomas Gordon in his classic book *Parent Effectiveness Training*, "Each and every time they [parents] force a child to do something by using their power or authority, they deny that child a chance to learn self-discipline and self-responsibility."

> ❝I believe the best thing a parent can do is lead by example and be the person they want their children to be. Then, establish a trust between parent and child so that there is a safety net for when mistakes happen. ❞
>
> —18-year-old male, California

I honestly believe it is wonderful to give clear rules and boundaries. Kids crave boundaries even when they pretend they don't. Because kids often think we make rules just to control them, it is important they know we make rules because we care about their safety and well-being. Research has demonstrated that kids who sense parental warmth and support alongside monitoring are more likely to accept parental authority, to call on their parents for advice and support, and to obey their parents' commands. Therefore, I think we would call adding clear demonstrations of warmth to your existing style a win-win situation.

Giving Yourself Permission Not to Be Permissive

At any given moment, kids might be happiest if their parents are permissive.

They'd get what they ask for. They'd have to follow fewer rules. From a child's perspective, this seems like kid heaven. And what parent doesn't want to be liked by their kids?

Sometimes we do things just because they are different from what our parents did. We vowed we would never repeat their mistakes. Many parents today were raised in homes that felt too strict, and we promised ourselves to be more laid back, friendlier, and possibly permissive.

This style feels good in the short run but doesn't pay off. Children raised by permissive parents may be more anxious because they monitor themselves through internalized fear—or guilt—over not disappointing their parents. When parents don't set boundaries, children set their own but without knowing where those boundaries should be drawn. We should not be surprised to learn the boundaries might be too loose and these kids tend to engage in more risky behaviors than we'd hope.

On the surface, a wonderful aspect of permissive parenting is that it allows for a great deal of affection, even friendliness. In my view, there should be no limits on affection. Friendliness, however, is not what kids need, at least not from their parents. They have friends for that. We are something much more important; we are loving role models who offer secure relationships that will survive life's invariable ups and downs. Don't get me wrong. Fun is good. Hanging out is good. Down time is great. Not every moment has to be teachable.

Parents who tend to be more permissive often tell me their son or daughter is their best friend. They feel secure in the knowledge that they have open communication because of their "friendship." They trust their child will come to them for everything; therefore, they worry less about undesired behaviors. If they were correct in these assumptions, I would be a strong promoter of permissive parenting. Unfortunately, several research studies have demonstrated that kids raised by permissive parents withhold information from their parents to avoid disappointing them or hurting their feelings.

Parents with a balanced style of parenting (lots of affection and fun allowed with some rules too) know the most about what is going on in their kids' lives. And, as we will discuss further in the next chapter, what you know is what your kids choose to tell you. If you have prioritized being your child's friend, I am certain you have done it for all of the right reasons, most notably to foster open communication. I think you'll be happy in the next chapter when we discuss proven strategies to encourage our kids to open up to us.

If you thought your parents were more authoritarian than you liked, you don't have to swing in the opposite direction. If you wished they had let you know how they felt about you, please make your feelings of affection for your kids well-known! But then leverage your close relationship by adding clear expectations about behaviors. Sometimes saying no is an extra way of showing your love. Your kids will gain a sense of security by knowing they are being protected with thoughtful monitoring.

" My dad had a lot of trouble balancing protective instincts and letting me and my siblings learn life lessons. Usually, if we wanted to do something he wasn't a fan of, the answer was, 'Do as I say. You live under my roof.' End of story. It's frustrating. I think parents should have an explanation and reasoning for their answers and choices regarding their kids. 'Because I said so' only pushes kids farther away. **"**

—19-year-old female, Texas

More Thoughts From Teens

My parents spent 17 years "protecting" me from all sorts of bizarre things. For example, I still don't have my license. They have spent so much time "protecting" me that they haven't actually had time to talk to me about the things they are doing on my behalf (in their mind). Honestly, parents need to communicate with their children, as it's all too often that they treat them as blind followers or outright forget to raise them. They should protect their teens only from situations that pose threats to the teen's long-term mental and physical health…. Kids should learn life lessons like accountability, responsibility, and the value of honesty as soon as they can. It's too easy to assume that kids will learn these down the line, to not teach them, and then to be surprised when the child turns out to be wildly irresponsible as an adult.

—17-year-old male, New Jersey

Children will be children. Sometimes no matter how many warnings are issued, they will still dive into danger headfirst. In my Spanish culture, there is a saying, "While you were going, I was coming back." This saying basically explains that what most children, especially teens, are going through or experiencing has been experienced by their parents. Sometimes when parents give advice, it is because they have been in the same situation and want to protect their children from it. What parents can do is first give a warning. Secondly, they can give a warning with an explanation or sample to help persuade [their children] into not doing the wrong thing. Thirdly, if [their children] still refuse to listen, the parent should explain to them the situation they went through (if they did or someone else close to them) and go over the consequences that have left an impact on their life. Parents should always protect their children from any life-threatening or illegal situations because those are the most dangerous situations. If they have tried everything mentioned and the child still refuses to listen, then it's time for them to learn a life lesson!

—16-year-old female, Pennsylvania

Parents may feel they know better (and it's possible they do!) and that their kids are making a terrible choice (and maybe they are!). But the ability to make a choice about one's life is a human right. To suppress people's will, to deprive people of their agency, should not be done lightly. Personally, I would first ask the children why they want to make that choice. Don't assume you know their reason and their thought process. If you think they're lying, at least hear their lie. Then ask them to hear your reasons. Ask, please. One of the things I find frustrating is that my parents can just call me to their room and lecture or scold for hours and dismiss me whenever they like. Ask, and if [your children are] reluctant, convey how important this is to you. If they agree to listen, persuade them. Use logic. Ask them to empathize with you (but do not use guilt, try to emotionally manipulate, or whatever). Don't rule out compromises. And if the child still refuses to change his choice, you have 2 options: one, you respect his choice, and let him do what he wills. Two, you respect his choice, but stop him anyway, keeping in mind that it is his right to make choices about his life. You're imposing your own beliefs on him (regardless of good or bad) and you are taking a liberty with him.…

—18-year-old female, Texas

Coming from extremely strict parents, I have been very sheltered. But I think what some parents don't realize is the more they shelter their children, the more curious their kids will be. As I am going to be a college freshman this fall, I worry about how overwhelming the whole new college scene will be. Hearing about things and seeing them firsthand are very different realities. I definitely remember feeling like an outsider of sorts in high school because I was the only one not allowed to go to parties, concerts, you name it. So I think some experimenting on the child's part should be allowed, but some guidance is best. Parents should not let prevalent teen issues be some kind of taboo. Communication is key.

—18-year-old female, Pennsylvania

Do NOT baby your child to the point where they are going to rebel, but also don't let them run free like they are feral; it isn't constructive. You need to know the difference between being a friend and being a parent, meaning no matter how hard it is, you have to lay down the law, or you WILL be taken advantage of. HOWEVER, there is no need to be a dictator; lay down the law (being a parent), but make it very clear to the child that you are open to talking without fear of reprimand (being a friend). The sooner you encourage your child to be open with you, the better. Same goes with enforcing your rules. In addition, being open works 2 ways. You have to be prepared to be open with your child when the time comes. Lastly, it is extremely important to [educate] your children [about] drugs, alcohol, and sex early. Again, do NOT cradle them; children are curious little devils and they will find out eventually, but by then it will be too late… inform your children of the consequences of using drugs and teach them to say no because they will be asked eventually. Teach them to not put themselves in vulnerable situations and that if their friends are doing it, find new ones.

—18-year-old male, unknown state

…ACTUALLY trust them! Give them responsibilities and consequences. "Hey, listen, sweetheart. I trust you and know that you can handle yourself with this phone. But we're all human, even I am, and so I just want to let you know that if you go over your minutes, there are going to have to be consequences." Raise your teens as teens who will someday have to take care of themselves and hopefully change the world. Prepare them for THAT! In regular everyday life, excluding strange occurrences, there are not many (if any) life-threatening situations. If it doesn't kill you, it's OK. Really. As a teen, I EXPECT that there will be things that beat me down, and as a teen of my upbringing, I almost LOOK FORWARD to and antici-pate working my way back up! But, also as a teen of my upbringing and of those accountable for my upbringing, I can't grow and satisfy those anticipations of learning how to face adversity, because I have not been entrusted with many of those responsibilities from which I will no doubt make mistakes and fail…. PARENTS, LISTEN UP, PLEASE: you may know this, or it may just be buried under the surface because you don't like it, but with absolute, 100% respect, I must let you know that teens HATE your explanation of, "Because I said so," or, "I'm always right." If you, yourself, as a parent, are not open to communication, how do you expect us to be?

We don't feel inclined or welcome to share things with you if you only offer back one-sentence reasons. No explanation. "Why should it matter that I lied to you?" "Well, son, not only does it hurt me because by not telling me you were at Julie's house and not Joe's, I was late for my meeting, trying to pick you up somewhere you weren't, but it also hurts YOU in the future when your boss expects you to be trustworthy. You need to learn to tell the truth; otherwise, it will be hard for you to stick a job and earn a living." It may be strange, but even if we won't admit it, we WANT that kind of communication. We don't want to be confused as to why you parents are angry with us or disappointed with us and for what reason you are. Otherwise, we'll think of you as parents who get angry for no reason. GIVE US YOUR REASON. TEACH US LIFE'S LESSONS. Don't expect us to learn it on our own—now or later.

—14-year-old female, Michigan

CHAPTER

13

Effective Monitoring

Thus far we have discussed setting boundaries as both a loving act and as one that guarantees your child's safety. Furthermore, we have underscored that kids with clear boundaries feel safer because they know they are protected and are more emotionally secure because they recognize they can test their limits and experiment within territory we have assessed as relatively safe. However, to this point we have made the simplistic assumption that if we set boundaries our children will follow them.

It is a kid's job to test her boundaries, to push for them to be expanded, and to occasionally stray beyond the lines.... This does not mean we should forgo setting clear boundaries. As one young person in Illinois explains to her parents, "Please keep giving me clear limits. It doesn't mean I'll always follow them, but I can promise you I'll at least stop and think at that point where I know I will be crossing your lines. I need your voice in my head."

Setting boundaries is only a first step toward assuring your child's safety; those limits only have meaning if you also monitor that they are followed. Until recently, the message to parents about monitoring was clear. We were told it was our job to ask a lot of questions such as "Where are you going?" "Who are you going with?" "When will you be home?" "What are you doing?" The who, when, where, what, and whys of parenting defined actively involved parents. When we asked questions, we were clear that we were being the good, attentive parents the public service announcements told us we must be. The problem is the strategy didn't work as well as hoped.

It is not what we *ask*; it is what we *know*. The limitation of asking a lot of questions is that the answers we get might not be truthful. To effectively monitor our children, we want to be the kind of parent to whom kids choose to disclose what is going on in their lives. We want them to look to us for a safety check-in as they consider if they might be straying too far (back to the lighthouse metaphor).

This chapter is about being the kind of parents who can monitor their kids because they know what is going on in their kids' lives. We'll know not because we make demands or hover but because we are considered helpful, as valuable resources who should know. We won't know every detail, nor should we; kids need their own lives. Our goal is to know what we need to know to effectively facilitate a healthy transition into adulthood.

Can't I Just Microchip My Kid?

Yes, for all practical purposes you can. You can put a GPS tracer on your car or on your child's phone. You can attempt to trace texting, social media, and computer usage, as well as send your kid's hair for drug testing.

I won't tell you where to place your limits on monitoring if you genuinely believe your child may be straying toward danger. Short of that, though, I far prefer you develop the type of trusting relationship where you have secured your child's desire to share with you what is going on in his life, particularly when it involves any issue that could approach your standards on safety or morality.

Being "Tell-Able"

When you have the kind of parent-child relationship where being honest with you makes sense to your kid, you are well positioned to be an effective monitor. The boundaries you set will be respected because it is understood they serve a protective purpose; they were not arbitrarily placed as a means of control. You will know what is going on when you are considered "tell-able."

In a nutshell,

- Parents who have a balanced parenting style know the most about their kids.

- Parents who listen well have kids who choose to talk.

- Parents who make it clear their concern is about safety have kids who appreciate their involvement.

- Parents who let their kids "win" when they present valid cases keep hearing their kids' thoughts.

- Parents who reward responsibility with earned privileges raise kids who do the right thing. Young people have less reason to fight against boundaries when they are not rigid; they learn all they have to do to expand their horizons is demonstrate the capability of being able to handle what is out there.

Balanced Parents Know Their Kids Best

Parenting style, or the interplay between warmth/responsiveness and monitoring/rules, affects both behavior and parent-child communication. Authoritarian parents do not know as much of what is going on in their child's life because communication is usually unidirectional (one way). "You'll do as I say." They have relatively rigid rules, and because there is not much flexibility, kids either comply or sneak past the limits. Children of disengaged parents might create behaviors to grab their parents' difficult-to-get attention because just talking usually won't be enough. In fact, they may go beyond where they imagine the boundaries should be just to make someone notice. Indulgent or permissive parents value communication dearly and have warm, open, and friendly conversations. They want to know what is going on in their children's lives, and they trust that they do. However, research has repeatedly demonstrated that children raised permissively often do not share what is going on for fear of disappointing their parents. On the other hand, kids whose parents are *both* warm and set appropriate boundaries share the most with their parents.

I can't say with certainty why young people are more likely to share their lives with parents who have a balanced style, but I believe it is about how much kids value guidance. Young people are striving for balance themselves. They need to experiment with life to grow, but they want to do so safely. Balanced parents appreciate the need their children have to test their wings and allow them to do so when they have demonstrated their capabilities. But balanced parents also sparingly offer meaningful limits. Kids are more likely to check in with parents who they know only set limits at the edges of safety or at least when they have a rationale. Kids want to learn from their parents' thoughts about why the limits are being set. They treat their parents as lighthouses, a constant source of guidance. They choose to share with their parents because it is the best way to get that valuable guidance.

“You shouldn't be so strict because it makes the child want to defy you more.”

—13-year-old female, Georgia

Listen Well, React Little

It may be that the first step in optimizing our ability to monitor our children is to first learn to monitor *our* reactions. When we react, children choose to stop telling us the details of their lives either to spare us or to avoid the discomfort our reaction engenders in them. On the other hand, when we act as sounding boards, always listening fully but offering guidance only when prompted, kids share their inner lives with us.

Listen Well

The key to keeping kids talking is for parents to learn to be effective listeners. Young people crave adult attention, even when they seem to be pushing us away. Listening is core to every respectful human interaction and the best way to offer someone your full attention. Listening, with well-timed reflection that briefly repeats back the problem and the potential solutions the person is considering, can be a powerful way of facilitating someone to hear his own internal wisdom and ultimately choose to do what he *knows* to be right.

The pivotal importance of listening is great news for parents. So many people find themselves at a loss for words when their children are troubled. They worry they'll give the wrong advice or be unable to offer a solution. We all need to free ourselves from the pressure to always have ready solutions. It is liberating to genuinely view kids as the experts in their own lives and to trust they possess internal wisdom. Sometimes that wisdom is untapped (or even suppressed), but it exists nonetheless. Our own guidance, therefore, will be far more effective when it is used to facilitate our kids to arrive at their own conclusions.

Sometimes there are no solutions, and only time will alleviate a problem or at least put it into perspective. Regardless of whether or not a solution is at hand, listening is a way of offering the gift of unconditional respect.

Listening without judgment and with respect does not mean we condone every behavior or agree with what our children are saying. But before we can offer meaningful guidance, we have to listen to the spoken words and try to grasp the emotions beneath them. Whether our kids come to us with urgent concerns or mundane matters, we create a zone of safety by listening without interruption or interrogation. This is part of loving our children unconditionally; there are no prerequisites to receive our love.

The bottom line is parents who listen are tell-able. Tell-able parents know what is going on in their children's lives and are positioned to protect them when necessary. They can steer their children away from trouble far before they approach the figurative cliff. And that is what monitoring is all about.

Part 4, Rebooting: Moving Toward the Relationship You Hope to Have, will offer a deeper discussion on how to best communicate with our children; there we will offer more thoughts on effective listening.

React Little

When parents react with quick judgment, concern, or condemnation, kids stop talking. Furthermore, when parents always try to solve problems, adolescents whose sense of control is linked to their ability to manage themselves may stop sharing the content and complexity of their lives. We all know that hysterical responses can shut down communication, so it is worth considering how and why our subtle responses also prevent further disclosure.

The most blatant offender is "the parent alarm." It blares, "My child is in trouble!" and we rush forward with a solution before our kid finishes a sentence. He shares, "Mom, I met this girl—" and you respond, "You're too young to date." This is a lost opportunity to talk about healthy sexuality. If he asks, "Dad, what do you say to a friend who wants you to get high with him?" and your response is, "I knew it! Brad is a terrible influence on you; I want you to find other friends," this is a lost opportunity to discuss drug use and navigating peer pressure.

We also react too quickly because of our discomfort with silence. We tend to fill the void with our own words. If instead we learn to say nothing, our kids will have the space to formulate their thoughts into words and we'll learn more.

We are also uncomfortable with our kids' making mistakes, so we jump in to rescue them. This is an example of protecting our children at the expense of preparing them. It also is at the expense of knowing what mistakes your child might be headed toward because she won't tell you when she might be headed for the rocks if your reaction is too swift.

We also can get in the way of further disclosure when we over-empathize with our children or catastrophize an incident. Often their pain becomes our own, and we become angry about hurtful situations from which they might otherwise easily recover. For example, a child might say, "Mom, I had a huge fight with Latoya and she'll never be my BFF again. I think I hate her!" If a mother's response is, "I don't blame you one bit, darling. I think she's a little creep and you were always too good for her. Honestly, I don't even like her mother," she'll never know that Latoya is her daughter's best friend again the next day. "Mom, Dad, I might get a D in algebra this quarter." "Don't worry, we'll get you tutoring. I'm sure it's the teacher's fault. We'll speak to the principal. We'll move if we have to." I'll bet these parents won't hear much more about this kid's grades until it's too late.

It is relatively easy to learn to limit our blatant reactions, but we may be unaware of how loud our subtler messages can be. Our kids have incredibly strong sensors that pick up on our signals. Their fear of disappointing us, or their frustration over our judgments, may hinder further communication. In routine exchanges, we can inadvertently, and usually unintentionally, convey that we're judging, moralizing, minimizing, negating, catastrophizing, belittling, or shaming. The following example demonstrates how a parent's various responses may be interpreted (or possibly misinterpreted) by a child and lead to decreased communication in the future:

Eleven-year-old Rosa comes home from dance class with reddened eyes and ready to burst into tears. Gradually, she reveals that her teacher has said she's improving but may never learn her routine well enough in time for the recital.

A mother's comment like, "What does she know?" will undermine Rosa's trust in her teacher, belittle the problem, and not encourage her to practice her skills.

If her mother says, "Darling, you will be the star of the show," Rosa will question her mother's assessment skills, doubt her mother's sincerity, feel increased pressure to perform, and conclude that her concerns were not taken seriously.

If her mother suggests, "Fine, quit dance if that's what you want," she is turning a temporary setback into a permanent catastrophe that needn't exist. Furthermore, she is clearly judging her child and expressing her anger.

If she says, "Don't cry, Rosa. It's not that bad," she minimizes a problem that is upsetting her daughter and teaches her daughter to hold back rather than express her emotions, creates a moral judgment based on little information, and undermines the teacher's ability to effectively coach her daughter.

All of these comments were intended to be helpful but may limit Rosa's desire to share the feedback she receives in the future. Instead, Rosa's mother will want to create a setting where Rosa feels relieved for sharing her feelings and secure in her mother's unconditional love. There is a good chance that Rosa's unstated need was to know her mother would not be angry or disappointed if Rosa did not perform in the recital. A statement like, "It's natural to be disappointed that you may not be ready for this recital. But I'm so glad you're improving. Keep up the hard work, sweetheart," accompanied by a hug, would offer support and security.

Make It About Safety

Our challenge is to give clearly defined rules and boundaries in a way our children will not reject. Judith Smetana's research, captured in her book *Adolescents, Families, and Social Development: How Teens Construct Their Worlds,* guides us how to do just that. She explores what adolescents consider parents' "legitimate authority" and has shown that we only know what our teens choose to tell us. Equipped with this knowledge, we are better positioned to frame our rules in a way that our kids consider legitimate.

Teens agree we have an obligation to be involved with their safety and a responsibility to prepare them to function appropriately in society. This includes teaching them to respect other people's rights and to follow the law. On the other hand, they do not believe we have the right to interfere with things they consider within their personal territory. If it is about their friends or a behavior they choose that doesn't challenge their safety or interaction with society, they will likely view our input as interference.

The toughest areas for setting rules and boundaries are those that involve your child's friends. Because kids may not believe you have the right to comment on their personal business, including friendships and what they do with their free time, rules and boundaries should be framed to be about safety whenever possible. I would argue that if a peer issue does not involve safety or morality, you should remain available as a sounding board but otherwise not enter these discussions. If you condemn or belittle any of your child's friends, you might just make them seem more intriguing or attractive. If you forbid them from being with particular friends, they may stop telling you who they're with and where they're going. They might even make up stories while thinking, "Who I hang out with is my personal business, not theirs."

Our strategy has to be to monitor and modulate peers' influence in a way our children find acceptable. First, kids deserve privacy when issues about their friends do not involve safety or morality. But it is OK to set general rules that offer protection from difficult situations or bad influences. There will be less rebellion against rules if kids don't feel like they were made to interfere with specific relationships. Curfew, for example, keeps kids off the streets when things may get out of hand. When your community makes it expected that adults appropriately supervise parties, teens will all be safer. Next, you can subtly promote positive relationships and make it easier to be with trusted friends by creating opportunities for kids to get together. Third, your child wants to do the right thing; he just needs the skills to follow his own internal wisdom. That's why it is so important to give him the tools to safely navigate the peer world, as discussed in Chapter 10, Navigational Strategies.

Finally, remember there is less to rebel against when teens understand that boundaries exist for their safety. Sometimes a peer's influence can lead to unwise decisions, and other times peers may innocently create distractions or emotions that make teens lose focus. Driving is a perfect example of the latter. Peer passengers substantially increase the risk of crashes for new drivers. But if you say, "You may not have friends in the car while you are driving," your teen will think, "You shouldn't even be talking about my friends." *(In other words, "You have no legitimate authority here!")* "Why do you hate my friends? I'll take them anyway, and you'll never know." Instead, set boundaries while clearly explaining your decision framed in your responsibility to protect your child from a very real danger. "I care about your safety, and research has proven teen passengers distract new drivers. You may not drive with teen passengers until you have at least 6 months' experience behind the wheel." Because it is unlikely your adolescent will accept this at face value; he will likely demand further explanation. This is a good thing, because remember, it is his job to expand his boundaries to the point he believes he can handle. He might say, "But my friends would never do that to me; that's probably because other kids act crazy in cars." Reinforce that this is a temporary rule, "It takes 3 seconds to avoid a crash. You have to see something, decide what to do, and do it all in 3 seconds. Kids get loud and excited when they're having a good time. It's too much to expect you to keep your eyes on the road, maintain control of the car, and manage your friends' behaviors. This is not open for discussion, but it's also temporary. When you have more driving experience and you've consistently shown you're a responsible driver, you'll be able to take your friends with you. In the meantime, I'll get you all where you need to go." He may even go further and ask, "But how come you can drive a carload of people?"

Your response could be, "Well, first you will notice I am always scanning the road for things that might happen. In fact, 999 times out of 1,000 if I looked away for a couple of seconds, nothing would happen. But 1 in 1,000 times, I'd miss the truck coming out of a side street or a kid on a bike. So I'm no different than you, and I always try to keep my focus on the road. But the difference between us is when I see something, my instincts will kick in. You need time to develop your instincts, and until then you'll need every fraction of a second to think."

The reason I played out the above driving example is to bring home the point that you should always be prepared for some mental and verbal wrestling when you set boundaries. You should be proud your child wants to thoroughly understand why you are setting boundaries. He *should* be pushing his limits and insisting that limits be properly set at precisely the point where they really do protect his safety.

Therefore, with any issue where you have to set and monitor boundaries, try to be prepared with your talking points on why and how the issue involves safety or the ability to interact successfully in society. If you can't come up with a good explanation that is framed in these contexts, you might reconsider if your rules are necessary. On the other hand, if there is an issue that is clearly about safety and your adolescent doesn't seem to grasp that and argues endlessly, you win. Period. It is about safety. Demonstrate flexibility elsewhere so you can't reasonably be described as rigid. Hopefully, over time, your son or daughter will learn from the realization and think, "Usually my mom or dad is reasonable, so there must be a reason they feel strongly about this."

Or Make It About Getting Along in Society

The young people in Judith Smetana's research also said it was legitimate for parents to prepare their kids for the real world and to protect them from breaking rules of society. Suppose your teen daughter comes to you and asks for some money to go to the tattoo parlor or shares she is going to get one of those really cool gauges to stretch her earlobe out. In your head, you might say, "Why would anyone need a hole big enough for a ping pong ball to go through her ear?" but instead you say, "Ewwwwwwwww, don't do that. No daughter of mine is going to disfigure herself that way." Don't be surprised by the hostile response, "Well, they're not your ears, are they?" because you have placed it squarely in personal territory. Try instead to frame your concern about getting along "out there." "I admire that you want to express yourself. My concern is people will judge you before they even know you. They are going to think they know who you are just because of what you look like. I know it's wrong, but that's the way it is. I'd hate to see you not get a job because of something so unfair. Also, that's a pretty permanent decision. Any way you could still express yourself but in a less permanent way?"

Let Them "Win" When They Deserve To

Many parents dread the endless arguments of adolescence, but these heated discussions are a key to effective monitoring. As long as our kids are fighting with us, they are engaged! As long as they are arguing, they are telling us something, and we are continuing to learn about what is going on in their lives.

Some teens seem to suffer temporary hearing loss ("What?") or constant fatigue ("I would talk, but I'm sooooo tired"). Therefore, parents miss much of what is going on in their teens' lives. Other adolescents argue with a vengeance for what they think is just and fair.

If you are fortunate enough to have a fighter (you never thought you'd hear it be described as fortunate, did you?), it is strategically important you reinforce that her arguments can pay off. Be willing to judiciously bend the rules or make an exception. This will reinforce that discussion works.

When our children make a reasoned case for an exception to our rules or for an expanded scope of freedom, and they have demonstrated responsibility, it is important we demonstrate flexibility. Nancy Darling and colleagues have shown that parents should be flexible around rules to keep their children continually engaged. This is part of the responsiveness considered central to balanced or authoritative parenting and absent from authoritarian parenting.[4]

Darling points out that our clear rules can sometimes generate discussion, even arguments. But this is far better than silence or lying. Arguments can be productive and lead to increased agreement over time. When our kids learn that reasonable negotiation pays off, they will continue telling us about their lives. As importantly, they will learn we reward open communication and demonstrated responsibility. These are valuable lessons that will serve them throughout life.

---

[4] Nancy Darling is a developmental psychologist and professor at Oberlin College whose research focuses on adolescents' social relations and changing relationships with parents and peers.

Imagine your daughter comes to you and says, "I got asked out by the greatest guy ever. I really want to go to this concert with him Saturday night. I'll be home after curfew, but you'll know exactly where I am. I'll stop in and let you meet him, but please don't say anything to embarrass me! Just smile, OK? Don't worry about my homework; I'll finish it all during the day. And I know you always worry about sleep, but I'll sleep late Sunday and still get up in time to babysit like I promised." If you respond, "You know curfew is 12:30; rules are not made to be bent," don't be surprised when she kisses you on the cheek on the way out the door on Thursday night and says, "Love you. Don't forget: I'm sleeping over at Courtney's Saturday night." Kids lie when they find there is no yield in talking to us.

Discipline Means to Teach, Not to Control

It is important to understand that the word *discipline* means "to teach"; it does not mean "to control." When we discipline effectively, we are increasing our children's sense of control, not ours. This can be done when they learn that the freedoms and privileges they receive are directly linked to the responsibility they demonstrate.

I wrote more extensively about effective discipline strategies in my book *Building Resilience in Children and Teens: Giving Kids Roots and Wings.* In this book, I want to highlight a few key points.

- If a consequence does not teach something, it is not discipline; it is a punishment.

- Most kids expect parents to tell them what to do. They think we want to control them rather than delegate control to them.

- Children gain a sense of control when they understand that they earn privileges. They lose their sense of control when rules are imposed on them.

- We should have as few rules as possible but be clear and consistent about the rules we set.

- Some limits are permanent, but most are fluid. The boundaries are set at the limits of where the child can safely venture. As a young person demonstrates more capabilities, those boundaries expand.

- We leverage children's natural desire for independence by giving them the privileges they can handle while keeping safety nets in place. *You* don't hand out privileges and freedoms lightly, nor do you use them as bribes. You have clear boundaries that demonstrate privileges are earned.

- Most issues you consider will probably be negotiable. It's healthy for children to negotiate schedules, rules, and consequences for not following them. By being part of the process, kids exert some control and may be more likely to follow through on boundaries they've had a role in creating. They also learn useful give-and-take skills for future negotiation with peers, teachers, or bosses.

- No matter what boundaries you set, problems will inevitably arise and merit an appropriate consequence. When your kids mess up, your message should be, "You've done something wrong, but I still love you." If we reinforce our unconditional love, even in the face of disappointment, kids will still turn to us when they find themselves in future trouble.

- Just as you expand boundaries as your child demonstrates growth, you can also retract them to the point that your child has proven he can handle. This approach to discipline also prevents you from needing to arrive at a consequence when you are angry. Consequences formulated in anger are often too harsh and not logically related to the infraction. When that is the case, the consequence will feel worse than the crime, and the young person will feel punished, not taught. Therefore, discipline does not occur. On the other hand, we can fairly return our children to the point of demonstrated responsibility. "You don't seem to be able to handle yourself well when you are allowed to stay out until midnight; therefore, you'll return to a curfew of 11:30, which you handled well. We'll see how you do there and talk again in a month." The consequence is measured, fair, and directly related to demonstrated behavior, making the young person highly motivated to earn back his privilege. More importantly, he clearly understands he controlled the outcome.

66 Parents should protect children when it comes to things like safety. But when it comes to stuff like friendship troubles or failures that they experience, children need to learn this on their own. When a parent hovers over every aspect of a child's life, the child becomes dependent and doesn't learn the lessons needed for life. This hovering can only make a child weaker. 99

—17-year-old female, Pennsylvania

Making It Easier on Both of You

Remember, kids are almost always trying to answer the question, "Am I normal?" They answer that question by looking around and comparing themselves to other kids. When your rules differ from those of other parents, you'll be seen as unreasonable, and your child may be more likely to rebel. If your community, or at least the parents of your kid's circle of friends, set up common rules and boundaries, your child can meet your expectations, stay safe, and feel normal at the same time. When boundaries are just "the way it is," kids will be less likely to generate tension.

More Thoughts From Teens

It's annoying when you say something like, "I like the high heels in this picture," and then your mom is like, "Not just no; you are never wearing those." It's also annoying when your mom says to stay away from a bad person and then talks trash about that person every single time that person is brought up.

—12-year-old female, Guantanamo Bay, Cuba

I've noticed that some parents feel a need to protect their kids from situations that could get them into legal trouble but ignore life lessons that are centered around ethics and responsibility. For example, parents might obsess over making sure their son doesn't smoke marijuana but forget to teach him to respect women. This is totally backward! Kids have to learn to keep themselves out of legal trouble, but parents need to give basic moral guidance.

—18-year-old, gender unknown, North Carolina

Parents should recognize the fact that as their children are growing up, they need to let [their children] be more independent. In terms of the child's social life, parents should give their children space when they're with their friends so that the child can experience growing up somewhat on their own. For example, parents should not be texting and calling their children 24/7 while they are trying to hang out with their friends, because that defeats the purpose. Set guidelines and curfews so that the child and the parents are very clear on what behavior is expected and what is appropriate.
—17-year-old female, Texas

Protect your child when they endanger themselves. Everything else should be something they figure out. Protect them from drugs, alcohol, and needlessly dangerous behavior. Give them the reins on everything else, and if they need help, be there, but don't push "help" onto them.
—17-year-old male, Illinois

Teens need to learn through their own mistakes, and parents cannot coddle them through every single one of [our] problems, because we have a lot. If parents do that, then later in life, when a teen is on their own, where they can't turn to their parents to fix every little problem, then they won't know how to deal with life. A parent can protect their teenager, but they can't cross the line of being overprotective. An example of how a parent should deal with this might be if your teen's having trouble in school (in an argument with friends), you need to let them deal with this on their own. Offer your advice. Say, "I'm here if you want to talk about it," but don't say, "Tell me what happened right now." Don't tell them to apologize no matter what; just let them handle it the way they think they should. Don't call up their friend and say, "You and my daughter/son need to make up right away." I don't want my parents involved in all of my personal business, but I do like knowing they're there if I need them.

Going through my phone or social networking sites is way crossing the line. Trust your teen to make the right decision, and if they cannot handle it, trust them to come to you for help. If my parents were to ever invade my privacy like that, even if they believed they were protecting me, I would just be very angry at them. That, to me, just says they don't trust me, and why would I bother telling someone my problems when they don't trust me? If you don't trust me, then I don't trust you. Teens need to know that their parents trust them no matter what, and that's when your teen will talk to you. Some kinds of situations parents should protect their teens from would be if they have suspicions [their teens] are involved with drugs, hanging out with some seriously wrong people, or are depressed and in danger of hurting themselves. Then parents can cross that line and need to figure out how to help their kid by any means necessary.
—17-year-old female, Pennsylvania

There are a lot of smaller things, especially things such as problems in school or struggles with self-identity, that should be a teen's job to get them through themselves, but that doesn't mean a parent shouldn't provide guidance. I think that parents should always be open to discussion and let their children feel welcome to speak up if they need help, but ultimately let them make their own decisions and reap their own consequences when it comes down to legal or non–life-threatening things. For things that are obviously illegal, life-threatening, or otherwise endangering the teen's health in any way, of course a parent should step in, even if the teen is against it. That is part of the responsibility of being a parent, to raise their child as a healthy, law-obeying citizen. I think that many times there are teens who want or need guidance in certain aspects of life, and the adults in their life should be open, happy, and willing to help from that standpoint but not be overpowering and controlling in day-to-day life.
—18-year-old female, Alabama

CHAPTER

14

Parenting Toward Lifelong *Inter*dependence

Amongst our most important roles is to raise our children so they will be able to venture forth to create and support their own families. For this reason, we are instinctually programmed both to protect our small children and to allow our older adolescents the latitude to explore varied relationships and experiences. In other words, we intuitively and subconsciously *know* we must allow kids increasing independence, even if it challenges our desire to continue to shield them.

The ingrained knowledge we have that we must support our children's capacity to explore the world is tempered with our desire that they not venture too far away from us (geographically or emotionally). Our parental bone marrow wants us to continue to be involved in their lives, even when they no longer require our protection. But our culture values independence so highly that it takes on a sense of urgency. This frenetic pace comes at the expense of our ability to find that comfort zone where we could both allow our kids to navigate the world increasingly on their own and convey our desire *and need* to remain close.

An overt emphasis on independence may not create the healthiest families over the long-term. For millennia, humans were sustained because we existed as *inter*dependent beings. We lived within extended families and clans. Our clans existed within larger communities and tribes. Generations needed each other. We venerated our elderly, and our elders bestowed wisdom on our children. We yearn for *inter*dependence. This explains why when you speak of your child growing up, you experience a lump in your throat; it gives away your natural, healthy ambivalence about your child leaving you one day.

Regardless of how much society glamorizes independence, many of us find it far too difficult to allow the stumbles that are part and parcel of moving toward independence. For those parents, the instinctual need to protect is dominant. However, for their children, that protection will be seen as *over*protection or may even be viewed as inappropriate attempts at control.

We *can* create those intergenerational relationships in which we all flourish over the long-term. When our teens leave our house knowing we supported, even celebrated, their growing independence, they will return to us after they have proven they can make it on their own. If, however, we install "control buttons" during their adolescence, we may undermine their desire to maintain a close connection.

Don't Install "Control Buttons"

Did you leave your childhood house shouting, "I'm free!" or thinking, "I'm going to miss it around here." Even if you adored your parents, you wouldn't have found the resolve to leave if you didn't at least fool yourself into being (occasionally) desperate for your freedom.

When you had your own child and were considering the level of involvement you hoped your parents would have in your lives, were you inspired to live in the same community? Or did you live farther away, hoping to keep the visits time limited and infrequent?

When you considered how much your own mother or father would respect you as a parent, did you worry they wouldn't let you develop your own style of parenting? Did you worry they would take over? Or did you believe they would be helpful when asked or genuinely needed?

I'd guess the answers to all of these questions would be largely determined by whether you felt controlled or supported by your parents when you were a teen. Our "control buttons" were installed during adolescence. If you want a long-standing healthy relationship, don't install these buttons now. Instead, be genuinely excited by your child's growing capabilities and supportive of her developing independence.

When our adult children know we honored their need to become independent, they will return to us for the *inter*dependence that defines loving, functional families across the generations.

> By allowing your child small freedoms, they will be less rebellious and less curious. Therefore, they won't feel a need to do things behind their parents' backs.
>
> —17-year-old female, Pennsylvania

Fostering Growth and Independence
While Assuring Safety

Everyday issues trigger many parent-child struggles and also offer opportunities for fostering independence. It's the common issues adolescents need to manage that will reveal to your children whether you are committed to preparing them or are overprotecting them. A teen might think she should be granted a new privilege just because she's old enough or because her friends are doing it, but she might not have mastered the skills needed to manage the situation. If you focus on preparing your adolescent to master those skills, rather than deny her the opportunity to have new experiences, she will feel supported rather than controlled. You will have turned potential sources of conflict and rebellion into opportunities for her to demonstrate responsibility and for you to partner in her growth.

Childhood and adolescence is filled with opportunities for trial and error and ultimately accomplishment. We must help our sons and daughters learn from day-to-day mistakes rather than view them as catastrophes. Simultaneously, we need to monitor them closely enough so we can help them avoid errors that could cause irreparable harm. While we remain vigilant for dangers, we must not be overprotective, lest they miss the opportunity to gain valuable life experiences. We also want them to make those mistakes that will teach them how to rebound, recover, and move on. We want both progress and missteps to occur under our watchful eyes so we can reinforce the life lessons that build enduring resilience.

Independence, One Step at a Time

When is your child ready to face a new challenge? When he is wise enough to know what he is dealing with and has enough skills in place so there are optimal chances for success.

A request by your 16-year-old for the car keys won't be as terrifying if your response does not hinge on his age. If he's demonstrated general responsibility and you've taught him how to manage different driving conditions while slowly exposing him to more challenging ones, and you've made it clear you will monitor his progress even after he is driving on his own, you'll be able to say, "He's ready," with reasonable confidence. Your stomach won't be turning when your 15-year-old daughter goes on her first date if you have raised her to have self-respect, the knowledge to protect herself, the ability to recognize pressure, and the skills to respond to it.

Each developmental milestone requires a different strategy. *Letting Go with Love and Confidence*, a book I wrote with Susan FitzGerald, helps parents consider how to approach a wide variety of specific issues. It is beyond the scope of this book to offer strategies for a multitude of developmental tasks or challenges, but there is a common path to support independence in a measured manner.

First, take time to observe, just as you did when you baby-proofed your home. The first step then was to get down on your knees and experience the world as your child saw it. Once you saw the world as he would, you knew to use the back burners, turn pot handles inward, and cover electrical sockets. Now, getting a kid's-eye view will heighten your senses about the challenges your child or teen may encounter. You'll never view the mall the same way again when you pass the scintillating images and seductive pulls. You'll never see the walk to school the same way after you've evaluated the dangers and distractions along the way. You'll be better prepared to phase in new privileges and put into place needed supports and monitoring.

Next, consider your child's temperament and unique developmental needs. Although this may sound like you need a professional degree, nobody matches the expertise you have on your child.

The next step is about listening. Listen respectfully and without judgment to what your child thinks she can handle, and ask what guidance or support she seeks. Invite her to develop a plan for mastery with you. Genuinely believe that even though she is young, she is still the greatest expert on herself and the challenges she needs to confront.

Finally, together with her, generate a road map that has broken the overall task into multiple manageable steps. Each step should build her skills and confidence to prepare her to successfully meet the overall challenge. Most critically, help her understand she will gain more privileges and opportunities for growth as long as she continues to demonstrate responsibility. When she stumbles, she'll stay steady for a while or even move a step back to the point where she remained safe and competent. Discipline delivered in this manner is consistent with its true meaning, to teach or to guide, rather than being about punishment or control.

6 6 If your parent is super controlling, you begin to tell them less and do things behind their backs. It's not that you want to lie to them, or keep secrets from them, but more that you want to live life.... 9 9

—19-year-old female, Texas

When young people know that our intention is to help them get to their goals, they'll be less likely to be offended that we are carefully monitoring the process. Most importantly, they will appreciate our presence in their lives. They will not feel overprotected, and no control buttons will be installed.

Our children may temporarily still push us away as part of the uncomfortable journey toward their independence. The operative word here is *temporarily*. When they are confidently standing on their own, they will return to us for the loving *inter*dependence we all need to flourish in this complex, fast-moving, and sometimes impersonal world.

Moments for Personal Reflection or Serious Discussion

It is easy to intellectually consider the fine balance between protection and overprotection. It is objectively clear that only life's lessons can prepare us for our journey. But the challenge is battling your instinctual need to protect. It is in those moments that offer real challenges when fear may take over, and preparation seems like something that can be considered tomorrow. There is no question that for circumstances that truly challenge safety, you should be driven by your "mama tiger" or "papa bear" instincts to fight for and protect your offspring. But sometimes it just feels like danger, and the real harm comes not from the situation but your overprotective interpretation of what is harmful. *Why do I feel like my child is in danger when my friends tell me there is nothing to fear? Why do I find myself in a panic when my spouse tells me to relax? Do I forbid my child to do something just because it keeps me calmer or gives me a sense of control over a world I fear is unpredictable?*

It is difficult, but you can gain awareness of the patterns you are repeating that may be based on fears or insecurity you can conquer. Equipped with this self-awareness and clarification of your real goals, you can change your approach. Because many of our discomforts may be deeply rooted, you may benefit from professional guidance. But a first step is certainly a discussion with your spouse and child on how you as a family can strike the balance between safety now and the long-term life skills gained by dealing with life's blessings and adversities today.

Some questions to consider include

- How does my child benefit from my protective instincts?

- Would a reasonable observer think I am sometimes overprotective?

- What message does my child receive when I offer protection?

- What message does my child absorb when I am more protective than necessary?

- Do I tend to believe the stakes are too high to allow my child to fail and recover? If so, what is that about? Is it related to my personal fear of failure? Do I feel as if I am inadequate or a bad parent when my child stumbles?

- Am I holding my child so tight, or imposing such rigid rules, that he feels controlled? Or am I letting go in a way that honors his developing independence, with an eye toward fostering long-term interdependence?

> ❝Adults should be open, happy, and willing to help but not be overpowering and controlling. ❞
>
> —18-year-old female, Alabama

PART

3

The Voice of Youth

Youth lack the wisdom of years but nonetheless are the authorities on their own lives.

It would be nice if kids came with instruction manuals. We would know the exact steps to prepare them for a meaningful and successful life. Also, it would have simplified this whole parenting thing if in the last 2 parts we had definitively come down on one side or the other of those 2 toughest of questions. For example, we could have said, "Love your child unconditionally; any attempt at placing expectations undermines the purity of that love." Or we could have emphatically stated, "Children learn best through experience, and our efforts at protection destroy their confidence." But the key word in the subtitle of this book is the one you likely did not even notice: *balancing*. It is the balancing act that allows us to craft our strategies to meet the needs and temperament of each child and to adjust them as he or she develops. We've offered some guidance on striking that balance, often based on the best of current social science. But to get it right, you have to look at and listen to your child.

Ideally, your child would be able to articulate precisely what is needed from you for him to flourish. Short of this idealized scenario, we are hoping that the more than 500 young people who participated in helping put together this book will help you better understand how your own kid might react to or be affected by your parenting strategies.

There are many reasons why our own children may not be able to give us the feedback we need to find that ideal balance of love and expectations, of protection with trust.

First, they might be too young. If this is the case for you, you are joining us at the best time. Listening to our teen participants now could have the greatest effect on your child because you are positioned to have fewer regrets later. (You'll still have them; they come with the territory of caring so much.)

Second, they might lack the insight to know how their feelings, behaviors, or performance are tied to their interactions with us. Insight is something that comes over time; they may not yet have gone through the developmental stages that allow them to gain insight.

Third, our children have only one set of experiences with parents (us!) and therefore can't compare how they are reacting to our efforts with how they might respond to adjusted strategies.

Fourth, the familiar is comfortable. When people are used to something and have learned how to manage it, for better or worse, it might be too scary to consider change. In this case, silence feels like the best option.

Next, sharing their frustrations, insecurities, and self-doubts might reveal they are not doing as well on the inside as they appear to be doing on the outside. It is tough to reveal problems when others think all is going well.

Finally, our children do not want to disappoint us. Their desire to please us sometimes gets in the way of telling us what they are feeling and often gets in the way of them giving us valuable feedback. I know you might be thinking, "Is he crazy? I get 'feedback' all the time, and it's not always so pretty." I get it. But the kind of feedback we are talking about now is different; it is in response to those aspects of parenting for which they absolutely appreciate that you have the best of intentions. They may not share that something is not working for them, because they do not want to hurt your feelings.

Now let's be honest: there are some barriers to communication from our end as well. It is hard to get feedback from our kids. First, most of us were not raised in families with parents who had "How am I doing?" check-ins with their kids. We were more likely to have had "My house, my rules!" one-way conversations. Consequently, we may not be skilled in how to create the zone of safety where our children will open up with us about their feelings. Next, they know how to push our buttons far better than anyone else, and we may not be eager to enter a conversation that might lead to conflict. They don't always have the skill set to deliver feedback kindly, so we avoid getting it. Maybe most importantly, their opinions matter so deeply to us that they are sometimes hard to hear.

I hope you will get to the point that you can learn from your own children. Part 4 offers some communication strategies for you and your son or daughter to get you there. In the meantime, I invite you to consider hearing from youth who have no relationship with you and therefore no barriers that might prevent frank, open communication. They also will not push your buttons as those who know and love us can. As a result, it may be easier to hear their views. Listening to them will help you see things that might be in plain sight but out of view. They may help you collect your thoughts to frame the kind of questions that will help your own kids better reveal themselves. When we know our kids, including how they are experiencing our parenting, we are better positioned to help them thrive.

How the Youth Views Were Used in This Book

Although this book is rooted in social science and expert opinion, the youth viewpoint assures that the points offered here have been "market tested" as ideas that kids care about and will likely therefore be responsive toward. The greatest influence the youth perspective had on this book is largely invisible to you. Their ideas have flavored much of the content, and some elements of this book were included entirely because so many youth felt strongly about them. For example, the idea behind Part 4, which offers you the skill sets to openly communicate with your son or daughter, originated with one of my 18-year-old daughters, Ilana, and was reinforced by the teen panel. Essentially the panel asked, "What's the point of telling parents what they might do better if they won't know how to approach their kids about it?" Ilana and Talia gave input on every principle and redlined ideas they didn't think would work for kids. Adolescent views were peppered throughout the book to reinforce key concepts and to ground the content in the understanding that kids are not passive recipients of parenting; they are deeply affected by our actions. Above all, their presence serves as a constant reminder that they want healthy close relationships with us and they care about being successful. We need this because we mustn't be swayed by popular culture, which wrongly implies parents matter little compared to peers and that young people don't care about their future.

This brings us to this part of the book, in which Ilana and Talia will briefly summarize the youth views. It is a tall order to do justice to more than 500 young people's views in a few pages, but as you will see the job was made easier because the youth were surprisingly unified.

CHAPTER

15

Eliciting the Youth Perspective

As a qualitative researcher, I have been eliciting the perspectives of youth for nearly 25 years. There are 2 things I have learned consistently in my research. First, we adults are often surprised by how much kids care about issues that affect their lives. Second, the inclusion of youth *always raises issues that adult experts haven't considered.*

This project was not conducted as a research study. Rather, it was an invitation for young people to teach adults about how to support them to thrive. Nevertheless, this process revealed how much young people care about issues that affect them. And, as usual, the adolescents enriched the ideas through their participation.

The Invitation

Young people were invited to participate as teachers. They were told,

We are looking for honest input from 12- to 19-year-olds on 2 questions that are critical to parenting. Your responses may be used in an upcoming publication for parents by the American Academy of Pediatrics and adolescent health expert Kenneth Ginsburg, MD, MS Ed, FAAP (www.fosteringresilience.com). We hope to use your answers to help parents understand how to give teens the right balance of support and independence. Your unique perspective makes you a great teacher to help parents think about how to strike that balance. We hope your thoughts will help other young people.

The Questions

The young people were asked to respond to the following 2 questions in as much detail as they liked and to include examples to illustrate their points:

- Many parents find it very challenging to balance the need to protect their children or teens with the need to let them learn from life's lessons. What advice would you give parents as they face these challenges? What kind of situations should they protect their teens from? When should they let them learn life's lessons?

- We know that children and teens raised with unconditional love, support, and acceptance grow up to feel more secure. We also know that young people are more successful when they are held to high expectations (in terms of putting a good effort into their school work and behaving well). The problem is that once a parent sets high expectations, the love may no longer feel unconditional because the possibility of failure or disappointment exists. Therefore, it is a struggle for parents to strike the balance between loving without conditions and making their expectations clear. What advice would you give parents about how to balance this issue as they raise their children?

Finding the Youth

Many of the young people were referred by their parents who saw an invitation placed on HealthyChildren.org, the official American Academy of Pediatrics Web site for parents.

We were committed to hearing the views of a geographically, ethnically, and socioeconomically diverse group of youth who had a high comfort level in offering their thoughts to adults. We anticipated that some youth who chose to participate were likely going to be those who felt particularly frustrated with their parents, so we wanted to be sure that we also included youth who had a history of working with adults to solve problems and who thought deeply about the power of parents in their lives. Finally, because we knew that we were interested in exploring the concepts of success and thriving, we wanted to include some viewpoints from youth who had demonstrated high levels of academic and extracurricular achievement.

Initial Groups Invited

I have been fortunate to work with organizations, youth, and families throughout the country and therefore was able to select groups of young people to invite as teachers. The groups below were selected to assure a wide range of young people who would meet the goals stated in the previous paragraph. After those initial youth were involved, they in turn invited their friends until we had more than 500 "teachers" from across the nation.

The Jack Kent Cooke Foundation Young Scholars Program

The Jack Kent Cooke Foundation Young Scholars Program supports youth from across the nation who are exceptionally promising students with financial need. Young scholars excel academically and demonstrate persistence, leadership, and a desire to help others.

SpeakUp!

SpeakUp! is a Pennsylvania-based program committed to improving communication between generations. Its unique events allow parents and youth to learn one another's perspectives on critical issues that affect health and well-being. Its small group sessions have a mixture of parents and adolescents, with the one restriction being that you cannot be in the same room as your family member. This allows everyone to more objectively listen to representatives from the other generation. Then it offers families the skills to continue their own conversations at home. Their approach is similar to the one taken in this book.

Girls to Women Health and Wellness

Girls to Women Health and Wellness is a Dallas, Texas, adolescent medicine practice who works with parents and their daughters to provide adolescents with the confidence, information, and tools to make positive life choices.

Youth Whose Parents Are in the US Military

Military-connected youth (eg, those with parents who are service members) have endured prolonged and frequent separation from one or both parents for more than a decade. Therefore, many of them are particularly thoughtful about the critical role of parents in their lives. The initial contact for our military youth was Chris Dickson, Regional School Liaison Officer, Commander, Navy Region Mid-Atlantic.

Youth Who Have Benefitted From the Family Action Network

The Family Action Network is an Illinois-based program and one of the nation's premier parent education organizations. Many of its programs focus on how parents can raise young people to be authentically successful in an increasingly competitive world. Our initial contact was Lonnie Stonitsch, Family Action Network Cochair and Programming Chair.

Trying to Understand More About Our Teachers

To learn more about the youth participants, we asked for some key descriptive information, being careful that none of it would identify the young people.

- We asked participants' age, gender, and state, as well as whether they would describe the area they lived in as a city, small town, suburban setting, or rural setting.

- We did not ask for race or economic status directly but recruited to assure that our goals for diversity were met.

- We were interested to learn the basic style their parents used to raise them. Although there are very complex surveys and measures that accurately explore and assign parenting style, we used 4 simple sentences to get a sense of how the participants were being parented. We asked youth to report which sentence best described the approach to parenting taken by their father, mother, grandparents, and stepparents.
  - You'll do what I say. Why? Because I said so.
  - We're like friends. I trust you'll do the right thing.
  - I care about you, and I'll give you the freedoms you earn, but for safety-related issues, you'll need to do as I say.
  - Kids will be kids. Do what you want; you'll figure it out.

- We also offered each participant the opportunity to write a sentence that described himself and another that offered a glimpse into the type of parent he hoped to be.

The Participants

More than 500 young people shared their views to create this book. Some took only a few moments to report their parents' parenting style, but most dived fully into the essay questions, some spending more than 2 hours sharing their views. Although we were able to get a diverse representation of young people (Figure 15-1), it must be understood that all of our teachers cared enough about this subject to commit their time and effort. In other words, youth who would not think that parents mattered very much would likely not have participated.

Our participants lived in 40 different states and 5 overseas military bases. Some states, however, were overrepresented: 19% of participants were from Illinois; 16%, Pennsylvania; 6%, Virginia; 5%, New Jersey; and 5%, Texas.

Figure 15-1. Youth participants categorized by gender, age, and community setting.

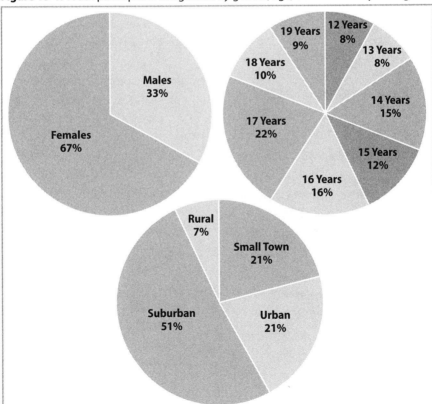

Youth Participants Categorized by Gender, Age, and Community Setting

Approximately half of parents were described as having a balanced approach to parenting: "I care about you, and I'll give you the freedoms you earn, but for safety-related issues, you'll need to do as I say" (45% of fathers and 53% of mothers). About a quarter of parents were described as taking an authoritarian approach: "You'll do what I say. Why? Because I said so" (28% of fathers and 25% of mothers). A smaller amount of parents were described as more permissive: "We're like friends. I trust you'll do the right thing" (13% of fathers and 17% of mothers). Young people described only a few parents as taking the hands-off, disengaged approach: "Kids will be kids. Do what you want; you'll figure it out" (5% of fathers and 3% of mothers). The percentages do not add up to 100% because 9% of our participants reported not having a father, and 2% stated they did not have a mother.

In addition to the approximately 500 youth who completed the questions were 2 other groups of participants. Twenty young people from Pennsylvania and New Jersey participated in 1 of 2 focus groups about parenting. In these groups, teens discussed ideal interactions with parents and how their mothers and fathers could be most supportive in helping them manage the pressures in their lives.

Finally, 16 young people participated in the teen expert panel. Our teen expert panel chairperson, 17-year-old Jakub Zegar from Pennsylvania, interviewed them. The panelists helped clarify points that were made in the surveys and focused on how to foster child-parent communication. You will know when a quote is from a teen panelist because teen panelists' names are used, but most of their advice is just folded into the book.

Teen Expert Panel

Jakub Zegar, age 17, Pennsylvania (chairperson)
Carolina Andrada, age 17, Florida
Sonni Browne, age 16, Pennsylvania
Kevin Cho, age 17, Pennsylvania
Amanda Farah, age 18, Pennsylvania
Lauren Furey, age 16, Pennsylvania
Cameron Gillaspy, age 18, Pennsylvania
Lizette Grajales, age 17, Pennsylvania
Stephanie Lefthand, age 19, Texas
Simone Levy, age 16, Pennsylvania
Sarah Schrading, age 18, Pennsylvania
Angela Sim, age 19, Pennsylvania
Seth Sugerman, age 14, Texas
Linton Taylor, age 17, Pennsylvania
Josh Toro, age 18, New Jersey
Nora Walsh, age 16, Illinois

Global Findings

The following chapters flesh out some of the young people's views. Let's underscore 2 key points here.

First, the youth genuinely cared about this subject. Granted, the youth voice here is biased by those youth who chose to participate, but they still could have easily concluded that parents didn't matter. Remember, some participants invested their energy in completing the survey precisely because they were angry at their parents. They might have said, "Who cares about parents?" But in sharp contrast, even youth who unloaded frustrations focused their energies on describing the relationships they desired.

Second, all of the various descriptors we gathered on the youth mattered little to how they believed parents could ideally support them. No matter how we cut and reshuffled the youth's responses, there was not a clear difference in their views. Age, of course, contributed to an increasingly sophisticated understanding of how parents' behaviors affected them. Otherwise, community size, participant gender, and region of the country did not make a noticeable difference to the core points the youth were trying to convey. Interestingly, it even seemed to matter little how the young people described their mother's or father's approach to parenting. My expectation was that this book was going to emphasize how youth reacted to varying parenting styles. My assumption was that the kids who were parented by more controlling parents would plea for more freedom and those who were parented more permissively would be hungry for more monitoring in their lives. Instead, virtually all young people called for the balance between trust and monitoring and *all* youth spoke of the overriding importance of unconditional love.

Therefore, the numbers given in this chapter are offered simply to demonstrate that our efforts to get a diverse sample paid off. Because the kids were fairly unified on their views means it is likely they are similar to the kids in your community or even share views with your own children. Now the hard work is left to you. As you hear the voice of youth, ask yourself, "Is this what my own child might be thinking?" Of course, if you want to be sure, you'll have to ask the expert on kids' views that lives with you.

Now for the details…

CHAPTER

16

The Youth Perspective: Love Versus Expectations

Ilana Ginsburg

We need your love to be given without conditions,
but we also need you to set the bar high for us, because
we want to know that you think we have something
important to bring to the world.

Love Must Never Have Conditions Attached

A theme consistently raised among nearly all teens who built this book is that parental love is critical, but it loses its meaning when it feels as if conditions are linked. Some teens shared that they felt parents sometimes expressed their love in a way that seemed conditional because it was related to their children's performance. They reported that as they grew older, they felt as though the attention they received, whether positive or negative, seemed increasingly tied to something they did or produced. Other youth contributors focused heavily on the pressure they felt from parents to reach certain expectations. They made it clear that the most painful part of parental pressure is that it seems to imply they are not good enough (or deserving of love!) "as is" and become worthy only if they are "as we (parents) wish you to be."

Many kids emphasized their plea for unconditional love, support, and attention by capitalizing the word *always* next to their statement, saying, "I believe that a parent's love should ALWAYS be unconditional," as stated by a 16-year-old young man from Pennsylvania who described himself as someone whose goal in parenting someday is to be "a loving and supportive father who will allow [his] kids to make their own decisions and mistakes." In framing the kind of father he hoped to be, he underscored the view from youth that their decisions or mistakes must not be tied to their parents' love, attention, or support.

Although most young people described receiving clear expressions of parental love, some kids spoke of how their parents did not express love often enough, if ever. These teens believed that their parents assumed the kids knew they were loved. However, the teens expressed that being reminded that their parents' love is present and, indeed, unconditional provides them consistent emotional support and offers confidence boosts when needed.

And When It Does Feel Conditional...

When love feels conditional—when parental affection is solely shown in response to grades, performances, or behaviors—kids experience an ever-present sense of pressure. This is especially true for those kids who know they cannot please their parent(s) in any other way than producing what is demanded of them. This can be a driving force toward perfectionism, insecurity, self-doubt, and even depression. The kids who spoke about having these types of parents were quite open about the negative effect it had on their emotional and psychological states.

A 17-year-old female who described herself as a "high achieving perfectionist who is trying not to worry about the small things in life" reported,

> ...as a high-achieving teen, [I feel] my parents' high expectations have affected me negatively. I am a perfectionist in all aspects of my life, and I am strongly affected when I don't achieve what I intend to. I also now have a very strong desire to please, working myself far too hard to gain the praise of others. This affects my home life, school life, and especially any relationships I enter. I wish my parents had accepted my achievements a little more instead of telling me that my best is perfection. They love me, but sometimes their demands can overshadow that.

One young person drove this point home with palpable pain, even anger. In her case, the expectations seem to have hurt her so deeply that she suggests parents should abandon expectations altogether. This is not the stance of teens generally, and certainly not that of my father, sister, and me, but we include this quote so you can see how painful expectations can feel when they are communicated in a way that implies a child is only acceptable under certain conditions. It is also included because this girl passionately reminds you that no measure of success matters more than your child's emotional well-being.

"Success is relative. I know many "successful" teens who deal with long-term mental disorders because of the pressure placed on them by their parents; I have panic attacks in school and severe depression because of this pressure. If you raise your child to be "successful,"… it says to me that you care more about their grades, more about the money they'll make, than how they turn out as a person and/or feel about themselves. That, to me, signals the ultimate parental failure: the idea that it's OK if she's an anorexic because she's a cheer-leader or it's OK if he's literally on suicide watch; he's going to be a lawyer. If that's what you want, fine. By the by, I'm not exaggerating here; I know people who've had this happen…. Love should be unconditional, always. Psychology counts the nuclear family as one of the most important things to a child's development. To not love your child is inherently selfish. You're sacrificing their mental well-being, making them feel bad, because...why? It's one thing if they hurt themselves or others, but love isn't support for actions. Love is caring for the well-being of your child and hoping that they are happy. Forget high expectations. They're corrosive and will just eat away at the family's relationships…."

Expectations Are Needed but Must Be Given Wisely

When expectations are connected to whether you show love, they are harmful and may separate you from your child.

Generally speaking, however, kids reacted well to expectations and were even asking for them. They felt as if parents' expectations helped them plan their lives and set goals for themselves. They requested a bar set for them that is neither too high to reach nor so low that it underestimates their potential. When it was set too high, they felt as if they could never please their parents and were just set up to fail themselves and to disappoint others. On the other hand, when expectations were set too low, they felt their parents didn't have faith in their abilities.

We would suggest that you watch your kids and speak to their teachers to see what they would be able to accomplish if they tried really hard. That will give you an idea of high, but realistically attainable, expectations. It is critical, however, that you have to be pleased by their effort and not be disappointed that some of your friends' children, or especially a brother or sister!, can reach a higher bar. Finally, we're not good at everything, and you have to know that the bar might need to be set at 2 different heights for different subjects or areas of our lives. Especially when school was discussed, young people spoke of their deep frustration and anger at their parents when they were punished for a lower than expected grade.

About 20 survey participants addressed parents using rewards as a strategy to assure their goals are met. Most kids suggested that the accomplishments in themselves needed to be viewed as enough of a reward. Some expressed shock or condescension that their peers were receiving rewards such as money, music, or electronics for something they should find satisfaction in accomplishing for themselves. Still, others said that rewards were welcomed as encouragement. Because of the differing opinions, we are not able to draw a conclusion on this youth viewpoint. However, there was clear consensus that an expectation must be placed to provide support and encouragement and absolutely not as something that needs to be accomplished as a means to avoid punishment.

Many youth spoke of how important it was when parents made it clear that expectations and goals were in place to benefit the kids, not the parents. We need parents to communicate clearly that goals are set to guide us in pushing ourselves a healthy amount that allows for our growth, accomplishments, and new experiences.

A 12-year-old boy from Illinois stated, "My parents often explain to me that they have unconditional love for me and who I am. But they also set high standards for me to strive for.... They tell me that their high standards are not set for them. They want me to succeed for my own good, not theirs. If I do not give my best effort, I am the one impacted by it. My parents know this and therefore have set my standards because they love me. This I know...."

Expect Effort, Expect Uneven Results

In a world that expects kids to be good at everything, we very much need someone on our side who wants us to find ourselves. We will never figure out who we are or what we want to do with our lives if we aren't able to figure out what we love and don't love. We also need to figure out what we are not good at. Even if we try hard, we might fail or, at the least, not do very well. We think parents have a right to insist that we try hard, but we do not need the stress that comes from our own families thinking we have to be perfect.

A 16-year-old boy from Pennsylvania who described himself as "anxious, nice, and funny" promoted the idea of creating realistic expectations rather than overwhelming ones that set people up for failure.

Make it clear to your child that you will love them no matter what. That is super important. I cannot overstate that. I think that would actually decrease the stress of a situation and therefore [allow them to] succeed more in a particular area of difficulty. This might seem obvious, but do not make your expectations exceed the capabilities of your child. Some kids are just plain bad in particular fields and should not be faulted for having a lack of skill. If Billy is not a runner, then do not expect him to join the track team. I have a friend who is absolutely abhorrent in chemistry. I'm talking like 24/100 on any given test. She is driven so hard by her parents to do well in that class, but no matter how hard she tries she just does not do well. I am not saying to ignore the fact that they are not doing well, but do not pressure your kids to get an A+ in a class they are not good at. So I am not very good at math. Not terrible but B+ to A- range. Most people are happy with that, but my parents were not particularly pleased when I came home with an 84 for the ninth-grade mathematics course (my lowest grade ever and, to date, my only B). In this scenario, I think my parents were way too harsh. They weren't overtly angry, but they would tell their friends about how I would not go for help in this class and how I was not trying to succeed. That really sucked. It hurt. A lot. This would have been a situation where some love could have helped. I understand that they're high expectations, but making it clear that they still loved me would have given me a great boost.

Many other young people wrote about this. Here is a sample of their thoughts.

> ❝ A parent should expect straight As, for example, all the time ONLY if that's what the parent knows should be the result of the child's best effort. Likewise, a parent should be satisfied with Cs if the child tried his or her best to achieve those grades. However, expecting straight As from a child who tries his or her best and achieves a lower grade will only negatively influence the child's learning experience and morale. ❞
>
> —19-year-old male, Pennsylvania

66 A parent should hold their child to certain expectations, like to do well in school, but…shouldn't be disappointed in them and show them different love. Love them through all their imperfections. It means a lot to us as teens. 99

—Anonymous

66 Everyone is capable of different things, and a parent should not treat each of their children the same because they are all different in their own individual way. For instance, if their child receives a C on a test and the parent knows that the child can do better, they should remind their child in a kind way that they could have achieved a higher score; however, they should not scream or yell or show disappointment because the child will feel as if they are unappreciated and they aren't good enough. 99

—17-year-old female, Pennsylvania

66 When parents raise their expectations too high, the kids/teens start to feel like their parents only love them when they meet their high standards…. One example is my dad. He has high standards for me. I read above my grade level and write well. But when I don't do well on a test, he gets mad. Parents shouldn't have standards where only a 100 is considered good. Another example comes from when I was at a high-level ski competition. There was a kid competing who I knew was really good, but when he didn't get first place his mom got really mad at him, which made him sad. Any sport should be done for fun and not to please your crazy parent obsessed with winning and having the best child out there. 99 —13-year-old female, Massachusetts

Expect Your Child to Be a Learner, A Student of Life

School offers only one type of opportunity for learning. There are plenty of small moments in life to learn life's lessons, and they shouldn't be missed. Expect your child to be open to the world and receptive to these lessons. For example, one time while traveling, my dad, sister, and I were exiting our hotel through the lobby when we witnessed a couple persistently complaining about the ambiance, lack of coat hangers, and placement of the bathroom in their hotel room. They were rude, and it seemed they were criticizing issues that were absurd to focus on. The manager patiently listened as the couple ranted about the unsatisfactory characteristics of the hotel. She offered the couple the option of viewing other rooms and free meals, but they refused to accept the gestures. Although it was obvious the couple was trying to swindle the hotel into a free stay, the manager remained poised. During this display, my dad had my sister and me sit down on one of the couches in the lobby, far enough away that it was not obvious that we were listening in, to observe the manager's skill in handling difficult situations with one set of guests while accommodating a growing line of others. After the scene settled down, we continued on with our evening and went to dinner. We discussed the scenario over our meal, and Talia and I gained the life lesson about interpersonal relations that my dad wanted us to take away.

To Understand Our World, You Have to Understand What School Is Like Now

You may have noticed that many examples explain how love feels conditional when revolved around school and grades. In fact, the overwhelming majority of comments in response to this question focused on school. It may be, therefore, that for you to understand us you need to have a better understanding of what school is like today. It is simply the most relevant component in our lives while we are still growing up under your roof, and it is likely to be the greatest source of pressure in our lives, even before parents' expectations are put into the mix.

We recognize that no general statement about the pressures school places in kids' lives could apply to everyone. In fact, there are schools where kids do not receive adequate educations; students may not feel the pressure to excel and are not challenged. In these cases, students need more resources, better education, and clearer and higher expectations from the educators. On the other hand, children who attend under-resourced schools might be dealing with particularly high levels of pressure. Their self-expectations and desires to excel may not match what their educational environment is able to offer them. In some communities, the pressure needs to be dialed down for kids to thrive, and in others resources have to be added and expectations raised. The young people involved in creating this book overwhelmingly spoke of the pressure in their lives to excel. You know your kids and your community best and whether or not this pressure applies to them.

Narrow Definition of Success

Much of the tension surrounding school in a parent-child relationship is sparked by the pressure of today's society and its view of educational success. From what I have gathered through conversations with my parents, as well as those of my friends' families, the pressure to do well in school and to get into a top college has intensified in our generation. I recognize that this societal pressure may be driving parents to push us, but please be aware that it can make you, the parent, part of the problem. We, as students, are feeling pressure from many places, and you can either support us to deal with that pressure or drive us to our breaking points. A 17-year-old female implores parents to "remember how it was when you [parents] were growing up, and take notice of how much things have changed since then." Success may not have been measured as critically in previous generations, or, at least, not as many kids were driven to excel in multiple areas.

Daniel Coffeen, PhD, offers a perspective on the current system by stating,

> *High school, it seems, has changed.... Young men and women— 13- to 18-years-old—must work more or less tirelessly to ensure their spot at a college deemed worthy to them and their families. So rather than living their adolescent lives—lives brimming with desires and vitality, with vim, vigor, and brewing lust—these kids are working at old age homes, cramming for tests, popping Adderall just to make the literal and proverbial grade.*

As a student at a top ranking, public, magnet school in Philadelphia, I understand the pressure to perform academically; it is ever present. It is commonly assumed that if you are not applying to, or planning on attending, an Ivy League (or other "name") school, that your academic efforts or desire for success is lacking. This outlook toward school and learning needs to come to an end. The pressure it produces, and the narrow view of success it conveys, threatens learning. Most of my viewpoints are clearly shared by many other youth involved in this project.

What It Takes to Get the Grade

Your child, and even what he knows, is more than the number produced on a piece of paper. There are so many factors that contribute to a grade. The student's effort is certainly key, but there are other contributing pieces to the puzzle. Maybe your child has a teacher with whom he does not get along, or an emotional complexity that is limiting his focus, that he is keeping from you. A grade is not always the full reflection of effort or knowledge.

When the grade is the end goal, the assignments are completed, but much is not committed to memory. One way to get the letter is to put in the hours…too many hours. Students transform into zombies with countless nights of little to no sleep. It is hard to focus the next day when we are exhausted. There is little absorbed and even less learned. Worse, perhaps, is that in some cases, integrity is compromised because kids feel cheating is a better option than "failure."

In case you think we are complaining about nothing, or too lazy to put in the work that your generation did, please take on a homework assignment for our sake. We need you to walk in our shoes to understand why many of us are lacking enough sleep and so many of us are stressed. You might view us as inefficient (and we may be), but do an hours–check-in on our lives. Consider first the time we might be putting into our sports and extracurricular activities after school. Then go to a parent-teacher night and ask each teacher, without revealing your point of view, how much homework he or she assigns each evening. Add it all up and see if it leaves much room for relaxation and sleep. See if there is space for us to answer that "Who am I?" question that is supposed to be the point of adolescence.

Teachers

We have spoken about kids being uneven. I'd go as far as to say that teachers can also be uneven, which affects our grades and learning. First, there are easy graders and tough graders. Everyone wants the easy grader because grades count. This can be a blow to learning because sometimes the tougher graders challenge us the most intellectually.

Let me be clear: most teachers truly care about the students, and I have been lucky enough to have many of these. Another reality, though, is that some teachers can sometimes be intimidating or dismissive, and when they are they can undermine kids' confidence. My own learning and performance, and absolutely my stress level, has increased when the teacher utilized this style.

On occasions when I arrived home from school very upset, my dad spoke to me about 3 types of teachers.

- There are the teachers who are primarily driven by their love for the subject matter they are responsible for passing on to the next generation. These teachers may not be as focused on the developmental needs of students or to the varied needs of pupils in the classroom. They certainly care about kids but may not always know how to show it. The key to learning from them is to appreciate that they know so much about their subject.

- There are teachers whose main focus is on the students. These teachers learn about a topic to gain the opportunity to work with young people.

- Then there are the teachers who are amazing with their subject *and their students*.

I, for one, learn more deeply and perform better with teachers in the latter 2 groups. For me, the relationship matters. That was key for me to know about myself as I selected the college that would best match the way I learn.

When a student comes across a teacher she connects with, she is reminded why she enjoys learning in the first place. However, if your child is not fortunate enough to receive a roster that she is comfortable with, please contact your child's school and see what steps can be taken to make sure she is in an environment in which she can learn. If your child is uncomfortable entering a classroom each day, or feels undervalued or judged by a teacher, then she should be removed from the situation in order to promote learning in a way that is the right fit for her. If the school does not allow for a change in your child's roster, please be open to the idea that your child may be struggling in a course because she is uncomfortable learning in the atmosphere provided by the teacher, which may heavily affect her grade if she does not get along with the teacher.

I know that some, including my father, may argue it is healthy for a child to stick out a year with a teacher he does not get along with to learn the art of self-advocacy and human relations. It is true the child may gain valuable life lessons in handling others over the duration of a year with a teacher with whom he is not compatible. However, a serious discussion may be necessary to determine if this is the case for your child or if he or she needs to (and can be) removed from the situation. Communication is key.

Peers

The pressure doesn't come from just schools, teachers, and parents. It can also come from other kids. Parents worry about peer pressure causing their kids to do drugs but may not realize that a lot of peer pressure is about performance. Kids often check in with each other to make sure they are not the last ones understanding something or to compare how they scored on an exam. This intensifies the pressure. I have heard my father speak to school audiences about the importance of changing school cultures from being places where kids ask, "What'd you get?" to places where students ask each other, "What'd you learn?" with the understanding that each of them had strengths that could be shared to help others gain knowledge. Such an environment would accept everyone's unevenness and build a collaborative spirit where all could reach their personal heights.

Top Ranked or Best Match?

I survived the college application process. I believe I found the right match, a school that prides itself on the kind of faculty-student relationships from which I learn best and where collaboration is valued over competition. It was not chosen from a ranking list but from real research. Many of my friends, including my sister, made the same kind of choices. I believe that the pressure on students and families would be lessened if they realized they were looking for a match rather than a name.

Here are some other points about colleges that, if you understand them, may help you feel less stressed, allowing you to support your child more in this process and pressure him less.

First, every school your child could potentially attend will be what he makes of it. Your child will receive the education he wishes to take away. There are some schools that have a reputation as a "party" school or a school for underachievers, and so on, but they have fabulous programs in certain areas. Or a school might have a high-ranking and a sterling reputation for academics but a weak program in your child's area of interest. A reputation is not always an accurate representation of a school. Please do not neglect a college or university based on what you or your child hears from peers or assumes about it. Your child needs to do the research to find the match for his interests and career goals.

A college or university essentially must appeal to the prospective patrons in the same way that applicants must stand out to admissions committees. To create or strengthen appeal, colleges heighten their reputations and may do what it takes to maintain their standings, including limiting the diversity of students (diverse in every way) that makes a great learning environment. (I attend one of the most diverse high schools in the United States and can tell you it allows learning inside and out of the classroom). Also, colleges naturally laud their strengths and may not focus on areas in which they do not excel.

Next, colleges can be competitive environments. If your child is pushed so hard, or tutored extensively to achieve grades, she may not thrive in a competitive environment. Put bluntly, if your child is pushed above or beyond her limits, she may go to a school that requires higher grades but falter when she gets there. When viewing the process from this perspective, you, as a parent, can reflect upon the situation and remind yourself to support the match. Do you want your child to arrive at a university already feeling intimidated, just to find out that it was unable to provide the experiences she was counting on?

About those life-determining tests: no single test or grade will ever determine a child's life or predict the future. If a child does not achieve the scores he likes, he may retake the exam if the opportunity is available or review more for the next exam. No big deal. Additionally, receiving a C or lower will not ruin a child's life.

Schools are often seeking to build their own résumés to gain a prestigious reputation. They will super score SATs (take the highest sectional scores from multiple tests and combine them to create an individual's score). This indicates that a student's scores may not need to be quite as high as your child thinks, and some pressure can be taken away for her. Additionally, the university's Web site will provide the average scores of the students they accepted, revealing that there were scores that were higher and lower. The average scores shouldn't scare you or your rising college student away. Taking a moment to mull these things over can reduce much of the pressure of school and make it easier to be supportive when you and your child are under these pressures academically. The key is to take a step back and analyze the situation.

Finally, you want to support your children to "find themselves" in high school so they can better find the match for the next stage of learning. Extracurricular activities should be chosen because they are interesting or meaningful, not to build an application. It must be hard for schools to sort through who really has the interest and who has learned to fill in the boxes. They do not want to accept a student they feel will add to their community in certain ways, just to come to the understanding later that they accepted a résumé rather than a passionate, caring, dedicated human being. Therefore, putting pressure on your child to participate in extracurricular activities that do not suit your child's happiness and ultimate success will harm him, by sending him to a school that is not necessarily the correct match for him, and the school, which will receive a person who does not contribute to their community as they predicted. On the other hand, if your child can pursue his genuine interests, the school and student will find each other.

Extracurricular Activities Should Help Us Learn About (and Enjoy!) Life, Not Make Us Feel More Pressured

    I've been playing soccer intensively since the age of 5. I've been pushed for over a decade to be the best at it. It's supposed to set my future by paying for my college. But being pushed so crazily with so much pressure doesn't make me play better; it makes me not enjoy the sport anymore. I love soccer so much, but I hate it so much too.

—Jakub Zegar, 17-year-old, Pennsylvania

When children are young, athletics, the arts, and hobbies are valued for personal growth and enjoyment. They are also great ways to manage stress and, in many cases, to learn self-expression. However, as kids get older, extracurricular activities can sometimes become sources of stress themselves. Sometimes, performance becomes such a source of pride or entertainment for a child's parents that she begins feeling the same pressure to produce as she does in school. The stress may be even greater level if a scholarship is at stake or a family perceives the activity as a ticket to college.

Although with good intention, parents may push their child too hard to do well in an extracurricular activity. This may be done out of pure love and admiration for their child's achievements and capabilities, but it might also take away the joy of the activity and cause stress or anxiety. This is one of those cases when, believe it or not, a child can receive too much praise and support from a parent. Even if a parent is just a cheerleader in the stands, or if the parent crosses the line into taking over for the coach or becoming such a fan that the activity becomes "our win" or "our loss," kids absorb the pressure. Your child must never feel his performance fulfills your own unrealized dreams.

As students approach the later high school years, it becomes increasingly apparent that extracurricular activities are vital for college applications. She must metaphorically paint a picture of the type of human being she is or plans to be. These activities are no longer solely for enjoyment but to display characteristics that are attractive to prospective schools. Admissions offices look not only for team players but also captains, as "proof" that the applicant possesses the characteristics of leadership and responsibility.

One of the best things a teen can do is invest his time in the lives of others through volunteer work. It gives kids perspective and makes them feel valued. However, these activities are so important that they must be done sincerely. There are opportunities on almost every corner to make someone's life better and to learn how much you matter. The problem is that even something as noble as helping others has now become part of the game and, for some, another place to absorb pressure. It becomes easy to feign dedication through a paid program or to travel to distant lands to beef up volunteer credentials. Volunteerism is too important to let it become a portfolio stuffer.

I am aware of the rat race of college admissions. But we must keep the emphasis on choosing extracurricular activities, athletics, and volunteer activities for stress relief and enjoyment, as well as an opportunity to learn the differences we can make in people's lives. Parents here have to be unconditional in their support of their child driving the choice of her activities. Consider this: a school that is unwilling to accept a child for pursuing her passions and would rather accept someone who did it all (packed her résumé) is likely not the place to offer the supportive environment that will promote her optimal success and achievement.

Behavior

Behavior is an area in which expectations should be high. These high standards don't threaten the unconditional nature of love; in fact, they might reinforce it. Unlike school, extracurricular activities, or other activities in which there might be a clear goal, behavior is reflective of one's character. If you raise your child to be a kind, caring, and empathetic person, it will not be hard for him to reflect that in his behavior. It will simply be him living as a reflection of who he is and who you've raised him to be.

Let me clarify what is meant by behavior. Parents should expect the best from their kids—to be good, caring people. Kids should be expected to display these positive character traits that predict they will be good parents, partners, and colleagues in the future, including honesty, integrity, compassion, and a desire to make a difference.

Kids should not be expected to be angels because experimentation is part of growing up. They should, however, be expected to be safe at all times. Parents cannot keep us in a box, so we have to be expected to hold the right values and to have reasonable decision-making skills regarding what is safe and unsafe. High expectations are good as long as imperfections are expected, as a child does not feel trapped or unable to express herself.

A 17-year-old from Virginia and daughter of Marine Corps parents offers the following guidance:

Let them [your children] know that you have high expectations, but also let them know that you recognize that they're humans, too, and will make mistakes and that is OK. Then when they do make those mistakes, stay calm. Remember that they're just teenagers and it's not the end of the world. Let them make these mistakes because they are necessary to learn from. I think that it only makes situations worse when parents go off on their kids and escalate a situation by yelling. The mistake has already been made and your child is already feeling bad. Yelling at your child isn't going to change what happened, so why do it? All it's going to do is make things worse. Make sure you listen to your child's opinion and take it into consideration. They're people, too, and they want to be respected just as much as you do. If they feel like they aren't being respected, then they'll wonder why they have to respect you. Obviously, make it clear what you expect out of them, what is acceptable and what isn't acceptable behavior, and that there will be consequences when certain rules are not followed.

Several youth pointed out that adult hypocrisy can undermine the message adults are trying to get across. A self-proclaimed "passionate, intellectual, and social" 14-year-old female from Illinois provided the viewpoint,

Respect is what every parent wants from their child and should have. Parents should have a deal of trust with their kids and that comes with setting a good example. I'm not saying that parents have to be perfect but, in my opinion, I usually don't trust and respect someone who constantly makes bad decisions.

This is not to say that everyone is perfect and will live flawlessly. We are all humans who make mistakes. And as teenagers, some people begin to experiment in many ways. An example of this is young people who test their limits with substances. If this is the case for your child, speak with him to ensure he has a full understanding of the effects the given sub-stance may have whether physical or mental and emotional. Additionally, try to understand why your child is resorting to this behavior. It may be for pure recreation or it may be to escape emotional turmoil. If this is the case, traditional punishment will not be the answer. If your child is comfort-able enough to open up to you, offer guidance through discussion or seek outside help, such as a compatible professional for your teen's given needs. If the substance is for recreational use, I do not believe pure punishment will do the trick in handling the situation. The best way to prevent the behavior may be to provide your child with examples, such as photos, of people before and after substance use or allow him to speak with someone who has been down the path he is headed. If scaring your child is the best way to prevent what you fear most, and will ultimately provide him with safety, do so. He will later realize your intentions and be thankful for your loving intervention.

Coauthor's Note From Ken Ginsburg: Young people, including Ilana, often suggest that scare tactics be used to make adolescents aware, as a step toward changing their behavior. However, research indicates that scare tactics may backfire. This may be especially true if kids are turning to a worrisome behavior to escape or manage stress. Becoming frightened of the consequences of their behavior may only intensify that stress. If left with no alternative, we might drive our kids toward precisely that which we fear. Making a young person aware of the devastating consequences of a choice may be helpful as Ilana has suggested, but it should be done in parallel with "telling them what to do." In many cases, that involves helping kids manage the stress with healthy coping strategies (see Chapter 11, Preparing Your Child for a Stressful World). But the most important point that Ilana makes is to "try to understand why your child is resorting to this behavior."

We Need You, This Wasn't About Pushing You Away

Our generation is terrified of messing up, not succeeding, and imperfection. What you intend as support may therefore be experienced as pressure. Your high expectations may feel overwhelming to teenagers who are then scared to perform at a lesser level in the future and disappoint. To quote my father, a child and adolescent parenting "expert," "This parenting stuff ain't easy."

But knowing your child and maintaining open discussions with her will help your family find the appropriate balance.

The good news is that the youth viewpoint on love, support, and attention is resoundingly *not* "Who needs it?!" It is "We *always* need it."

Although it may not always feel like it, your child needs you and wants you in his life. This part of the book only reinforces that point. If children did not feel they needed their parents, they would not have invested so much time in sharing their thoughts and opinions about how much your love matters to them, nor would they have framed such a clear message about how much parents' actions truly affect their lives. Many teenagers have made statements essentially stating, "If my parents had handled (this situation) in (this manner), it would have provided me with the needed support and I would have been able to get through (that situation) a lot more easily." This should strengthen your confidence that your children truly rely on you for help and support throughout their lives.

It may be that you are parenting very much as the teens here are suggesting, with clear unconditional love and expectations that we are good people who try our best to perform at our highest levels. If you have a strained relationship, please consider that we have raised issues which, if addressed, will draw you closer. Kids appreciate parents who will take a fresh look at something in an effort to improve our relationships. With a few changes to the approach of handling given circumstances, your child will grow to understand that you are there for her and are trying to put your greatest effort into supporting her endeavors.

CHAPTER

17

The Youth Perspective: Protection Versus Trust

Talia Ginsburg

Whan is it right to protect your children, and when is it right to allow them to learn from life's lessons? The young people who helped write this book universally agree that parents have the responsibility to protect their kids. But how do we define protection? To what extent should protection be given? Children and parents are inevitably in different stages of life and, as a result, will hold differing views on these matters. As parents set and monitor limits, children will push against them, naturally setting families up for conflict.

This chapter was written with the hope that the voice and perspective of youth would be properly represented and understood in a way that supports families to strike the proper balance that will allow children to grow within safe boundaries.

We Need You but Not on Top of Us

The wrong, but stereotypical, view of the average teenager is that he wants as little adult oversight as possible. However, the youth who answered our question regarding parental protection versus learning life's lessons do not call for total independence. To the contrary, the teens absolutely want their parents' involvement in their lives. Their parents' presence increases their sense of security and makes them understand that they are loved. However, they also strongly believe that they need to deal with many of life's issues independently and that parent's should be involved simply when asked. However, many times your child will not take the time to explain this to you, and as he grows older, you may feel yourselves becoming distant.

This is important to remember so that you do not misconstrue your teenager's actions. A common misconception arises when attempting to understand some teenage actions. Just because your child pushes you away does not necessarily mean he no longer wants you in his life. You are needed despite your child's noticeable and growing independence. However, the form in which you are needed is changing. Your children are becoming more dependent on their expanding social lives. This means they are receiving guidance from not only you but other sources such as friends, teachers, and coaches. You should not be offended or hurt, but realize that it is a part of growing up and expanding one's horizons. Your involvement remains crucial, even if it feels as though you are just facilitating their engagement in activities at school, or with friends, and nothing else. How should you be involved? This will be touched on later in the chapter.

- Expression and experimentation is a big part of a teen's life. Trying new things allows us to truly decide who we are and what our likes and dislikes are. Unless your teen is in a completely harmful situation that is either life or death, let them go through it; simply guide them when asked. Trust your child; allow him/her to make smart decisions based on the guidance that you have provided for them over the past few years.

—17-year-old female, Pennsylvania

Life Is an Important Teacher

Although you may want to equip your child with a full understanding of the ins and outs of life before she reaches any rough patches, or prevent any tough times from occurring in the first place, remember that life itself is an important teacher. Allowing your child breathing room also means that you are giving her permission to, at times, stumble and fall. It is much easier to pick yourself up from a stumble at a younger age, and the consequences are less severe than they might be as an adult. Life is full of failures, as well as successes. Your child needs to be well versed in handling each to thrive during adulthood. See Chapter 9, on the importance of allowing your children to fail; we couldn't agree more strongly. This doesn't mean we will find it easy to fail, but that's the point. Our generation has a fear of failure, and we must get past this. We'll only rise past our fears when we grow in response to lessons provided by life.

Some Areas of Our Lives Require Oversight, Others Don't

The teen participants were remarkably clear that certain areas demand parental oversight and guidance, whereas in others parental assistance is not welcomed unless requested. However, parenting is not black-and-white. The need for intervention, at times, depends on the circumstances.

Areas in Which Teens Need or Want You

Generally speaking, kids expressed that parental intervention is invited when dealing with issues that *threaten safety,* such as unsafe sex, safe versus impaired driving, and serious substance use. Additionally, many teens categorized mental health challenges as needing parental support and recognized that professional intervention may be needed in relation to this issue as well. Although the teens did not necessarily see mental health as a threat to safety (although it can be), they did recognize that internal conflict is not an issue all kids can overcome on their own.

Areas Where Space Is Needed

The teen participants clearly stated that they did not want parental involvement in *social aspects* of their lives, such as social media, dating relationships, and friendships. These are areas where children feel parents should not interfere because it is better to learn from life's natural lessons.

Gray Areas

Subject matters such as casual drug or alcohol use, sexual relationships (after safe sex was taught and understood), and school were all discussed with either individual ambivalence or markedly mixed views. Some teens felt strongly that, for example, school was either a subject parents should or should not interject in. However, most felt that parental involvement should be dependent on the kid, parent, or specific circumstance.

Should parents become involved in gray areas? This circles back to knowing your child. Know the correct distance for your child, and wait there until support is necessary. Be attentive during daily conversations to pick up on experiences your child is having; know his environment, and assess the situation. If you know you have a more adventurous child, you may want to openly discuss these topics or create a comfortable environment in which he will feel safe coming to you for advice. This environment should be a judgment- and punishment-free zone. Remember, your child wants your guidance. Punishment will only prevent him from seeking future advice and, consequently, create too much space in your relationship.

If you feel your child may need less advice in these categories, be there when needed, but don't force the topics upon her. Children need guidance to be protected from anything that may create enduring harm and to know they're supported. This support and guidance may come in many levels, as exposure, to a certain extent, is a healthy part of growing up. Children must obtain experience to learn resilience and skills that will allow them to face life on their own in the future.

The youth participants additionally stressed the importance of trust and implied that their likelihood of positive and good decision-making goes up when trusted. Trust allows freedoms, and with the freedom of exposure comes personal choice. You should raise your child in a manner that will allow you to have the confidence to trust his decisions and decision-making skills. A lack of trust may affect your child's confidence and trust in you. If you do not trust your own parenting skills, why should he? However, along with the freedom of exposure comes personal choice. You should raise your child in a manner that will allow you to have the confidence to trust his decisions and decision-making skills. A lack of trust may affect your child's confidence and trust in you. If you do not trust your own parenting skills, why should he?

- … Every teen/kid still needs a little guidance. For example, parents need to remind their kids to do their homework and do the best that they can in all of their classes. Sometimes, though, kids have to learn some lessons for themselves. A hard lesson I learned was not to procrastinate. After a couple of nights of working on projects until midnight, now I always finish them early. My parents had warned me not to procrastinate, but that was a lesson I had to learn the hard way.
  —14-year-old female, Maine

- … Situations vary and different kids respond in different ways. Obviously, a situation involving drugs, alcohol, etc, is definitely when a parent has to step in. However, it is also important not be to overprotective. Personally, my parents are constantly texting me when I am at parties, asking if there are drugs or alcohol and whether my ride home is drunk. Another situation where protection can be needed is mental health. This is something that is less obvious but still important. As a person who has struggled with depression and anxiety, I would not be where I am without the support of my parents. I do not think any kid can deal with depression without a strong support group. This is probably the worst situation to allow a kid to deal with by themselves. So, like, watch your kids and make sure they are healthy. It can be tough to detect but not impossible. Let your kids fail at school. It will make them a stronger person. Everybody fails sometimes, and letting your kid have no ability to cope with failure is unhealthy. Every kid will get a bad grade, and those kids who cannot deal with it are not going to succeed. Hand-holding your kid through every obstacle is not going to set them up to be successful. In fact, quite the opposite.

—16-year-old male, Pennsylvania

- In social problems let them learn on their own, but with things that could cause harm physically then you need to get involved. For example, with drug and alcohol awareness, and unhealthy sexual relationships, parents need to get involved. If it's like a teasing social thing, where a kid needs to learn to stand up for themselves, the parent should point them in the right direction but not step in and do it for them.

—Anonymous

- …An example of how a parent should deal with this might be if your teen is having trouble in school (in an argument with friends), you need to let them deal with this on their own. Offer your advice; say, "I'm here if you want to talk about it," but don't say, "Tell me what happened right now." Don't tell them to apologize no matter what; just let them handle it the way they think they should. Don't call up their friend and say you and my son/daughter need to make up right away… I don't want my parents involved in my personal business, but I do like knowing they're there if I need them. Going through my phone or social networking sites is crossing the line. Trust your teen to make the right decision and if they cannot handle it, trust them to come to you for help. If my parents were to ever invade my privacy like that, even if they believed they were protecting me, I would just be very angry at them.

—17-year-old female, Pennsylvania

Make It Easy on Yourself: Ask Us

A hugely important factor that will help ease the anxieties of parenthood, as well as the child's struggle of transitioning into adulthood, is meaningful communication. The teens were clear about the topics for which they felt your guidance and oversight is needed and those for which it is not. However, there were also quite a few topics that received mixed views and could go in either direction. **If you're unsure of how to be the authority in certain situations, evaluate who your child is, and ask her opinion.**

Communication and guidance is a 2-way street and must recognize that both perspectives are valid. Discuss ground rules, such as curfews, and seek advice. It's OK to not always have the answer. Of course, with open discussion will come differing opinion. Explain why you made a certain decision; it will be appreciated, even if it goes against the desired outcome of your child. Communication permits trust, freedoms, and understanding, and it results in parental decisions that conflict with a child's desires to be mutually understood. Even more importantly, communication allows for parents to thoroughly understand who their child is and to adjust their actions and boundaries to their child's needs. Knowing your child's needs requires being engaged and understanding the environment he is in. This does not mean interfering in his personal life and relationships (unless invited to do so), but it does mean that you are aware of what new pressures, circumstances, substances, and other teen concerns he may be exposed to as he becomes a young adult.

- …Understand that a 'talk' with your child is not when you as the parent/guardian do all the talking and the child does the listening. The only way for the child to completely understand is if you make them feel equal to you. Not lesser, or superior, but equal. Always let the child have some input into the conversation and do not interrupt.
  —15-year-old female, Oklahoma

Make It Easy on Yourself: Give Us Skills

It must be difficult to grant your child independence when you're worried about her having to navigate an unpredictable world, but she's going to have to deal with it sooner or later. You'll feel better about giving your child freedoms if you know that she has the skill set to deal with peers and school, as well as to manage the stressors in her life. Some ideas on how to provide your child with these skills are covered in Chapters 10 and 11. An example skill is the use of a code word that allows you to put the following advice into action:

- Keep both yourself and your teen educated about risks and benefits of each decision (for example, if they want to go to a party, who it is with and what their reputation is). Make sure you have some plan in case the risks develop into an unacceptable situation (but let the teen decide when it is unacceptable). Make sure they know that they can contact you in case of an emergency or another situation, and be available to them.
—16-year-old male, Colorado

Overprotection Hurts Us

Although overprotection often results from genuine, deep-rooted love and the desire to keep your child safe from harm, it is not received well. Overprotection suppresses your child's ability to make decisions and function on his own. Additionally, it may add to your child's insecurities and be harmful in the short- and long-terms. This way of displaying love is often misinterpreted.

It Makes Us Feel Incompetent

Overprotecting your child communicates a lack of trust. It suggests that your child is incompetent, incapable, or does not have the skill to navigate life on her own or even that she is too fragile to handle life's lows. These unintended messages have the ability to create self-doubt and additional insecurities within your child. As children transition into young adults, they should gain exposure that will give them a growing comfort with the world they are about to enter on their own. Children need to learn, in a hands-on manner, that their own decision-making can successfully guide them. Any insecurities, or lack of self-sufficiency, gained from overprotection may hinder one's ability to smoothly and confidently enter adulthood. This may create unnecessary hardships during the transition of leaving one's home.

It Isolates Us

Yes, overprotection does have the ability to prevent unwanted or harmful occurrences, but it also shields from those experiences that allow for growth. Growth comes from even the smallest interactions with life. Protecting your child is valid to an extent, but when it prevents learning from failures, experiencing successes, and making social progress, it is no longer a positive barrier within your child's life.

Social interaction is pivotal for growth; teaches how to have a future family, coworker, or boss; and serves as good preparation for the world at large. It is natural for a parent to fear the influence of peers. There certainly may be poor influences, but allowing your teen to hang out with a group of friends is not equivalent to allowing him to immerse himself into trouble. Give your teen the benefit of the doubt, and trust that he knows right from wrong. Realistically, the teenage years are a major time where experimentation will take place; however, that does not mean all teenagers will experment, nor does it mean teens should be cut off from social opportunities. Many times, a teen or child has the capacity to learn purely through association. If a friend made a bad decision, your teen may observe the consequences, as well as social repercussions, and learn not to follow in those same footsteps.

Childhood is a constant cycle of lessons. If a young person is restrained from experiencing life at this time, it will only cause her to feel isolated from, and have a lack of understanding for, those who have had a wider variety of opportunities. In addition, it may cause her to crave life in unhealthy doses.

- …Another friend of mine has helicopter parents. This causes her to stay in a lot. She actually doesn't leave her house at all in fear of upsetting her family. She doesn't want to disappoint her father. She doesn't do anything, not because of worry that something might happen to her but rather [because of fear of] how her dad will react to what happened to her. This causes her to be overprotective of her brother as well. This makes her always worry about her brother. All of this causes her to have really bad anxiety.
  —Anonymous

- I'd say that feeling overprotected is like being confined to a life raft without having an anchor. You have nearly no freedom and then everyone else around you is doing the things you want to do; suddenly your friends can drive, then they can stay out late, then they can sleep over at each other's houses, and because of all this they form bonds and become closer while you just drift away. It becomes very isolating.
  —Carolina Andrada, 17-year-old, Florida

- …Coming from extremely strict parents, I have been very sheltered. But I think what some parents don't realize is the more they shelter their children, the more curious the kids will be. As I am going to be a college freshman this fall, I worry about how overwhelming the whole new college scene will be. Hearing about things and seeing them firsthand are very different realities. I definitely remember feeling like an outsider of sorts in high school because I was the only one not allowed to go to parties, concerts, or you name it. So I think some experimenting on the child's part should be allowed, but some guidance is best. Parents should not let prevalent teen issues of everyday be some kind of taboo. I think in this situation and many others, communication is key.

—18-year-old female, Pennsylvania

It Makes Us Rebel

When a child's desire to gain experience and need to prove that she can handle herself is suppressed, you mustn't be surprised when she responds with rebellion. Your child may act out to test her footing. If your parental presence is too overbearing, your child's actions will reflect her need to find herself. These actions might be positive (eg, finding creative avenues for expression). However, she may also dabble in experimentation with negative substances, drugs, or behaviors. Your initial positive intentions create a feedback loop of overprotection leading to defiance. In turn, parents respond with punishment, and further suppression of opportunities for growth occurs. This will cause even more rebellion and a chain reaction. However, not all kids rebel; some will just internalize the emotions and be riddled with self-doubt.

- Being overprotected is like being trapped inside a glass box. You can see everything that's going on around you, but you're confined and stuck. Any chance you get to leave the glass box is like a luxury. So you take as much of the world in at once as you possibly can, sometimes in unhealthy doses, before you're cooped up again.
  —Sarah Schrading, 18-year-old, Pennsylvania

Under-protection Leaves Us Feeling Uncared for or About

Although set boundaries may sometimes feel like frustrating limitations, they reflect guidance, safety, and love. Under-protection leaves a child with the sense that his parents don't care about him. Children and teens with no boundaries are at a point of loss and confusion within a vast amount of freedoms. It is at this point that a child may feel hurt, lost, and uncared for.

Additionally, experimentation may take place for the teen to try and create his own boundaries and find his limitations.

Don't assume that under-protection communicates your trust in your child's ability to navigate the world. Your nonchalance may be interpreted as a lack of support rather than the presence of confidence. Know and listen to your child to figure out how much structure she needs. Be prepared to create the foundation she can work and flourish off of. This comes full circle to the main point: keep communication open and safe to create opportunities for your children to share their thoughts and a foundation.

We Want You in Our Lives...at the Right Distance

As your child matures, it is natural for him to try and create distance between you. Although this may send the message that you are no longer needed, that is untrue. You are simply needed differently, at a further distance, which will allow for your child's personal growth. He needs to learn that he is capable of facing the world—with or without parents. Even though your role as a parent will become less hands-on, your involvement in your child's journey is still very much desired.

Children need boundaries. Boundaries provide safety and communicate that your child's well-being is cared for and about. It is easier for kids to test their personal limits when they are aware that a parental authority is monitoring to reinforce safety. However, these boundaries have to be set at the right distance—far enough to allow for growth but close enough to protect from dangers that really challenge safety.

Your children, although it may not appear as though they do, watch and listen to you. You can be a forceful presence in your child's life by simply leading through example. Hypocrisy lacks assertion. If you want your child to obtain certain standards, live by those standards yourself. If provided with a good role model, guidance, and protection, children will learn how to act, what safe and unsafe environments are, and how to navigate the world. Ultimately, protection is a balancing act.

You can keep a distance and still be an impactful figure in your child's life. Figure out the right amount of space between you and your child. Be supportive when needed, and allow growth through experience. Ultimately, both ends of the spectrum, overprotective and over-lenience, are problematic. Find the balance that is right for you and your child. Because this will change as she grows, it is critical that you keep channels of communication safe, nonjudgmental, and open.

PART

4

Rebooting: Moving Toward the Relationship You Hope to Have

"I'd like to think of myself as a lighthouse parent—reliably there, totally trustworthy, making sure he doesn't crash against the rocks, but committed to letting him learn to ride the waves. Sometimes, though, I'm not giving him the space he needs to find himself."

"I knew exactly the kind of parent I wanted to be. You know, the kind whose kid would always come to me. I don't know what happened, but there's a distance there, and I want that closeness back. We spend so much of our time focusing on what's going wrong now that I wonder if she still knows how deeply I love her and that she can always count on me."

"How do I offer the unconditional love central to my child's well-being while also conveying my expectations are high? How do I protect without overprotecting? How can I sit by while allowing my child to sometimes fail? But if I don't, will he be prepared for life?"

The 3 of us hope that through reading this book, you have solidified your understanding that although we wrestle with these issues—love versus expectations and protection versus trust—they are not in opposition to each other when you choose to be like a lighthouse for your children.

In addressing these topics, we had to challenge some of society's assumptions about what leads to success. We may have taken you out of your comfort zone at times. But we suspect, in most cases, we reinforced what you already felt was true, and we hope to have built your courage to do what you know is right, even when your thoughts or values lead you to swim against the prevailing tide of what others (mistakenly) say good parents should do. We hope you are motivated, and better prepared, to do what it takes to help your children thrive in an increasingly challenging world.

Part 4 contains brief chapters that hopefully offer reflection points and communication skills to support you in being the kind of parent you want to be. This book focuses on key questions fundamental to preparing our children to thrive. But we do not want to assume these issues are the only ones you are working to get "right" as a parent. Families are complicated, and some go through serious struggles. No matter the issue, safe and respectful communication is the opening point of all positive change, and it is critical to healthy relationships. If you have deeper concerns in your family, let these strategies get you on the road to improved relationships by reminding you how much you cherish each other. Then, consider professional guidance to get to the place you deserve to be.

The teen panel offered a lot of advice in crafting Part 4. Remember, youth are particularly close to parenting. They know best how different approaches to communication support them and which approaches unintentionally undermine them or even drive them away. Our kids are critical partners in our efforts to prepare them to reach their potential. In keeping with this philosophy, the last chapter in Part 4 is written for them. It briefly prepares them to communicate effectively with us now and therefore with their life partners, colleagues, and families in the future.

CHAPTER

18

Getting Started: Laying the Groundwork for Productive Communication

Change is hard. It is a series of back-and-forth movements and trial and error. Change is harder when people around you expect a certain pattern of behavior from you and act in a way that elicits it, even as they claim to resent or reject it. In other words, even when our kids dislike a certain way we react or something we say, they will still draw that behavior out of us because they crave our attention. This creates an uncomfortable, but predictable, cycle that can be difficult to change. For this reason, motivation is only a starting point toward progress. It may be time for a reboot, an opportunity to allow for changes in your family interactions, so you can better prepare your child for lifelong success and your family for healthy *inter*dependence.

Prior to considering changes, or communicating your plans, you will want to do some groundwork to prepare yourself. This will increase your resolve as you take important steps to help assure your tone, expressions, and body language match your intentions.

Defining Your Goals as a Parent

Our generation endures a lot of pressure to get parenting "right." This is tough because no one knows what right really is. Furthermore, no one can clearly define it for you because your child and family are unique from all others.

Honestly, you'll never get it right, but your commitment to trying is what makes you a good parent. You'll make mistakes, but you'll model resilience and flexibility as you recover and redouble your efforts to get closer next time. A first step along the journey, though, is to clarify your goals, define success, and determine which external forces are important to you and which you will need to ignore.

We've tried to raise, and in some cases answer, key questions to help you clarify your goals as a parent. Here are a few questions to revisit as your first step toward a reboot. Remember, you are the expert here, not us. Because we don't know your child, you'll know which of these questions speaks to you and which critical ones might be missing entirely.

- How will I define success? Will I consider only happiness today and college admissions tomorrow? Or will I think about the future 35-, 40-, and 50-year-old I am raising? What can I put into place now so she will have a sense of meaning and possess the key traits of compassion, tenacity, creativity, and resilience, among others?

- How can I assure his strongest abilities will have room to flourish? How can I demonstrate that I know all people are uneven and only want him to commit the effort to finding himself?

- How will I give my child the security and protection needed to thrive today but also prepare her for tomorrow by allowing the space for failure and recovery?

- How will I create the type of home where communication is safe and feelings are valued?

- How will I communicate clearly what moral behaviors I expect?

- How will I raise a child who is able to be independent but will choose to be interdependent?

Finding Your Own Lens

There is a reasonable chance we have asked you to change some of your underlying assumptions about what good parenting should look like. Our recommendations might generate anxiety in you, especially if they stand in contrast to what other parents in your community are doing.

We parents need to understand the external forces that are pushing on us and find the confidence to push back. Media, community members, and even our extended family have produced pressure to raise our kids a certain way. We feel like failures when we act differently, so we may have sometimes made choices that were not best for our child. Ultimately, we need to do what is best for our children, even if it is different from what others suggest or insist on. Just recognizing these external forces in our lives gives them less power.

As you choose to be different, reassure yourself with your thoughtfulness, but allow for occasional ambivalence. Lighthouse parents offer oversight and guidance, but understand that an occasional hands-off approach better prepares children for the future. It is understandable, however, that in any moment, you'll feel safer protecting your child by guarding him closely. Holding tight offers us a more immediate sense of security than letting go does. The risk of overprotection feels more abstract than the palpable danger of allowing your child to experience life's lessons. Take a breath and remember that lighthouse parents do *not* allow their kids to crash against the rocks; protection has its time and place. But protection over the long-term is about building skill sets that can only be acquired through experiencing life's challenges.

Lighthouse parents absolutely want their child to be headed toward success. They just know that charting the course too narrowly will backfire and impede their child's achievements. Nevertheless, in any moment, it may feel like a leap of faith to understand that *not* pushing your child may produce better academic results than hovering over her.

Anxiety before change is expected. Standing against community norms, even if they are wrong, almost always makes people second guess their choices. We suggest you create your own lens through which you will judge success. Once you reach the point of confidence that these strategies will genuinely benefit your child, you are ready. Prior to that, your child will sense your mixed feelings and be left confused.

Getting Off the Treadmill of Anxiety

Many times, our poor parenting choices result from a perception that our kids need to be turned around. Because people often see bumps in the road as catastrophes rather than opportunities, others may tell you, "Do something!" This external response may cause you to impulsively overreact. It may cause you to intervene before a lesson can be learned. It may cause you to push your child toward perfection instead of allowing an opportunity for him to discover his "spikes." To create space for the kind of communication that can offer you a reboot, you need to get off the tread-mill others have designed. Often our kids are just fine and nowhere near a crisis point. It is a crisis if your child is suicidal or addicted to drugs such as heroin. It is not a crisis to get a C in algebra. Understanding the difference and putting it into perspective allows you to take a breath and be the kind of parent you want to be.

Forgiveness

Parents and kids bring the same struggles to the table. We are working hard to be better parents, and our kids are working hard to grow up; we will all make mistakes. We need to know it is OK to not be perfect parents because there are no perfect parents! Life throws us so many different situations that we cannot prepare for everything, and at times we are going to get it wrong, just as our kids will make mistakes. And sometimes our messy lives make it difficult to be the ideal parent. A parent is ill. A parent loses a job. This adds to the guilt and pressure. Yet it is in these moments of adversity when our children can learn resilience from us.

As you work to have the healthiest relationships within your family, it is important you let go of lingering guilt or anger. As long as you harbor anger, winning or proving a point may seem like the most important goal. As importantly, guilt can leave your emotions so wrapped up in knots, they are not freed to move you forward.

To initiate your reboot, **start by forgiving yourself.** If you overprotected, it wasn't because you wanted to smother; it was because you loved so deeply that the thought of any harm coming to your child seemed unbearable, and you chose to overshoot in the other direction. If you haven't been a perfect role model, it wasn't because you didn't want to be the best parent, it was because you may have been working through, or avoiding, some of your own baggage. Assuming you have not always acted as you'd wish, it certainly was not because of malice or even intent. More likely, you had your own buttons installed and were reacting to them. This is part of being human. Free yourself of guilt; self-condemnation is a barrier to engagement.

Next, forgive others. They may have been managing their own discomfort, and it is unlikely they were trying to hurt you. Until you forgive, there will always be a part of you that will want to prove your point or reiterate the righteousness of your position. You may even want to get even rather than keeping your eye toward progress.

Anger eats at us. Guilt leaves us in a state of emotional paralysis, whereas forgiveness heals us. Forgiveness allows us to achieve the calm state necessary for effective communication.

> Kids have to realize where their parents have come from and how much they have worked. But parents need to understand that times are different, and it is different for their kid. The past is the past, so a parent has to be conscious of what the 'now' is. This does not mean to be disrespectful of the past, just for both sides to realize each other's struggles. Share your experiences with your kid; don't force them upon him/her.

—Kevin Cho, 17-year-old, Pennsylvania

Getting on the Same Page as Your Spouse

Life is not always like *The Brady Bunch,* the TV show on which wife and husband Carol and Mike and even housekeeper Alice parented in glorious harmony. There is a good chance your views on parenting differ from your spouse's. It may be that reading this book has brought your differences to consciousness or even magnified them.

It is not realistic to expect 2 individuals to come to agreement on everything. But for the sake of your children, and their relationship with each of you, try to portray a united front. If you are inspired by this book to shift some of your parenting practices, don't take your spouse by surprise. A first step is to sit down together, wrestle through some of these ideas, and come to a place you can generally agree on.

Peace in your home is more important to the well-being of your child than any strategy offered in this book.

It is not that I believe the contents of this book will likely trigger an argument between you. Rather, if you act alone you may be setting your spouse up to look badly, and that is not good for any relationship within your home. Suppose, for example, you begin to parent in a way that diminishes your child's academic anxiety by acknowledging all people are uneven and all you demand is effort. In the meantime, your spouse continues, with the best of intentions, to focus on grades. Suddenly, your spouse seems out of touch or less caring. Or imagine you allow more freedom now, knowing your child needs to learn from life's lessons as long as she remains in safe and moral territory. Your spouse, however, remains overprotective, not out of tyranny but from concern. Suddenly your spouse looks unreasonably strict. In these cases, your desire to be a more effective parent could inadvertently harm the relationship between your children and spouse.

It is better to approach your children with a unified compromise than to parent with polarizing styles. When you share a position, you will spare your child any anxiety resulting from having to process potential messages that are at odds with each other.

66 When I hear my parents fighting, it kind of sucks. It's just annoying and discourages the child. Take it somewhere else; there is no need for me to be involved in your fight. 99

—Anonymous

Solidifying Your Intentions

There is a lot of parenting advice out there. We have tried to put together a body of work that draws from behavioral and social science, expert opinion, and the wisdom of youth. We hope it has given you a good sense of how to approach parenting in a balanced way that will steer your child toward emotional security and academic success. We also hope you have clarified your goals and feel excited about implementing some of the philosophies and strategies consistent with lighthouse parenting. However, we urge you not to dive in while excited. We invite you instead to continue your research if necessary, and discuss this with trusted friends and relatives. When your intentions are well entrenched and your enthusiasm is tempered with a solid commitment to shift strategies, you are ready to approach your child.

CHAPTER

19

Creating the Space for Change

The first step in changing your parenting (or relationship) patterns is to signal your desire to do so. However, this also might be the hardest step to take. It might feel like a risk to suggest you'd like to do things differently. "Will I look weak?" "Will I be taken advantage of?" "Does this fly in the face of that 'consistency' every parenting expert says I have to display?"

I'd like you to reframe your decision as a gift you are going to give your child. You are modeling growth. You are demonstrating flexibility. You are showing you are willing to consider new evidence instead of being entrenched in comfortable, possibly ineffective, routines. You are acknowledging that children are the experts of their own lives and should be part of decisions that affect them. You are looking at your children—really seeing them—and noticing they are not thriving as you hoped they would. You are recognizing that healthy relationships in your home are the bedrock of happiness and success. By signaling a desire to change patterns in your relationship, you are showing very clearly how deeply you care.

The Opening Words

If your child is young, you may not need to say anything. He may or may not notice the changes you're making, but you'll see the positive effects in your household and his improved well-being. However, if you have an older child or an adolescent, chances are he is entrenched in predictable patterns of behavior that are tightly tied to what he has grown to expect from you. Remember, your child may no longer like everything you say or do, but he still cherishes your engagement. That means he will follow a pattern of behavior precisely because he knows it will elicit familiar responses from you. If you want a reboot, your child has to be on board. But he also has to trust that the change you are advocating for is real. Otherwise, he won't take the chance to make changes himself. This is why it is important you solidify your intentions before you attempt a conversation.

The challenge is to make this conversation feel like a big deal without making it feel like a big deal. Kids love drama from their friends. They can't stand it from their parents. If you sit down for a heart-to-heart on all of the hopes and dreams you hold for them, the pressure might feel overwhelming. If you share all of the reasons why you are worried about them, it might lead them to wondering (and worrying!) if everyone sees their insecurities or problems as well as you do. If you make it about how much you believe parenting in your community is going wrong and how you refuse to be part of the problem, they might grow concerned you are going to make them different from all of their friends. If you reveal how badly you feel about some of the things you might have said or done, you might position them to have to take care of your emotions. All too much drama.

Instead, be clear about your desire to have your children become their best selves, and say you want to be supportive in their journey. It is OK to say you've been thinking (or reading) and realize that some of the things you have said or done could have backfired. (Go ahead; blame this book.) Tell them you want to support them, and blow them away with, "I'll need some of your help to tell me how I can best do that for you."

I don't know your kid, so there is no reasonable way I can devise the perfect script that will strike the right balance that signals a change without seeming like you are responding to a crisis. But here's my best shot at putting together some scripts that are serious but not dramatic, warm but not smothering, and ask for guidance without making you seem helpless.

Literally just sit down [with your child]. Everybody tries to avoid it because it just feels raw. But that's what makes it so important. Everyone tries to divert attention away from problems or pretend they never happened. Then everything just gets worse. Instead, just say we messed up and this isn't going the way we had hoped. Then, after presenting the problem, ask if they want to fix it. Explain that the first step is for you to hear their opinions.

—Carolina Andrada, 17-year-old, Florida

Script 1

I think kids today get so much pressure to perform that it is hurting their ability to figure out what they want to do with their lives. Believe it or not, there is a lot of pressure on parents too—people telling us exactly what we should do if we want to be good parents. I may have done some of the things I was told to do, but it may not have been right for you. All I want is for you to find out for yourself what you want to do in the world. I may need your help on how I can best support you to do that.

Script 2

You're growing up, and I like what I'm seeing. I think sometimes I still see you as my little girl, and I might be protecting you too much, without noticing how much you've grown to be able to handle. I think I'm going to trust you to make more of your own decisions. Don't get me wrong; I'll never let you do anything that's not safe or to make choices I think are immoral. But that'll leave you with lots of opportunities to learn on your own. I'm sure you'll make mistakes. I sure did. But I think I'm the person I am today because of how I learned to get past those mistakes. Let's be honest; I may not turn off my overprotective instincts too easily. I'm counting on you to help me by telling me when I need to back off.

Script 3

It's no secret that I don't always like some of the choices you make. I feel like most of the time I'm just yelling at you about one thing or the other. This is not the kind of parent I want to be or the relationship I want to have. I want you to know I don't see you as a bad kid, even if it seems like I do sometimes. I know what a good person you are, but I don't think I show you that often enough. I'll make you a deal. You show me more of who you really are, and I'll work hard to stop focusing on your mistakes. I'll tell you a secret: I've made plenty of mistakes myself. I may need some help here, so feel free to tell me if I seem stuck.

Sarah Schrading, an 18-year-old from Pennsylvania and one of our teen panelists, suggests that what you propose needs to be quickly reinforced. She says it is critical you back up your words with action. That action will be particularly powerful if it is unexpected. For example, if you have been overprotective, follow your stated desire to allow more freedom with, "Therefore, I am going to let you _____, because I trust you. I know if you need me, you'll let me know." If it is about behavior, you might follow up your statement with, "Let's just go out and _____. I promise not a word out of my mouth will be about correcting you. I just want to be with you."

You can construct the best script, and your child still might not want to have a discussion. It may be she doesn't trust you really want a reboot. Don't be surprised if your child even tests you by trying to push you away first with, "Why do you care all of a sudden?" Stay calm and respond with, "I care because I love you. I always have and always will. I just want to make sure I am showing it in the best way." If your child turns it up a notch with, "Just go away; get out of my life!" say something like, "I'll step away for now, so we both have time to think. But the one thing you can never ask me to do is get out of your life. I love you too much for that." As the conversation heats up, remind yourself you are being tested. The way to pass this test is to be resolute in your love and firm in your continued presence.

Saying "I'm Sorry"

You're human. You may not always have been the parent you dreamed of becoming. Life may have gotten in the way. Perhaps you were stressed and weren't always your better self. Your patience has certainly worn thin at times, and it is likely that during those times you were less flexible than you'd have liked and retreated into patterns from your childhood, even if you didn't like them. It also may be that your relationship with your partner went sour and therefore the connection with your children may have suffered.

Any of these situations could have left your children legitimately angry. Worse, they could have left you wondering if you have the right to be the kind of active, effective parent you'd like to be. Either way, a statement alone of your desire for a more effective relationship may not suffice.

There is nothing that earns a reboot like an apology. Put it on the table. None of us are perfect, and the only thing we can hope for is we will grow from our experiences and make it right with the people who may have been hurt along the way. You are asking forgiveness and an opportunity to move forward. Your behavior did not reflect all you wanted to be. Nothing matters more to you than having a good relationship with your children/partner, and you are asking for a do-over. You still won't be perfect, nobody is, but with open communication, you'll all grow together.

Let me emphasize that an apology is not an explanation or justification. Telling someone why you did something may be helpful, but it can also be interpreted as an excuse. Really saying you are sorry is healing, because it helps the other party understand that you *know* they were hurt.

It may be that from your perspective, you've done nothing that merits an apology, but your child would disagree. Remember, it matters less how a message is intended and more how it is received. If your child is hurt or angry, it may have more to do with his reception than anything you did, but as the adult in the family, you can model how to move past bad feelings.

One of the most effective strategies to defuse tensions in families is with a heartfelt apology. Because parents rarely apologize, it can really create change. Even if you believe you've done nothing wrong, you can always apologize for the experience your child had and how your words were received. If there is tension in your home that you cannot explain, it can be helpful to try out an apology. "It seems like you're upset about something. Is there anything I may have done, or not done, that I could make right?"

You might even consider highlighting how much you care about being a good parent by acknowledging you might not always get it right. "I'm going to make some mistakes as I try to be the best parent I can. If I miss a mistake that I've made, please tell me. You can tell me I got it wrong. And we can work to fix things together." This is a great way of reinforcing that relationships take work and back-and-forth communication, a lesson that will last a lifetime. On a more basic level, it emphasizes you are receptive to your child's feelings, and that will certainly prove to be valuable, even lifesaving, in the future.

Carolina Andrada, a teen panelist, wanted to highlight that kids are listening to parents, even when it's not obvious, and they hear apologies. She said even if your teen storms into her room to hole up, it is still worth going to check in and even apologize. She might keep yelling at you, but after you leave the room she'll say, "Wow, Dad came to say he was sorry." When she calms down, she'll be more prepared to talk it out. I'd add to Carolina's point that kids are going to feel good just knowing you wanted to talk and you cared about their feelings.

> ❝ …before you start ranting or yelling or anything like that, acknowledge your own faults. Maybe say something like, 'Hey, I want you to know that I'm really proud of you, but I also want to talk about how we can improve our relationship. Sometimes I feel like I can improve my parenting; how do you think I can change?', Try to be casual but assertive. ❞
>
> —Lauren Furey, 16-year-old, Pennsylvania

Getting Back to High-Yield Interactions

A starting point to *really* knowing your child is to return to the kind of interactions that allow thoughts and feelings to surface. This involves taking a breath and backing away from the frenetic way of thinking that suggests our sometimes-too-rare face time has to focus on high-yield topics such as grades, performance, reprimanding about behavior, or even discipline. Instead, *be.* Enjoy each other. Create spaces where listening happens. I assure you, if you do, talking will follow. You'll still have the opportunity to monitor how your child is experiencing school and his behavior, but you'll also know who he is.

This is a 2-way street. Your child, especially during the teen years, has likely stopped sharing parts of her life with you. Pulling away is a normal developmental process. Normal doesn't make it less painful. Remember, your child's withdrawal from you, alongside her maddening desire to have you be invisible (or at least silent), represents her discomfort with how intensely she loves you in the context of her understanding that she will, in time, need to separate from you. No matter the reason, the fact remains that she will share less.

When I speak to teens, I explain that they remain largely in control of the pressure they receive from their parents. Teens need to understand that if all they show us is their report card and other performances, that is all we will know about. Of course, then, it is all we can focus on. We'll work with what we have. This is not the way to earn our compassion or help us understand the complexity and nuances of their lives. It is not the way to help us learn where encouragement and expectations end and pressure begins. It is not the way to teach us when they feel our loving protection becomes undermining to their development. It is only when we understand their feelings and experiences that we can learn how we need to shape our parenting to meet their needs. It is only when we are exposed to what is going on in their inner lives that we can offer the compassion and empathy at the root of our capacity to hold them as they face life's challenges, without smothering them as we do so.

So first we must create spaces where our children remember the depth of our love for them. Nothing will create higher expectations for them than us seeing them as they have always been. Nothing will free them to show themselves more than a pressure-free zone of emotional safety and security. Nothing shouts, "I respect you!" more than creating a space where a person can truly be himself. When people are respected, they can safely reveal themselves. So please consider redefining high-yield time as moments together that remind your family why you matter so much to one other.

Have a conversation with your child about how much you want to know her. Explain her role in this 2-way street. Share how much you want to know her and that you can only be the parent she needs if she shares with you who she is. Don't overpower your child with your request; make sure she knows you have no interest in interfering with the details of her personal life, only interest in being there when needed. If you struggle with choosing the right words to say, please let your child read Chapter 23, A Chapter for Young People: First Steps Toward a Better Relationship With Your Parents, which is written just for young people.

Seeing the Strengths

You knew exactly how to parent when your child was 2 years of age. You caught him being good and offered redirection when necessary. Then, as your child became older, you may have taken the good for granted and focused more on redirection or even punishment. You also may have redefined *good.* As a younger child, it was about *being,* the joy with which he experienced life, ideally while behaving well. It may have transformed into *performance.* It may also have become more focused on *discipline,* as we adults too often stop noting the miracles of development. These miracles may be more subtle in our school-aged children and adolescents than they were in our toddlers (standing for the first time is more dramatic than the development of an abstract understanding of life), but they are miracles nonetheless.

One thing that does not change is your child's overwhelming desire to please you. All children, regardless of age, want their parents' approval and attention more than they hope for anything. And if they do not get approval, they will settle for attention.

If your child's behavior is worrying you or you feel she is making unwise choices, there is a good chance most of your interactions focus on what she is doing wrong. The problem is our children are not inspired to do better just by being made aware of their faults. They learn that the behaviors we don't approve of are what get our attention. I am not saying kids don't need clear boundaries and, at times, stern corrections. But we must never forget that what inspires kids is being held to the high expectations that only you can really have for them. When you see the beauty you know is there, your kids will see it within themselves. We must see our children as they really are, not as how they sometimes choose to behave. As importantly, they must know that is how we view them. Kids want to feel respected. Seeing a person as she deserves to be seen is loving and respectful.

If you came to my office and began to unload your concerns about your child, I would ask you to place them in the context of his strengths. I'd say, "Tell me what you absolutely love about him. Tell me the best things about (your child's name). This will help me better understand why you care so deeply and about the potential you see." Just doing that changes so much. Parents' faces soften and eyes moisten as the love of their child overcomes them. They sometimes realize their concern isn't the catastrophe they had assumed when they see it amidst a sea of existing strengths. Most importantly, the young person transforms from being angry and defensive into understanding that his parents' concerns are deeply rooted in love.

You're not in my office right now, but doing this for your own child is useful before you approach any topic. You don't want your child walking away from an interaction with you feeling she is a disappointment or problem. No one in the world loves your child more than you do. Even if at any moment things are not going as you'd wish, write down a list of everything you love and admire about your child. If you're struggling to flesh out that list right now because your child is in a stage of adolescence when she is not always as kind to you as you'd like, ask her teachers or friends' parents for their thoughts. It is likely they are seeing who your child really is, despite the (temporary!) treatment you might be getting at home. Save that list as a reference to keep your thoughts, words, and actions in perspective. Use it as a touch point before you address any concerns.

> [Parents should] start off by telling their child that they are proud. Point out something the kid has done well lately. It has to be something that you haven't said in awhile. This will make the kid willing to listen…. As long as you both are alone, calm, and not preoccupied.
>
> —Nora Walsh, 16-year-old, Illinois

> Constant, harsh comments will wear teens down and will make them self-conscious. It's just going to make the teen only think about him/herself in a negative way.
>
> —Simone Levy, 16-year-old, Pennsylvania

Seeing the Strengths...in Yourself

It makes a lot of sense to see the best in your kid as a starting point for moving forward, doesn't it? Now here's a crazy idea. What about applying this same approach to yourself? It is too easy to feel inadequate; guilt is not in short supply with our generation of parents. Forgiving yourself was a first step before being able to come to the plate. Now how about thinking about all you are doing right as a parent and person. It is your existing strengths that assure you will succeed in an effort to restore your relationships to where you want them. I don't know you, but if you've read this far, I already know you are a committed parent who has a deep reservoir of love within you. You also deserve to be seen through a strength-based lens.

Picking Times and Places

The car is a great place to launch a conversation, because you have a captive audience. You also pass scenes that can spark a discussion, which allows you to bring up tough topics without getting personal. You'll be able to talk about important subjects while avoiding eye contact. This may be especially important for boys, who feel intensely but don't always do well with "Tell me how you FEEEEEL" conversations. (Don't do this if your teen is the driver, because it is too distracting.)

Ideally, you would be able to have office hours for your kids, so you could meet their needs or have the "big talks" at designated times convenient to you. Or you could have nicely scheduled family meetings (which truly are a good idea), just like the perfect TV families. But in reality, especially as your child enters the teen years, you're the one who is going to need to be flexible. The same child who is screaming at you at 3:00 pm, or asking you to wear your invisibility cloak as you chauffeur her friends, will come to your room at 11:30 pm and need to cuddle because she is overwhelmed. The timing is often abhorrent, but these are the most cherished moments of parenthood.

The teen panel had a few ideas they wanted to make sure you considered.

1. Keep conversations low-key, at least at the start. If you start out too emotional, it makes your children uncomfortable. It also positions them to need to take care of you, which makes it harder for them to problem-solve.

2. Never have these conversations in public.

3. Never have these conversations in front of friends.

4. Don't start these conversations when your children already have a lot on their mind or if they are already nervous about something such as a big homework assignment. They'll just explode when you approach them, and they may not be able to regain focus.

5. If they are finally relaxing after a long stretch of work, it is not the time to approach them. (This admittedly makes it tough to find the "right" time, but you are looking for a time that is more neutral.)

6. It is easier to talk with one parent at a time. Otherwise, it can feel like your children are being ganged up on. (This is another tough one because it remains important to stay on the same page with your partner. Nevertheless, this idea was offered repeatedly by teens.)

> **"** There is definitely a wrong place. Don't confront them in front of friends. And never in public. Teenagers feel embarrassed enough because of their parents, so doing it in public will just anger them and be cause for poor communication.... It always has to be one-on-one. Having 2 parents can make the kid feel as if it is going to be a battle of 2 vs 1. **"**
>
> —Kevin Cho, 17-year-old, Pennsylvania

Sometimes the Words Are Hard to Say... or Difficult to Listen To

It may be you've read some of the ideas about initiating the conversation and thought, "I just can't imagine saying that," or, "She'll never listen long enough for me to get the words out." It may be you should do some advance groundwork, even before you have a sit-down conversation. Those high-yield moments are a great start if you can create them, and they'll make words easier later. Letters can also be useful tools to reboot relationships when spoken words don't seem like the best or most feasible option. Some thoughts about letters include

- Follow the same general rules outlined throughout Part 4, including keeping the drama down, focusing on the present rather than the past, and operating from a place of strength.

- Letters can be a powerful tool to state how deeply and unconditionally you love someone. Feel free to pepper in some anecdotes you find amusing or special as a personal reminder of the depth of your love. It will give the receiver motivation to keep reading.

- Make a clear statement on what you want rebooted and your commitment to moving forward.

- Letters are a wonderful place to offer a heartfelt apology.

- Do not use the letter to offer criticism. Express your concern in general terms only. When people are hurt or angry, they might focus on only the one negative sentence in a 3-page letter, as well as use that sentence as a reason to avoid further engagement.

- Consider having an objective reader review the letter before you send it. Have the reader check for thoughts that could be misinterpreted or phrases that could trigger anger or resentment. If anything has even a chance of backfiring, remove it.

More Thoughts From Teens

It would be nice if parents would make clear that discussion of awkward topics like dating or even extreme things like smoking or drugs is fine. It is helpful to be able to talk to parents who won't judge and are understanding. I wish that parents would remember that coming up to them about an issue, no matter how wrong or unacceptable it is, takes a lot of courage in itself, and that just being willing to talk with them shows that you understand what you did was wrong and that you want to fix things too.

—16-year-old female, Illinois

A good place to start an important conversation is when you are chauffeuring your kid everywhere. There's something nonchalant and casual about it. Teenagers will shut down if you seem like you care too much.

—Simone Levy, 16-year-old, Pennsylvania

Start slowly; don't just pick the biggest details to talk about out of nowhere.... It should be more of a how and why it got to this point, not just pointing out that it got to this point where there is no communication.

—Linton Taylor, 17-year-old, Pennsylvania

As a parent, you can't get mad regardless of what your child says. As soon as you get mad, he/she will not want to talk anymore. If you want them to talk, reassure them that you won't get mad.

—Kevin Cho, 17-year-old, Pennsylvania

One-on-one is good to start the conversation. Never both parents at the same time. But it has to be a moment when you guys are OK with each other, because if anyone is angry, it won't work. Heart-to-heart and when everything is just OK. And by heart-to-heart, I mean just being completely honest and expressing your true feelings.

—Lizette Grajales, 17-year-old, Pennsylvania

CHAPTER

20

Communication 101: Listening and Talking

The importance of listening in a respectful, loving manner, and of being thoughtful about the words you choose, has been discussed in various ways throughout this book. This chapter is a landing page that will allow one space to underscore the central importance of these ideas. A bit of detail, and a few added skills, have also been included here.

Listening

Listening is by far the most important part of communication. It suggests openness to others' views and informs us of what needs to be addressed. It conveys respect like nothing else can do because it says that what you think and feel matters. It also creates the space for talking. People will not speak if they fear they will not be heard. They may yell in a vain effort to assure they will be heard, but they will not talk; thus, listening sets the calm tone for real communication.

The overriding importance of listening unloads the pressure of finding the right words. Thinking about what to say can be tough; knowing it is more important to listen can build your confidence in your ability to be an effective communicator. Don't get me wrong; listening does not always come easily. Sometimes you have to settle yourself before you can draw the inner strength to just listen. Because listening doesn't feel intuitively natural, especially when you are worried or stressed, there are some skills you can use and some communication don'ts to follow.

Listening Without Reacting: The Key to Keeping Them Talking

In Chapter 13, I covered the importance of listening in the context of monitoring. All of the points made count double for restoring trust. Briefly, I covered the importance of listening without reacting as the key to being the kind of parent kids choose to disclose to. Simply put, listening keeps kids talking, and reacting shuts them down. Reaction includes the parent alarm that blares impulsively in an effort to protect our children, essentially saying, "No you don't!"

We also shut down communication when we catastrophize our kids' concerns and even when we over-empathize. All reactions teach our children that they better think long and hard before they talk, because they lose control of their decisions once parents worry. When we act as sounding boards instead, listening attentively but offering guidance only when asked, kids are more likely to share their inner lives with us.

Listening as a Demonstration of Unconditional Love

A barrier to listening while reserving judgment is our fear that it implies approval. It communicates approval of the child but does not condone the behavior. That unconditional love is exactly what makes you "tell-able," and tell-able parents know what is going on in their children's lives and are therefore able to protect them when necessary.

> 66 Understand that a 'talk' with your child is not when you as the parent/ guardian do all the talking and the child does the listening. The only way for the child to completely understand is if you make them feel equal to you. Not lesser, or superior, but equal. Always let the child have some input into the conversation, and do not interrupt. 99
>
> —15-year-old female, Oklahoma

Talking

The following short points are about things you should or shouldn't do as you talk:

Talking in a Way That Allows You to Monitor Well

In Chapters 12 and 13, I also covered the importance of talking in a way that allows you to monitor well, which positions you as an ever-watchful lighthouse.

In a nutshell,

1. Balanced (or authoritative) parents know best what is going on in their children's lives. They essentially communicate through words or actions, "I love you, and I trust you. I'm going to give you roots that will make you feel secure and wings that will allow you to explore the world. But for those things that involve safety or morality, you'll do as I say."

2. Kids shut parents down when they approach personal issues (eg, friends, styles of dress, romantic relationships).

3. Parents who make it clear their concern is about safety will have kids who appreciate parental involvement.

4. Parents who let their kids "win" when they present reasonable, well-thought-out cases will keep hearing their kids' thoughts.

5. Parents who make it clear that responsible behavior is rewarded with earned privileges will raise kids who choose to do the right thing.

Talking in a Way That Promotes a Growth Mind-set

We discussed the importance of the growth versus fixed mind-set in Chapters 5 and 6, primarily in the context of promoting academic success. Growth may also be critical in allowing the kind of intellectual and emotional flexibility that can break unhealthy patterns of interactions. Every time we talk in a way that implies our kids *are* something, we reaffirm our expectations that they will remain that way. You *are* selfish. You *are* unreasonable. When we focus instead on what they *do,* we remind them they are capable of changing and in control of choices they make.

The "I" Statement

In Chapter 10 we talked about preparing your child to navigate the world by teaching her the basics of self-advocacy skills. One of the concepts we focused on was the "I" statement as a means of getting your views across without escalating tension and as a means to draw out another person's empathy rather than defensiveness. That very basic skill is also useful as we parent. Think about it: we are advocating all the time with our kids. We are advocating for the kind of relationships we hope to have with them and for the kind of healthy and responsible choices we hope they will make.

Recall that many arguments start by telling others what they have done wrong. *"You did this!"* The "I" statement prevents a person from feeling blamed and therefore reflexively holding his position more rigidly or becoming hostile. Instead, we draw out a person's empathy by talking about how we (the "I") experienced the situation. Please return to Chapter 10, the "I" Statement section, for examples as you consider how you might benefit from using this technique to avoid pushing your kid's buttons and to draw out his empathy and compassion for you.

Never Belittle a Feeling

In an effort to reassure others, we sometimes say things like, "Don't worry about it." "Just get over it." "It's really not that big a deal." This attempt at reassurance often stops communication, because it belittles the other person's concerns. It diminishes the importance of her emotions. Instead, let your child know you hear her concerns and want to be supportive. Simply saying, "I hear how much this means to you," may be enough. If not, ask how you can best be supportive.

Never Say "I Understand"

You don't. An upset young person can respond angrily, "How could you understand? You've never been in this situation before!" Instead, try, "Help me understand," or, "This has really hurt you; tell me what it's been like for you." Ask for your child's help in guiding you to know what she needs, such as, "Tell me what I need to know to be a good parent for you right now."

66 My mom…starts with a question. She asks her question to get my opinion on the topic. Regardless of my opinion, she will never flip out.… If she comes in with her opinion just yelling at me…, she knows I'd shut off right away and go into my mood of, 'Yeah, whatever you say, Mom.' 99

—Amanda Farah, 18-year-old, Pennsylvania

Helping Youth Express Their Emotional Thoughts

Some young people, especially smaller children, do not yet have language for the feelings they are trying to express. Offer some options, so you don't have to guess their feelings. For example, "I don't know what you're feeling, but I could imagine, based on what you're saying, you might be feeling hurt, angry, worried, confused, or scared. Do any of those words fit with how you are feeling?"

This is about building emotional intelligence in children, which is a powerful means for offering them the tools to understand and express themselves. If you are interested in exploring this idea more deeply, I suggest starting with the 1998 classic work on emotional intelligence, *Raising an Emotionally Intelligent Child: The Heart of Parenting*, written by John Gottman, Joan DeClaire, and Daniel Goleman.

Check Your Assumptions

We all make assumptions about what others mean by the words they say. We also might believe that our intuition correctly interprets nonverbal communication. However, we are often wrong and therefore can misread a kid's mood. For example, your daughter sitting with her arms crossed and gazing into the distance with squinted eyes might be angry at you. But she also might be replaying a difficult day at school in her mind, as well as feeling intensely fragile, doing everything she can to hold it together. Your assumption could leave you feeling angry and defensive when what your daughter needs from you is support. Check your assumptions, "It seems you might be feeling upset. Am I right or totally off base?" Or it can be more productive to stay open ended, "I sense something's going on. Can you tell me what you're feeling now?" Or if it seems as if asking about feelings will put her over the edge, try, "I don't know what's going on, but I'm here to listen, now or later."

Don't Bring Up Things From the Past, Focus on the Current Issue

It is easy once you have someone's attention to begin adding other problems to the list or to use past infractions as justification for why you feel strongly about something. This is almost certainly going to bring out a person's defensiveness. It is hard not to feel ganged up on or piled up on, even in a one-on-one conversation, when accusations build on one another. It also reinforces you have noticed a pattern. In other words, you have grown to expect a certain behavior. Remember, kids live up or down to your expectations of them. The last thing you want to do is suggest their behavior is just what they are like. Furthermore, it is hard enough to change a course in the present. It is impossible to alter the past, so there is no yield in remaining stuck in it.

66 As teens, we overthink things way too much. If we are insulted, even if not on purpose, we'll take it to heart. We need words of encouragement more than we need to be criticized. If we are criticized too much, we just want to give up. 99

—Nora Walsh, 16-year-old, Illinois

Be Prepared to Offer Solutions

As you approach your child with a desire to change directions, it is important you are prepared to say in which direction you would like to be pointed. Otherwise, you run the risk of stirring up frustrations or sensitivities for no purpose. Change is almost always scary, even if nobody thought the old patterns were working. Therefore, everybody should know what the new plan is and why you are proposing it.

The solutions you suggest involve steps both of you can take. You'll note that I have used the words *proposing* and *suggest* instead of *choosing* or *demanding*. Therefore, at the least your kid's first action step is reacting to your thoughts and plans. Ideally, after you have moved forward, he should continue to offer feedback on how your new strategies are working. Note the word *feedback*. Feedback is not veto power; it is a voice, a voice that in most circumstances should be listened to carefully, because nobody knows better than your own child if your strategies are offering the right level of support.

You Don't Have to Let All Your Feelings Out

Talking about feelings is good. It models sharing and reinforces you are in a trusted and safe environment. But remember, kids don't like drama from parents, and they'll turn off when it gets too heavy. It also makes the discussion about you instead of them or your relationship together. Furthermore, you don't want them worried about you or to begin seeing you as fragile. They'll learn to keep things from you to protect you. Remember that you don't want them acting like "good little boys and girls" to spare you, because that can be at the root of perfectionism.

CHAPTER

21

Communication 201: It's More Than What You Say

Y ou'll have a better chance of guiding your child, without triggering reflexive resentment or rebellion, when your body language matches the words you say. Although we can shift our body language, it is harder to control than the words we say. Therefore, it is important to do our work prior to communicating so we sincerely believe the points we hope to make. When we deeply hold the beliefs we verbalize, the sincerity of our convictions assures that the messages our bodies and our words convey will match.

In general, words represent about 20% of what we communicate. The rest comes through our body language and facial expression. This means what we say tells only a fraction of what we mean. In fact, when our words don't match our movements or expressions, others tend to trust our words less and our faces most.

If anybody knows how to read meaning beyond your words, it is your child. You trained him to do so. Remember how you used your eyes or a displeasured frown to say no, No, NO? Your raised eyebrow, tilted head, and serious look communicated, "Don't you dare," when you were in a public setting and needed to subtly signal your expectations. Similarly, your child learned to look back at you quickly to get your approving nod as he considered venturing forth into the world. He also picked up on your ambivalence when you spoke about how excited you were on his first day at school but grasped his hand tightly as you walked in.

Nobody knows the meaning behind your every gesture and look quite like your children do. Their sensitivity toward your nonverbal cues heightens during adolescence. By the early teen years, our kids might know what we feel before we do, or at least they will say they do.

Adolescence brings an explosion of emotions and empathy. This is a wonderful phase of healthy development, although sometimes as parents we become victims of this extreme sensitivity. Although their emotionality often expresses itself in a way that makes our kids seem anything but empathetic, it is also the basis of their developing compassion.

Our kids' emotional volatility is about more than hormones; it is about healthy brain development. The teen brain is a subject of intense interest, and our understanding of neurologic development is expanding rapidly. In simplest terms, emotions are largely affected by 2 parts of the brain. The amygdala, or reptile brain, is the part that holds our instinctive responses and reactions such as fear, anger, and comfort. It drives our emotions, whereas our frontal cerebral cortex regulates those feelings by giving meaning and rationale to our emotions. Prior to puberty, these 2 brain structures are developing at a nearly even pace. Then, at puberty one of them gets a jump start and matures at a quicker rate. You guessed it, the driver of the emotions gets supercharged, while the regulator stays relatively behind. It is critical to understand that the emotionality of adolescence is a sign of developing maturity, not meaningless irrationality.

Unfortunately, the emotional charge can sometimes present challenges for teens themselves and for those of us who love them. It takes until the mid-20s for the cerebral cortex to mature to the adult level, but you can trust it is catching up as adolescence proceeds.

The development of empathy is rooted in our emotions, but another aspect of brain development comes to play as well. How do you look at someone and intuitively know how she feels? You assess her body position, facial expression, and words. You likely even sense the cadence of her speech, the depth of her breathing, and perhaps even her pupil size as you determine whether or not she is calm. Your sense of whether a person you are communicating with is composed, agitated, or frightened can be literally life-saving as you assess potential danger and determine how vigilant you need to be. These assessments are largely intuitive or automatic; this is not the time for you to consciously think through the meaning of another's unspoken signals.

Many scientists believe mirror neurons help us determine what another person may be feeling. A parallel set of neurons resides alongside your motor strip, which is the part of your brain that regulates your body and facial movements. When you see something, that set of mirror neurons mimics what you see but without your needing to do anything. Other parts of your brain then determine what you would be feeling, as if you actually were moving your body or twitching your face. For example, you see a man with folded arms, clenched teeth, and an arched brow. The mirror neurons associated with those same movements and expressions in you fire. However, rather than sending signals to the nerves and muscles in your body that would make you fold your arms, they transmit impulses to other brain centers, helping you process, "If I looked like that, I would be angry. I'll bet that man is feeling angry now."

Mirror neurons are developing rapidly during adolescence. Our kids are suddenly getting the meaning of others' signals in a way they never had. This is at the root of empathy and is something worthy of celebration. However, it also explains our children's extreme sensitivity to our every gesture, movement, and look. They are feeling everything so deeply, and that can sometimes get in the way of reasoned discussion. This also explains, to some extent, why kids are so self-conscious during adolescence. They are so attuned to others' every signal that it is hard for them to imagine they are not also under constant scrutiny.

An understanding of the teen brain offers us wisdom in how best to communicate with our children.

First, we should take every step possible to not activate our children's reptile brains. Their hyper-attention to danger signals means we have to do our best to assure our body language, facial expression, and verbal tone remain calm.

Next, we need to give our children time and space when they are agitated. When we grasp that reasoned thought takes extra time during adolescence, we learn to give them the moment needed to release and suppress their impulsive reactions and collect their thoughts. When we charge in with our responsive anger or even offer our rational explanations too soon, we are communicating with a person whose reptile-"reactive" brain is in charge. Space and time allows the calming part of the brain to prevail, which will assure our conversation yields higher results.

Third, we have to approach important or meaningful conversations *after* we have done our own work to be able to sincerely convey what we hope to communicate. If your words are ahead of your feelings (ie, you know what you *should* say but remain doubtful or conflicted), it is not the time to communicate. Our children's empathy sensors are on fire, and our ambivalence will be trusted more than our words. For example, take time to work through your own angst before saying to your child, "It'll be OK; you'll get past this." Until you believe that yourself, your words won't be believed, and you could inadvertently heighten your children's fears, as they may believe you are covering something up. Similarly, don't say,

"I really think you deserve counseling, because it will build on the strengths you already have," if you haven't worked through your own feelings of inadequacy for not being able to solve your child's problems and your uneasy sense that mental health care is stigmatizing. Finally, don't say, "All I want is your very best effort," if you will only be satisfied with the A.

Once you have done the work, your body will communicate that your words are to be trusted.

CHAPTER

22

Guiding Our Kids to Own Their Solutions

A valuable strategy to improve our relationship with our children is to make a shift from a style of communication that unintentionally belittles them, the dreaded LECTURE—to one that positions them to solve their own problems (with our respectful and supportive guidance). When we tell our kids what to do, they may listen. They might even do what we say, but they will not learn what to do when we are not there directing them. Furthermore, it makes them feel "small" when they understand that we think they are incapable of knowing what to do on their own. If our goal is for our kids to thrive, we must acknowledge them as the experts in their own lives and learn to facilitate them to arrive at their own conclusions and ultimately plan and take ownership over their solutions.

66 Teenagers are very sensitive, regardless of how tough they act. Don't just yell; talk to me, discuss with me, and converse with me, heart-to-heart. 99

—Lizette Grajales, 17-year-old, Pennsylvania

Trust

A first step is to trust that our children also want what is best for them. Kids' behaviors sometimes suggest they think little of consequences and choose to do what feels good. In these cases, their behaviors seem, irresponsible or to be driven by laziness. We must know, however, that their actions are often not an accurate reflection of their thoughts or desires. It was long thought that children, adolescents especially, believed they were invulnerable. This myth has been widely disproven. In fact, young people worry a great deal. They sometimes *behave* as if they believe they are invulnerable (especially in groups), but those actions (or lack of actions) are often a cover for very real, far more complex, feelings. We hope as we continue to see the best in them, they will learn to see and then reveal the best in themselves. Operating honestly from their own place of strength, they are more likely to select the wiser decisions. After all, they need ultimately to be steering their own ships as they ride the waves. Us telling them what to do won't prepare them to do so.

Why Lectures Backfire

It's easy to launch into a lecture when we see our children headed toward a mistake. We want to offer advice based on our own experiences. We want to solve problems and make sure our children don't even get close to the rocks. Our intentions are noble, but lectures don't work and, worse, can backfire. First, when we lecture, we usually do not create the space for our children to express their concerns, so they feel cut off, unheard, and disrespected. Assuming our lecture is in response to their behavior, they may even feel ashamed. They understand our anger and, perhaps, our condescension, but they rarely grasp the content of our message. For these reasons, they tune out before our second sentence is complete. Driven to frustration, they might become hostile or defensive or even rebel against our messages.

As the first step to shifting toward more effective communication strategies, it is important to understand that kids don't grasp the content of our lectures. To appreciate why children can't comprehend our well-reasoned cause-and-effect lectures, we need to first understand how they think. Children think concretely. Concrete thinkers see the world precisely as it appears. They don't think about future consequences, only how something affects them right now. Don't believe me? Ask a 5-year-old whether she'd prefer using her dollar to buy an ice cream sandwich or invest in her college education.

As children grow, they become more open to abstractions, ideas they do not have to see. Abstract thinkers can visualize the future and consider how varied choices will lead to different outcomes. Most late adolescents are abstract thinkers, but it is important to know that up to 20% of people will never move beyond concrete thinking. It is also critical to understand that all people think concretely during times of extreme stress, and we place our children in stressful thinking patterns when we yell at them. Under stress, their ability to problem-solve is undermined.

The transition from concrete to abstract thinker occurs throughout later childhood and solidifies in late adolescence. During the teen years, new brain pathways are activated that allow young people to process information differently. Remember how during adolescence you sometimes couldn't stop thinking? Things began to make sense as they never had before, but other things made no sense at all. Here is an example from my own adolescence: "If the universe is infinite, it means it goes on and on; there is no end. But how can something be infinite? It must end. But if it does, what's there?" My head spun with confusion and excitement.

In parallel, our experiences teach us consequences and therefore help us make connections between cause and effect. The young person begins to anticipate unintended consequences, as well as to understand the complexity of people's underlying motivations. ("Oh, he pretended he cared about me just so that he could _____." "I did X because it was fun, but Y happened the next day. I never thought that could happen.") We learn through our mistakes, especially those that are painful. We learn people are more complicated than just being good or bad. The newfound understanding that people can be manipulative is both hurtful and protective. As abstract-thinking adults, who have learned painful lessons, we want our kids to learn from our experiences and travel through life as painlessly as possible. Forgetting there may be no better way to learn than from experience, even failure, we easily slip into lectures.

Let's listen to a typical lecture. "What are you doing?! Your thoughtless behavior, behavior A, will very likely lead to consequence B. What were you thinking? Then consequence B will go on to consequence C. I never even imagined you doing C, but now I wonder what's happened to you. Is it your friend's influence? If you do C, almost always you'll end up with D happening! Look at me when I'm talking to you! I'm not talking for my own good. At this point, you'll lose control and probably end up doing E. Then, depending on circumstances now completely out of your control, consequence F, G, or H will happen. No matter what, a disaster could happen! You could even die!" Or you might be more familiar with a parent (maybe even you) saying to a child, "If you don't study _____ or finish _____, you'll never get a _____, and you'll never get into a good school. You'll end up amounting to nothing."

The catastrophic tone of lectures can lead to anxious thinking and therefore undermine a young person's chances of thinking clearly when he needs to perform.

The lecture has a somewhat algebraic tempo; variables affect outcomes in all sorts of mysterious ways. Algebra isn't taught to preadolescents for a reason; their brains aren't ready for abstract thinking. Similarly, we don't teach algebra to a young person running from a tiger. If we lecture a person not yet intellectually equipped for abstract thought or one who is extremely stressed, she grows frustrated because she can't follow our algebraic logic. She hears our frustration, understands our belittling tone, and absorbs our threats, but she does not learn from the content of our message. We sound like the adults in the *Peanuts* comic strip, "Waaa waaa, waaa, waaa," but with the added twist of urgency, "Waaa waaa, waaa, waaa,…and then you die (or fail)!"

We lecture our children to spare them the fate of learning painful life lessons on their own. Our intentions are noble, but we undermine our kids gaining the maximal benefit from experience. We interfere with the learning that comes from recovering from mistakes, and we may diminish their motivation to avoid those mistakes in the future. Don't get me wrong: I do not think kids should learn entirely from experience, as that can sometimes be dangerous. I believe we should steer them away from true dangers while letting them learn life's lessons from less risky situations. But we have to learn to guide wisely, in a way that kids can understand and that helps them draw their own conclusions.

A Better Way

Effective guidance looks more like facilitation than a lecture. It honors the intelligence a young person has rather than puts them in a position of feeling intellectually incapable. Long before puberty, children understand simple concrete math, such as $2 + 2 = 4$. Even a stressed person knows what happens if you add 1 more to 9. If we switch from an algebraic/abstract tone to a simple mathematic cadence, all kids can better understand our reasoning. Even a 7-year-old or stressed 16-year-old can grasp that one thing added to another can make something different happen. Instead of a litany of abstract possibilities (A to B to C to D), we need to break our reasoning into separate steps. "I am a bit worried about your doing behavior A, because sometimes that can lead to B. Can you imagine how A could go to B? Do you have any experience with something like that? Tell me about that experience. I'd feel reassured if you had a plan to make sure that B doesn't happen to you." Only when the young person fully understands the control they have over whether or not B can occur, can the parent move on to point C. "Do you see how B might lead to C?" and so on. This will allow your child to "get it" one step at a time and draw his own conclusions on why certain actions need to be taken.

66 If a parent just yells for 5 minutes, the teen will stop listening after 2. You have to sit down with your kid and talk to them before anything else. Don't point out what the teen is doing poorly; rather, ask them what they could do better. 99

—Nora Walsh, 16-year-old, Illinois

When we facilitate youth to reach conclusions by speaking to them in ways they understand—short, concrete phrases—kids feel respected as the experts in their own lives and competent to make wiser choices. They think through possible consequences step-by-step with their own ideas rather than those we dictate. They own the lessons well because *they* have figured them out. They learn how to generalize the lesson by breaking problems down into multiple steps and therefore no longer have to learn only through experience. They do not need to rebel, only to listen to their inner wisdom.

I offer several detailed techniques to put this strategy into action in my book *Building Resilience in Children and Teens: Giving Kids Roots and Wings*. In this book, I only want to briefly introduce you to 2 of those strategies, so you can imagine what they look like in real life. Choreographed conversations can be an effective way to teach problem-solving and build competence. These are casual conversations between parent and child, but the parent has a hidden agenda, to steer the child through a problem so she can come up with her own sensible solution. Just as in choreography, the "dance" is well mapped out in advance, but it should feel spontaneous and natural. We can also role-play to get children to their aha moments. The term *role-play* is used loosely. It doesn't mean you have a script or announce, "Role-play time!" (That is a guaranteed way to have your child run out of the house.) It's simply a way to consider a what-if situation and see where it leads, a step at a time. If the scenario doesn't lead to a successful conclusion, that can be an even more effective teacher because it can show the various possible results of unwise decisions and actions. When doing these role plays, keep them casual and informal, and try to stay away from the personal territory that is certain to trigger resentment. In other words, don't say, "I am going to pretend I am your friend David pressuring you to take drugs." Instead, notice real life situations around you, or on TV, and spin them out by considering where the situations might lead if…

Interdependence as a Goal

In Chapter 14, Parenting Toward Lifelong *Inter*dependence, I spoke of how when we install "control buttons" during adolescence, our children run toward independence without wanting to look back. Lectures are more than controlling; they are disempowering. They communicate clearly, "I know what is better for you than you do." A step toward our goal of *inter*dependence is acknowledging that the person in front of us is the expert, while we are loving guides, available as needed. Our children are ultimately in control of their lives and should plan their actions with that in mind. Knowing they can control their lives, they are freer to *choose* to share theirs with us.

CHAPTER

23

A Chapter for Young People:
First Steps Toward a Better Relationship
With Your Parents

If your parents are suggesting you read this chapter, take it as a positive sign. It means they want to have a good relationship with you, and they want to take some active steps to make that happen. It may be the relationship you have is already great, and they want to keep it that way or make it even better. Or maybe you have not been communicating as well as they'd like, and they want to change that. Most parenting books only talk to parents, but we think parent-kid relationships can only change in partnership with young people. This chapter is about preparing you to be a full partner in discussions with your parents about how to have the kind of connection you both want.

This Book and Our Philosophy

Your parents just read a book called *Raising Kids to Thrive: Balancing Love With Expectations and Protection With Trust.* Feel free to read the whole thing; after all, it is written so you will be healthier, happier, and more successful. But here's a brief summary. The book focuses on the importance of loving children unconditionally while also holding them to high expectations. We said expectations should be focused on the effort you put into your work and the kind of people you choose to be. It emphasized that too much academic pressure can backfire and that all people are uneven. Rather than being criticized for being uneven, young people should be celebrated for their strengths and supported to understand their limitations. Put simply, everybody is good at some things and not as good at others. People get stressed out when they falsely believe they are supposed to be good at everything. On the other hand, you are most successful when you learn to focus on your greatest strengths while also learning enough about other things to stay balanced and interesting. The book also covers how overprotection can hurt kids because it prevents you from learning your lessons through living and even from recovering from your mistakes. It emphasizes also that it still remains a parent's job to keep kids safe, moral, and prepared to exist in the real world.

What makes this book different than all other books on parenting is that more than 500 kids from 40 states helped write it by giving their thoughts on balancing love with expectations and protection with trust.

Another thing that makes this book unique is it includes a "so you want to change" section for parents. It tries to teach parents how they can best let you know they are committed to a healthy relationship and to changing course, if necessary, so they can better be supportive of you as you think about being the most successful you.

What's in It for You?

Lots. First, your parents want to be supportive without being overprotective. You are being invited to help teach them how to strike that balance. If they get it right, they'll be able to give you the kind of support you need. Second, your parents want to have a good relationship with you and are willing to take active steps to make that happen, including listening to you! That makes you pretty fortunate. Third, if you leave your house with a healthy relationship with your parents, that connection with them will only grow throughout your lives. Finally, and maybe most importantly, the relationships in the home you are growing up in are practice for life. Families are complicated. So are relationships at work. So are the ones you will have with your future partner and own children.

Complicated doesn't mean not worth it; in fact, our relationships are the most important aspects of our lives. They are so important that they deserve the work we put into them to constantly improve on them and figure out how to be most supportive to each other. What you learn now in optimizing, or at least improving, the relationship with your parent(s) will be lessons that will last a lifetime and be critically useful at many different times, with many different people. So as you read on, every time you see the word *parents,* think to yourself, "Or teachers or coaches now and the people I work with or my own family later."

Your Role in Building the Best Relationship With Your Parent(s)

A lot of kids complain that parents only seem to notice what their children produce—grades, scores, trophies. They feel badly that parents don't seem to notice how kids feel or care about who their kids really *are* inside. Parents, on the other hand, are saddened that kids don't share their lives in the way they used to when they were smaller. These concerns stem from the same problem, a lack of communication.

It is normal for kids to pull away from parents during the teen years. How else could you reasonably get ready to leave home? However, when you don't share important parts of your lives with your parents, you can't reasonably expect them to know what is going on.

Parents want to keep you in their lives. If the only thing you allow them to see is what you produce, such as report cards and soccer goals, don't be surprised if they focus on those things. They'll work with what they have. This can lead you to feel your performance is all they care about. This cycle intensifies the pressure in your life and strains your relationship.

You have control. We are not suggesting you share every detail of your lives with your parents. Space is good, and privacy is essential. However, when you allow yourself to be more open with your feelings, including the things that challenge you, or stress you out, you'll see a different side of your parents. They'll want to support you, and you'll see the compassion you knew as a smaller child. When you spend time with them and have new enjoyable experiences together, it will allow you to have more to talk about. Choosing to share your emotions (some of them) and your time (some of it) with your parents is a win-win situation that can break the cycle of pressure so many kids feel from their parents.

A Second Chance

You may be stuck in a rut. Maybe your parents, teachers, and even friends think they know who you are, but they really don't. Maybe you've chosen behaviors that aren't so healthy or particularly wise. Maybe you're doing them for fun, but now your friends expect you to continue doing them, even though you'd like to stop or at least slow down. It may be you're doing those things to manage stress. Or, if you are like a lot of kids who are reacting to pressure, you've decided that it isn't worth it. You've chosen to "not care," maybe exactly because you care so much. It may be you don't even know why you are doing what you do, but you wish you weren't.

No matter what, there is a reasonable chance people have grown to expect you to act a certain way. If some of your behaviors have not always been healthy, there is a good chance most of your parents' time with you is spent nagging or yelling. If, on the other hand, you've been a "perfect" child, people expect you to not make mistakes. Being expected to be studious all of the time, or a star athlete, can be just as burdensome as someone expecting you to be troublesome. It's hard to break the mold and be who you want to be—good, healthy, *and* imperfect.

This is your opportunity to reboot your relationship with your parents. Real communication allows you to express your needs and them to see you as you'd like to be seen. It's a second chance.

Know Yourself...and What You're Asking For

Before you can have a real conversation with your parents, you should know what you are asking from them. To tell them how they can be most supportive, it is important to know what you need. It is helpful for you to have a sense of when encouragement feels like pressure to you. To ask for privileges you think you can handle responsibly, it is valuable to know where you want to spread your wings.

Insight, or the ability to see within oneself, is something that is developed over time. So no pressure here. We are not asking you to "figure yourself out" before you talk. It may be what you need most from your parents is the support to do just that—figure yourself out. It may be this is too heavy for you right now, and you prefer just having time with your parents again, nothing more. That's OK too. We just want you to know what you are asking for.

Be a Teacher

It is rare in life for people to genuinely ask how they can best be supportive to you. If your parents are doing this, you want to seize the opportunity. A good starting point is for you to help your parents know what it's really like for you. This doesn't mean you have to get really personal or too deep; just guide them a bit about the realities of growing up today. They've been kids, so they are starting with experience. But they can't possibly know what your school and community are like now through your eyes. And until they do, they can't be there for you as much as they'd like to be.

Communication 101

Whether you start the conversation or one of your parents does, there are some general rules that will make it more likely to go well.

Be Forgiving

If you go into a conversation with a grudge or angry, it's not going to go well. You'll be more in the mood to get even or teach a lesson than you will be to make progress. People make mistakes. Even your parents. Even you. Do the work beforehand, if possible, to forgive.

If someone comes to you suddenly while you are still angry, chances are you're going to have trouble staying calm. Ask for some space. During those moments, remind yourself the person is coming to you to make things better. That is a huge step that takes a lot of bravery and always comes from a place of caring. When you take a moment to think that through, it might be enough for you to be able to be forgiving.

It may be the person who needs forgiving is you. We all have done things we wish we hadn't. We've all had selfish, thoughtless, and mean moments. We've all had ample opportunities to disappoint ourselves. Guilt is not a healthy emotion to retain when you are trying to move forward. Let it go. The actions you choose to take should free you from lingering bad feelings about the past.

No Feeling Is Wrong

In life, meaningful relationships are those in which feelings can be shared and solutions can be developed. Never tell anybody their feelings are wrong. You can disagree with them, but the feeling itself is never wrong. Learn to respond with phrases like, "I hear that you are feeling _____," or, "Thanks for trusting me enough to let me know you are feeling _____." This also gives you a free opening to say, "Sometimes, I feel _____," but don't end with, "Because you did _____," which will just start a fight. These kinds of statements are a first step toward assuring thoughts and feelings are shared. Without thoughts and feelings on the table, conflicts rarely get settled.

The Power of an Apology

There is nothing that earns a reboot like an apology. Put it on the table. None of us are perfect, and we can only hope we will grow from our experiences and make it "right" with people who may have been hurt along the way.

You are asking for forgiveness and an opportunity to move forward. Your behavior does not represent who you really are. You still won't be perfect, nobody is, but you'd like another chance.

An apology is not an explanation or justification. Telling someone why you did something may be helpful, but it can also be interpreted as an excuse. Really saying you are sorry repairs relationships, because it helps the other party understand you *know they were hurt.*

It may be you are not even sure you did anything wrong. Remember always that it matters less how you intended something and more how what you did was received.

One of the most effective strategies to lower tensions is with a heartfelt apology. If there is tension you cannot explain, it can even be helpful to try out an apology, "It seems like you're upset about something. Is there anything I may have done, or not done, that I could make right?"

Give Them an A for Effort

Sometimes when other people try to make things better, they don't quite hit the mark. That can increase your frustration and therefore even make things worse. Rather than allowing your thoughts to get away from you, take a breath and give an A for effort. At least your parents are trying. Knowing they are putting in the effort might be enough to help you give them that second chance. It also might be worth considering that if they didn't do or say what you needed, you may have to be clearer about what you need.

Parents care deeply for their kids. Most mistakes they make are with the best of intentions. Rather than starting from a place of frustration or anger, try to begin by reminding yourself you are dealing with people who have loved you from the moment you were born. Give them that presumed A.

Seeing Your Parents' Strengths

It is common for young people to sometimes see their parents as annoying. When you are having disagreements, you might feel they are being unfair or controlling. You also might feel they are putting too much pressure on you or overprotecting you. You are entitled to any feeling you have, but if negative feelings are all you bring up in a conversation, you can be sure it's not going to go well. Again, take a moment to reflect. Be thoughtful, especially when you are frustrated or angry, about all of the qualities you appreciate about your parents too. It will literally change the way you come to the conversation and therefore the results. This strengths-based approach you practice now with your parents will be useful in every challenging conversation you have throughout your lives.

Seeing the Strengths...in Yourself

It makes a lot of sense to see the best in a person as a starting point for moving forward, doesn't it? Now let's practice this skill on yourself. That's part of self-advocacy. If you are down on yourself, that's not a good position to start negotiating. You have to think about why you have value and are worthy of the chance to prove yourself. You should come to every interaction throughout your lives knowing you have something to offer the other person.

Stay Calm

Enough said. Things almost always go badly in conversations when you don't stay calm. Deep breaths really work. So does removing yourself from a situation, burning off your frustration or anger (sometimes with exercise, other times by talking to a friend, and sometimes just with space), and returning to it when you are calmer.

Choose the Time and Space

You know yourself, and you know where you are most likely to think clearly and when you are most likely to have the headspace to think something through. We already told your parents to follow the basic rules listed at the end of this paragraph. Feel free to add others that fit you better. If your parents want to start a conversation at a time that is not good for you, calmly give them the A for effort and ask them to choose another time.

- Never have important conversations in public.

- Never have important conversations in front of friends.

- Don't start important conversations when you already have a lot on your mind. If you are already nervous about something such as a big homework assignment, you'll be angry when you approach your parents, and you may not be able to regain focus.

- If you are finally relaxing after a long stretch of work, it is not the time to approach your parents.

- It is easier to talk with one parent at a time. Otherwise, it can feel like you are being ganged up on.

Listening

Listening is by far the most important part of communication. It suggests openness to others' views and informs us of what needs to be addressed. It shows respect like nothing else can do because it says that what the other person thinks and feels matters. It also creates the space for talking. People will not speak if they fear they will not be heard. They may yell to try to be heard, but they will not speak; thus, listening sets the calm tone for real communication. The fact that listening is the most important part of communication lowers the pressure on all of us, because we don't have to always find the right words to say. We can offer our respectful presence and our listening ear.

This advice is nearly the exact advice we shared with your parents about how to respect you. The best way to forge the deepest and most productive relationships with your parents (or anybody) is to listen.

Don't Assume, You May Be Wrong

We all assume we know what others mean by the words they say. We also think we can judge what they are thinking by the expression on their face or movements of their body. However, we are often wrong. For example, your father may come home and barely say anything to you, grunting instead. He may sit with his arms crossed, have a tight furrowed brow, squint his eyes, and breathe quickly. You may assume he is mad at you. But he also might be fuming over his boss being dismissive of his work. Your assumption could leave you feeling angry and defensive when nothing would have helped your father regain his footing more than an, "I love you, Dad." Check your assumptions. Try saying something like, "I can tell something's going on; I'm here if I can help. I love you." If it seems like whatever your parents are feeling involves you, ask for clarity. "You seem (angry/confused/frustrated) about something. Am I right?"

Focus on the Current Issue, Don't Bring Up Things From the Past

It is so easy once you have someone's attention to begin adding other problems to the list or to justify your behavior by bringing up something the other person has done in the past. This is almost certainly going to put the other person on the defensive and possibly overwhelm them. This can bring an abrupt stop to communication. When you pile up the accusations or list of problems, it also points out you have noticed a pattern; in other words, you have grown to expect a certain behavior. The last thing you want to do is to suggest to a parent that his or her behavior "is just what you are like," because that undermines someone's belief that he or she can change anything. Remember that the whole reason you are having the conversation is because you are hoping for an improvement in your relationship. Finally, it is hard enough to change course in the present. It is impossible to alter the past, so there is no use in remaining stuck in it.

Be Prepared to Offer Solutions

When your parents come to you asking for a new behavior or you go to them requesting they consider doing something differently, it is important the conversation moves beyond complaints and toward solutions. Otherwise, the conversation will stir things up with no purpose. Therefore, the goal has to be to come up with a new plan. Offer solutions that involve steps both of you can take, so nobody feels labeled as the problem. Before you approach your parents (or your boss or spouse in the future) with problems, you should think beforehand of the actions or strategies that could make things better. If your parents come to you with a problem that needs changing, buy yourself time and space by saying something like, "Let me think about this and get back to you on how I can work on this and maybe on where I'll need your support." To avoid them thinking you are trying to get out of the situation by stalling (or hoping they'll forget), clinch the deal by saying, "Why don't we talk about this again in 2 days?"

You Don't Have to Let All Your Feelings Out

Talking about feelings is good. It shows you trust somebody, and that often draws you closer. In the world of friendships, trust has to be earned over time. We've all been hurt by friends who spread our business around. A good strategy is to have 2 levels of personal information. The first level includes things that are personal enough to share but you wouldn't be devastated if they appeared on the evening news or got blasted out in social media. This is the kind of stuff you have interesting conversations about, build friendships through, and with which you test your relationships. The second level is the deeply personal stuff about you that nobody but your most trusted people, and perhaps a professional, should know. People have to earn your trust over time to be deserving of this piece of you.

Hopefully your parents fall into the category of having deeply earned your trust. Nevertheless, it is OK to keep some feelings to yourself as you wrestle with them. It can reduce the drama as you work on problems with your parents. But remember there is nobody on earth who will stick with you "no matter what" like your parents will. So if a problem feels intense to you, they are likely the ones who need to know. If you need a bridge to them, professionals such as your school counselor, teachers, religious leaders, or health care professionals can be helpful.

Be an Effective Self-advocate: Invite Others to Become Part of the Solution Rather than Blaming Them for the Problem

A first step to learning self-advocacy is knowing how to present your viewpoint in a way that is less likely to make someone else defensive. The "I" statement is a lifelong skill you can use now with your parents, teachers, and coaches and in the future with your spouses, children, and colleagues. It allows you to discuss meaningful issues while lowering the temperature. When any of us are angry, frustrated, or worried, we tend to blame the other person for causing a problem. When people are blamed, they feel judged and become defensive. This makes them hold their position more rigidly or even become hostile.

Many arguments start with people telling others precisely what they are doing wrong. These statements often begin with the word *you*. The natural response to, "You did this," is a defensive-offensive, "I did not, you caused it!" Instead, using "I" statements like, "I feel this way when…," or, "This makes me think…," may encourage the other person to problem-solve or even feel empathy, because the natural response then becomes, "How can I help you feel better?" or "How can we solve this?"

For example, if you are frustrated with your coach, you might want to say, "You are so unfair! You know I deserved to start the game. Why are you punishing me?" Instead, you might say, "I tried really hard to train for this game and felt really disappointed to get so little playing time. Can you help me understand what I can do to start the next game?"

Or if you are angry with your teacher, you might feel like saying, "You know I deserved a B on that paper. You are totally unfair. You give the kids you like better grades!" Instead, you might say, "I was really disappointed that I got a C on my paper. I thought I did a good job. Can you help me understand why you thought I deserved a lower grade?"

You might want to shout to your mother, "You are totally unfair! You are always punishing me for being born, and you obviously like (insert your brother's or sister's name[s]) better than me." That will make your mother defensive and angry, only making things worse. Your strategy is to bring out her mothering side, the part of her that wants to care for you and make things better. So instead, you might say, "I really feel like I wasn't treated fairly, and it makes me sad and frustrated. Sometimes I even feel like I am not as loved as other people around here." That will have her explore why you might feel that way.

Regaining Trust

It may be that the difficult conversation you have with your parents is about something serious you have done, which has made them lose trust in you. Your first impulse might be to deny you've done anything wrong. If, however, you have made a mistake or behaved in a way that is not acceptable, the strategy of denial is unlikely to work. It is far better to begin with an apology, as discussed earlier. Then it is a matter of re-earning that trust. If you've learned a lesson, explain that in a detailed way, so your parents can see the lesson hit home. If you need ongoing support, or further explanation, say that too. If you do all of this, you have set the stage to earn back their trust.

To regain and hold trust, though, it will have to be earned. The best way to do that is to demonstrate responsibility moving forward. Feel free to negotiate here. Say exactly what you are willing to do, over time, to prove you are deserving of their trust. Even say you expect to be watched more closely, but they will not be disappointed by what they see. We can't tell you what it will take to regain your parents' trust; it depends on their personalities, your general pattern of behavior, and how dangerous your actions may have been. The more dangerous, the more protective instincts will be activated in your parents and the more detailed reassurance over time they will need. What we can tell you is trust is always something that can be regained when your behaviors prove you are learning to be more careful or responsible.

Take control of this process by putting out there what you know went wrong and what you're willing to do. For example, "I know coming home late and drunk was not OK. And I don't blame you for taking away the car keys. But I wasn't drinking and driving. If I were, I wouldn't deserve them back. I parked the car at my friend's house and walked home; that's why I was late. I promise I'll call you if I ever find myself in a risky situation, so you can arrange for me to get home and at least not worry about me. I guarantee you I will never drink and drive. Driving is really important to me. Assuming I show you that I will always be on time for curfew, and that I don't repeat this mistake, how long until I get my keys back?"

Sometimes the Words Are Hard to Say... or Difficult to Listen To

Maybe you've read some of the ideas about holding productive conversations and thought, "I just can't imagine saying that," or, "She'll never listen long enough for me to get the words out." Maybe you feel your parents need to change their approach to supporting you, or you should do some advance groundwork, even before you have a sit-down conversation. One great strategy is to let your parents get to know the whole you again, as we discussed earlier. Letters (or notes or e-mails) can also be useful tools to reboot relationships when it seems too tough, for one reason or another, to start a conversation. They can smooth everything out for when you need to address something important later. Some thoughts about letters include

- Follow the same general rules outlined throughout this chapter, especially focusing on the present rather than the past.

- Start with something positive. Nothing softens up parents like reminding them you love them. Feel free to add why you respect them or a recent lesson you appreciated.

- Make a clear statement on what you want rebooted and your commitment to moving forward.

- Letters are a wonderful place to offer a sincere apology.

- Do *not* use the letter to offer criticism. Express your concern in general terms only. When people who are hurt or angry read a letter, they might focus on only the one negative sentence in a 3-page letter, as well as use that sentence as a reason to get angrier or avoid hearing what you are trying to say.

- Consider having an objective reader review the letter before you send it. Have the reader check for thoughts that could be misinterpreted or phrases that could trigger anger or resentment. If anything has even a chance of backfiring, remove it. Ideally, that reader will be another trusted adult, because they are more likely to know how your parents will interpret things.

Will These Strategies Solve All Your Relationship Issues?

No. Life is complicated. There are no perfect relationships, just those that are worth working on. One day, you may fall madly in love and choose to settle down with someone. You might think he or she is perfect for the first few minutes, but soon enough you'll learn about things you wish were different. If you try to change that person, he or she will never feel secure and your relationship will be undermined. But if you communicate well and create safe spaces so you can both express what you need and explore how you can be supportive to each other, you'll have healthy lives together. Then together you can work on how some behaviors or actions might change without changing the person.

At the workplace, you'll be spending countless hours with people you haven't chosen as life partners, but you'll still need to have productive, enjoyable relationships. That often takes a great deal of strategizing and compromise. It can't involve hostility, and it can't include holing yourself in your office.

Practicing effective communication strategies with your parents will build a stronger relationship with them. As importantly, it will prepare you for a happier and more successful life.

Parting Thoughts

Our love is undoubtedly the most protective force in our children's lives. Parenting has to be driven by the heart but informed by the mind. A child loved, but raised without expectations, would never learn his potential. If we allow ourselves to be guided only by our feelings, we might hold our children so tightly they would never learn to function in a complex world. They would feel protected but not learn to trust in their abilities. A child protected, but never allowed to experience life, would likely never learn self-control or how to reach the heights that only second, third, and eighth tries produce.

Balance

Truly, the most important word in the title of this book is the one you least likely noticed when you picked it up. Lighthouse parenting is a way of framing *balanced* (or authoritative) parenting. Balanced parenting is not a new or passing strategy; it has been shown to reduce risks and produce emotionally healthier and more academically successful young people. It emphasizes that children need love and warmth to gain the security from which humans develop and flourish. It recognizes that while children must test their limits, they must do so under the watchful eyes of parents who effectively monitor clearly understood boundaries. Indeed, those limits make exploration within the boundaries safe, offering the opportunity to make and recover from errors, to test limits, and to learn to expand upon them during development. Balanced parenting is loving without smothering, protecting without stifling growth, and guiding without directing.

We should be like lighthouses for our children—beacons of light on a stable shoreline from which they can safely navigate the world. We must make certain they don't crash against the rocks but trust they have the capacity to learn to ride the waves on their own.

Restoring Balance

I try hard to stay away from overtly controversial statements, because although they get attention, they distract from the work that needs to be done. However, I would like to leave you with a thought that may be radical in early 21st-century America. Our overemphasis on independence is backfiring. The American dream of success is too tightly linked to rugged individualism. The focus on individual success is a relatively new experiment that may undermine what has allowed us to thrive through-out the millennia. We thrive best, and indeed survive, even through the worst of times, when we remain connected to and supportive of one other. Although we raise our children to fly on their own, we must also prepare them to understand that maintaining strong connections to family is critically important. We do this neither by blanketing them with over-protection nor by demanding their full attention. We do this by taking care not to install the control buttons from which they must flee. We do this by honoring their growing wisdom and development. We do this by recognizing them as the experts in their own lives and by sharing our own experience when needed. We do this by backing away from believing every moment with our children must be productive and by returning to what has always worked, being together. Just being. Yes, they will fly away, and the launching may even have its painful moments. But ultimately, we want to raise children who choose *inter*dependence, knowing that nothing is more meaningful or makes us more successful than being surrounded by those we love.

A lighthouse remains stable and predictable. We leave it as we travel independently on the waters. But it remains a welcoming beacon of safety and security that we look forward to seeing time and again.

INDEX